3-3-67 LC 12-10-68

The Author

A writer on jazz since 1935, Dave Dexter, Jr. is today an executive producer with one of the world's largest recording firms. Born in Kansas City in 1915, he served his apprenticeship as a jazz writer with the *Journal-Post* during the wild period of Tom Pendergast's rule—the era of Count Basie, Joe Turner, Mary Lou Williams, Pete Johnson, Jay McShann, and Andy Kirk's Clouds of Joy. Every jazz performer of national renown played Kansas City frequently, and Dexter met them all. In 1938, he moved to Chicago to become associate editor of *Down Beat*, followed by three years in New York for the same rowdy, brazen publication, which he personally made into a twice-monthly bible for musicians and jazz buffs. In 1942, he joined the Jimmy Dorsey orchestra as a radio script writer and soon settled in California to become a writer-reviewer-critic-producer, frequently serving as a disc jockey with Al Jarvis and Gene Norman. For more than twenty years, he has continued to record, write, review, and occasionally participate in radio-television panel shows from his home base in California, meanwhile travelling widely to meet and write about jazzmen from Paris to Tokyo. A member of the Hollywood Museum records committee, he also writes and produces the official *Surface Noise* house organ for the National Academy of Recording Arts and Sciences.

HEEBIE JEEBIES

As Recorded by LOUIS ARMSTRONG on Columbia Records

By BOYD ATKINS

Bb INSTRUMENTS

thejazzstory

*from
the '90s
to the '60s*

by Dave Dexter, Jr.

with a foreword by Woody Herman

Prentice-Hall, Inc., Englewood Cliffs, New Jersey, 1964

To My "Team"

Little John
Mary
Janny
Marjorie
Davey
Patrick
Eddie
Mike
Sally

Foreword

Jazz is slowly gaining stature throughout the world. It is bigger and better than ever. So are the books about it.

No two persons ever hear jazz the same way. It is a highly personal music. It is complicated. All of us, musicians and laymen alike, enjoy or dislike a performance because of an infinite number of intangibles—our background, listening experience, knowledge of vocal and instrumental skills, even our age. Part of the charm of American jazz lies in its variety. We all like different aspects of it. Each of us has his own bag. *The Jazz Story* is about as objective, unbiased, and complete as a book on jazz can be.

I first met Dave Dexter in the late 1930s when our original "band that plays the blues" was appearing at a ratty, overcrowded, smoggy little basement joint on New York's West 52nd Street called The Famous Door. As I remember, he swept into the club one wintry night on a visit from Chicago, where he was a sort of one-man writer and editor of *Down Beat* at a time when it was the most violent, colorful, and irreverent monthly publication in North America. He thought the Herman band was great. He knew every note on every record we had ever made. And his odd Kansas City haircut and remarkable enthusiasm left some sort of an impression, I guess. Unlike a lot of young Ivy Leaguers who frequented the Door, Dexter roared out into the night determined to do something about our band. In Chicago, he egged radio stations into playing our records and he must have written a million words about us via feature articles, news stories, record reviews, and picture captions.

Eventually, of course, we started to move better: our record sales jumped a hundred fold, we made several Hollywood films. I like to feel, looking back a short quarter of a century, that the raw, unsophisticated, no-strings-attached efforts of Dexter and a few other hustling young friends who believed with violent passions in our music helped give the Herman herd an emphatic boost at a time when we—a group of naive refugees from Isham Jones' dance band —needed it most. Something that never ceases to amaze me is that these friends, not so youthful now, are still in there working for our band.

Then a couple of years later Dexter drove out to Hollywood from New York with our mutual buddy, Carlos Gastel, just to be present for opening night at the world's nicest ballroom, the Palladium. He and Gastel broke their 3,000 mile drive only by catching a jazz combo or two for a few hours in Kansas City. The least I could do was sit them at a table with Lana Turner and Bing Crosby. Down through the years we met often; I recall a fine summer evening at Detroit's Eastwood Gardens when Dexter hopped out of Glenn Miller's chartered bus and joined our band for a weekend. At the old but unforgettable Panther Room of the Hotel Sherman in Chicago we met frequently, Dave invariably enjoying a combination of black coffee, ice cream, and Budweiser. After he moved to New York to open a *Down Beat* editorial office and make the controversial musicians' newspaper a truly national publication, he was always near to encourage and help publicize us.

Along about 1953-54 we got together on a closer professional basis when he became producer of our records. Now he sported a new California crew haircut, and worked in Hollywood, but he still doggedly mixed beer and black coffee with impunity. The Herman orchestra was vastly different, serving up a considerably more modern, adventurous, and perhaps daring calibre of jazz. Some of it, Dexter charged, was "incoherent" and only distantly related to music. Yet he moved in and out of the control booth agilely, swiftly setting up proper balances and trying to make the finest possible records. I think we succeeded. We enjoyed every minute of our collaboration in the studios despite sporadic arguments over where jazz was heading.

The Jazz Story is a good book; it doesn't require a thesaurus to understand it. I might recommend in particular the chapters on the big band era and Kansas City jazz. Dave's acquaintance with Charlie Parker and his recollections of some of the Bird's eccentricities have never before been recorded in print. They give a rare insight into the tragic saxophonist's early days in the Middle West.

For all of its ups and downs during the last half century, jazz continues to become a more powerful and popular force in our society. Not just here in the U.S.A., but in civilized nations throughout the world. A well-written, accurate book like this will help spread the gospel even more. To our democratic way of life, jazz and the men who make it are more vital than ever before. Keep swinging. Onward, always, onward!

Woody Herman

CARNEGIE HALL BOUNCE

By ART TATUM

Preface

It has been nearly twenty years since my first book on jazz was published. *Jazz Cavalcade* (New York, 1946) was written as the swing era was expiring. Since then, hundreds of musicians who were unknown in 1946 have entered the profession and made good as jazzmen. The entire rebop, bebop, and bop period with its lively controversies has come and gone. The cool era, likewise, has swept in and out. But both movements have left indelible imprints on today's jazz.

And now, in the 1960s, the more progressive jazzmen regard Dizzy Gillespie's and Charlie Parker's revolutionary solo styles of the middle 1940s as almost quaint. Even the easy, unemotional, cool trumpet style of Miles Davis is considered passé by certain musicians. However inept the label, the latest in jazz is simply called "the new thing" and is led by Ornette Coleman, Eric Dolphy, and Charlie Mingus. A surprising number of young musicians and youthful jazz buffs are enamored with its unconventional aspects.

This book covers not only these recent developments but the entire *jazz story*, from the primitive New Orleans bands right on up to "the new thing." It is a compilation of the important facts behind that story—enhanced, I hope, by a running commentary drawn from three decades of personal observations and interviews.

A third trip to Europe in 1963 following treks to Mexico and the major South American countries, and another of some 28,000 miles around the world in 1959, have helped me acquire information and meet musicians personally for the *Internationally Speaking*

chapter. Jazz is like science. No matter where one is, it is compre-
hensible, disposing of language and cultural barriers instantly. It is
heartening to report that jazz continues to grow and prosper, improving the image of Americans and the U.S.A., in every nation
I visited.

To Charles Delaunay in Paris, who conceived and authored *Hot
Discography* with the assistance of Walter E. Schaap and George
Avakian, and to Leonard Feather, author of the formidable *Ency-
clopedia of Jazz* and my neighbor in the San Fernando Valley of
Southern California, I gratefully acknowledge use of their invalu-
able works.

To my publisher and to my editors, George K. Evans and Glenn
Laughery, I owe special thanks; also to Ruth Liberman, whose un-
enviable task it was to see that hundreds of ineptly typed pages were
accurately transcribed, and finally to my patient family, my thanks
and appreciation.

D. D., Jr.

Contents

LESTER YOUNG'S TENOR SAXOPHONE SOLO
HI HECKLER

As played and
composed by
LESTER YOUNG

Illustrations

SALT PEANUTS

As played by DIZZY GILLESPIE

Bb INSTRUMENTS

Transcribed by
FRANK PAPARELLI

By "DIZZY" GILLESPIE
KENNY CLARKE

1

The Scene Today

The life of a musician has changed drastically since World War II. Extreme changes have taken place in the sites where a musician can work. Television and taxes have nearly killed night clubs. No more than a half-dozen luxury ballrooms remain from the scores that flourished twenty years ago. A week's job in a theater is a rarity. And unlike the turbulent '30s, today very few radio stations employ staff orchestras, or trios, or even a solo pianist.

Yet, like the alley cat, the modern musician is a durable specimen who somehow manages to survive periods of unemployment, incompetent managers, apathetic booking agencies, hunger pains, occasional highway accidents and, invariably, untenable working conditions.

Many professionals turn to the easy life, to jobs with Mickey-Mouse, ricky-tick, schmalz, or dull "hotel" orchestras, with their simple instrumentation featuring three tenor saxophones. Others join what musicians call "combos," small bands of three or more musicians, most of which specialize in working *bar mitzvah* receptions, cocktail lounges, Little League fund-raisers and neighborhood socials. A pitiable minority accept seasonal employment in symphonies or chamber music groups; chairs in such prestigious organizations go almost without exception to older, even

ILLUSTRATION: Woody Herman. (Reproduced by permission of Woody Herman–Philips Records.)

elderly, legitimate musicians with long years of experience playing classical music.

Yet, for all the limitations and difficulties facing any musician in this
second half of the twentieth century, there exists a fascinating breed that
chooses an even more risky and circuitous course.

He is the jazzman.

He plays a highly specialized music. Millions and more millions haven't
the slightest interest in his talents, and will never pay to enjoy them. He
faces a life in which countless of his fellow citizens openly regard him
as an eccentric. Even insurance companies force him to pay higher pre-
miums than his fellow man pays. But he bears his stigma well. Many
thousands of today's professional musicians—jazz musicians—happily
manage to conform to today's complicated social mores.

Not many seasons back, a jazz concert was a notably newsworthy
event. Benny Goodman's 1938 Carnegie Hall appearance is even now
regarded as an epochal night in the history of jazz, and still remembered
is the Paul Whiteman Aeolian Hall concert on February 12, 1924, at
which George Gershwin's *Rhapsody in Blue* was performed for the first
time.

Concerts are, forty years later, a commonly accepted and popular form
of jazz presentation. Almost every college and university presents at least
one a year. New York's Town Hall is frequently used, as are stadiums,
theaters, auditoriums, and baseball parks in a hundred American cities.
Abroad, jazz concerts are often held in the old Olympia Music Hall in
Paris, the sleek Festival Hall on the bank of the Thames in London, and
in various other settings in such cities as Tokyo, Rome, Rio de Janeiro,
Hamburg, and even Moscow. Benny Goodman's appearances in a half-
dozen Russian cities in 1962 resulted not only in an American cultural
triumph, but in an entertaining record album (RCA-Victor LOC-6008)
as well.

Young jazz musicians and fans have helped make today's concerts universally successful, in large part simply because they are able to attend
them. Long gone are the days when Muggsy Spanier and George Wettling had to stand on apple crates in an alley outside Chicago's old Lincoln
Gardens to hear heated Joe Oliver-Louis Armstrong trumpet duets. Today, youngsters can sit comfortably inside auditoriums and applaud their
favorites.

And so the contemporary scene is radically different from even the jazz
world of 1950. Ballrooms are almost nonexistent, a full week in a theater
is rarely available to even the top attractions, and night clubs employing
jazzmen are rapidly disappearing. The musician, however, has never had
it so good in one broad, lucrative area.

The record studios have become the El Dorado beckoning to all. The instrumental soloist, the singer with a style, the combo, the big band, even the comedians are all in demand in a market which, according to the Record Industry Association of America, had retail sales in 1962, for example, amounting to $570,250,000 in the United States alone—an all-time record for records.

Recording sessions are held every day in many cities. Carefully placed microphones feed the music into tape machines, from which the mastering and pressing of albums and singles follow. Record dealers from Montpelier to Laguna Beach are then inundated with so many discs that only a fraction of available labels can be carried in stock. On the average, one jazz album in sixteen proves profitable to the company that produced it. Most are never heard. Many that are carefully recorded and lovingly collated are never placed on sale.

Contrast the situation with the depression year of 1932.

In a year made memorable by the election to the presidency of Franklin Delano Roosevelt, the "bonus army" and its march on Washington, Amelia Earhart's solo flight over the Atlantic, the Olympic games in Los Angeles, and the gala opening of New York's Radio City Music Hall, a hit record sold 10,000 copies—and there weren't any hits.

A musician almost had to be a star sideman in Paul Whiteman's troupe to obtain a record date, or so it appeared. Only the songs that had already been played into hits via Broadway musical shows, or by coast-to-coast radio broadcasts, were recorded. Today it is different. Only a record can make a song a hit. And the recording fee for musicians has been increased from $20 to almost $60 by the union, the American Federation of Musicians.

Jazz on records was hard to find in 1932. But because so many Negroes remained loyal, avidly purchasing platters in the face of incredibly difficult economic conditions, blues and Harlem-styled jazz enjoyed their own specialized markets. Victor, Okeh, Brunswick, and Columbia were the major labels. Some recorded and sold certain artists for certain specific markets, records called "territory" releases that were unavailable in other areas of the nation.

In the '60s, jazz singles have disappeared, and the easily breakable 78-revolutions-per-minute shellac discs that served so well for so long have vanished as well. Long-play records, for more than a decade, have dominated the dealers' shelves. Individual bands, or tracks, may run as long as fifteen minutes. There is no time limit, anymore, to an artist's performance.

There are, moreover, more than 500 active labels, all seeking the fast-selling entry—the big smash hit. And although several hundred companies have expired since the first record boom of the 1940s, just as many remain active because new labels are constantly launched.

Record companies (several operating out of kitchens, garages, and outdoor sheds) are to be found in Saukville, Wisconsin; Media, Pennsylvania; Desplaines, Illinois; Bergenfield, New Jersey; Tarzana, California; Coeur d'Alene, Idaho; Luray, Virginia, and a hundred other towns and hamlets. The quickest way to start a donnybrook among musicians is to ask what labels are the majors. Once there were four. Today, forty, perhaps? All record music. All provide jobs for musicians. Most important, all attempt to advance the jazz art.

A sizable group of jazzmen today fare extremely well. Louis Armstrong's nightly fee is the highest. Still, of all the veteran musicians working, he enjoys fewer nights off, and his recent payroll and travel expenses in comparison to the old days when he carried five saxes, six or seven brass, a singer, pianist, drummer, bassist, guitarist, valet, road manager, and baggage boy, is modest at best. For Louis, with his mobile combo and girl singer, can and does work Munich and Melbourne, Honolulu and Helsinki, Geneva and the Gold Coast of Africa, as easily and frequently as he works Chicago.

Ella Fitzgerald is another performer whose yearly income and world itineraries are astounding. In neither category does the President of the United States equal her.

Since 1960, the blind pianist and singer Ray Charles has merited top guarantees on every personal appearance. For a taped guest role on Dinah Shore's television show, in which he sang four songs, Charles was paid $15,000.

The St. Louis trumpeter, Miles Davis, is another big box-office winner. And so are Duke Ellington, Count Basie, Stan Kenton, and Woody Herman with their large, hard-swinging orchestras.

George Shearing, Julian (Cannonball) Adderley, John (Dizzy) Gillespie, Dave Bruebeck, Lionel Hampton, Peggy Lee, the Modern Jazz Quartet, Erroll Garner, Stan Getz, John Coltrane, Sonny Rollins, Sarah Vaughan, Pete Fountain, Gerry Mulligan, Oscar Peterson, Roland Kirk, and Ornette Coleman—also draw well because of successful jazz records.

A Dixieland band, or a ragtime pianist, offers simple, nonintellectual jazz of the lowest aesthetic order; yet both can provide charming, entertaining and emotion-packed performances if they are offered by first-rate musicians. Appreciating the more complicated jazz conceptions of a Horace Silver or Joe Harriott, however, is a different story. Advanced jazz requires study, as does all art.

Today, there are accredited courses in jazz available at numerous universities and colleges in the United States. Stan Kenton and other articulate spokesmen often are heard as guest lecturers. There are, in addition, four professional schools that attract young students seeking a career in jazz: the Berklee School of Music, Boston; Westlake College of Music, Hollywood; the Advanced School of Contemporary Music, Toronto; and the School of Jazz, Lenox, Massachusetts.

More and more young artists are well-educated, highly literate, and capable of arranging as well as playing one or more instruments proficiently. This trend probably got an impetus from the success of graduates and former students of North Texas State College, notably the guitarist Herb Ellis, the clarinetist, saxophonist, and composer Jimmy Giuffre, the arranger and composer Gene Roland, and the bassist and 'cello virtuoso (and, for a time, my benevolent landlord) Harry Babasin. All four now reside and work in the Los Angeles area. All studied on the Texas campus together.

Since 1959, the University of Notre Dame at South Bend, Indiana, has sponsored an outstanding Collegiate Jazz Festival every spring. Many promising young amateurs have thus been given a start.

While night club opportunities for the musician, and the jazzman in particular, decline with the years, the increase in recording jobs, educational facilities, and concert and festival "gigs"—the musicians' term for engagements—tend to balance up for the aspiring professional.

But let the fledgling student musician beware the path he has chosen to pursue. Working conditions for musicians are never, and have never been, more than merely tolerable. Almost constant travel is mandatory, and it is rarely under optimum conditions. Payment for services rendered, despite the union, varies from city to town to village to campus, and until one becomes a "name" performer on records, even modest jobs at union minimum scale are sometimes hard to find. Personal managers and booking agencies are not all trustworthy, nor do they unerringly work in behalf of every client they have under contract. Many artists must fend for themselves, then pay a commission for work they find on their own.

Any professional musician you talk with will readily agree that a musician's life is difficult. But he will add that the rewards can be immense. More people are enjoying jazz now than at any previous time. More musicians are playing jazz than ever before. Jazz has spread and won acceptance throughout the world, including the Soviet Union and its many satellite nations.

The scene today is far from ideal, but never has the future of jazz appeared brighter.

To one who has produced many exciting record sessions on Royal and Canal streets in the atmospheric Vieux Carré of New Orleans—and a book might be written about those experiences alone—there can be no doubt as to the African roots of jazz. Musicians in New Orleans still recount the stories they've heard since childhood of the pioneer musicians, the slave block in the Crescent City's Congo Square, old rag and jazz melodies that have undergone subtle changes with the years and emerged with new titles, and colorful marching bands in spectacular uniforms wailing the blues along with the national—or Louisiana—anthem.

Much of that climate of the early 1900s still exists in New Orleans. To the visitor, the humid river city comes into focus as a pleasing blur of hot gumbo, boat whistles, slide trombones, sugary pralines, shrill open-bell trumpets, chicory coffee, aggressive female night-club hostesses with accents perhaps too heavily laden with grits and cornbread; yet, for all the sounds, smell, and color of night life it is the city's music that dominates the senses.

All play in the same style. There are no big bands. And unlike the preponderantly youthful orchestras in other cities, in the fabled Crescent City it is common, perhaps even traditional, that elderly artists in their sixties and seventies play alongside youngsters.

The older musicians are fast dying out, however.

No longer may one sit at the Paddock Bar on Bourbon Street, savoring a cold Jax and the hot ante bellum clarinet wizardry of slender, dignified

ILLUSTRATION: Edward "Kid" Ory (left) and Thomas "Mutt" Carey. (Photograph by Charlie Mihn.)

Alphonse Picou. Born in 1878, Picou was 72 in 1950 when I last enjoyed his odd solo style in Oscar (Papa) Celestin's unit. Both Picou and Celestin were playing professionally before 1900 in New Orleans; both were pleased to reminisce fifty years later. Celestin died in 1954. He had recorded his first sides thirty years previously.

Jack (Papa) Laine went back even farther. A master of bass, drums, alto horn, and piano, he was born in 1873 and still performed at jazz concerts and special events in the Crescent City as late as the 1950s. Old Papa once confided to me, in the studios of WDSU, that he organized his first band within a mile of the radio station in 1887 when he was but 14 years old. Who today would have the temerity to doubt him?

Younger than Picou, Celestin, Laine, and other early practitioners with whom I talked was Sidney Bechet, who deserted New Orleans early and became one of the first Americans to play and help popularize jazz in England, on the continent, and even in Russia. He also played less exotic places like the Fairyland Ballroom in Kansas City with Noble Sissle's orchestra in the middle '30s. Bechet modestly recalled how he was playing "fair" clarinet at six—in 1903—and spoke of his ambition to live and play permanently in Great Britain. He missed it by the width of the English Channel. Instead of London, Paris became his home for about ten years, and it was in the City of Light that he died in 1959, greatly beloved as an entertainer and public figure.

Louis Armstrong, three years younger than Bechet, preferred to talk food ("can't find them good redbeans 'n' rice in California, man") rather than trace jazz roots in our interviews, perhaps because he is himself such a vital and king-sized figure in any history of the subject.

But Armstrong, Bechet, Laine, Celestin, and Picou all agreed on the origins of the music in their discussions with this inquiring reporter. All spoke reverently of the "old days" in New Orleans and of how the Creoles dominated the pop music movement that soon crystallized into jazz.

With the growth of the Louisiana Territory, and as generation succeeded generation, African harmony, rhythm, and melody were synthesized with the folk music of the booming Southern states—a mélange of French, Spanish, Italian, and English songs. Then came the Civil War and the Emancipation Proclamation and a violently revolutionary change in the lives of everyone in the bankrupt and disconsolate South.

Robert Goffin, the Belgian-born jazz authority who spent many years in the United States researching jazz and its makers, relates in his *Jazz: From the Congo to the Metropolitan** how, in the post-Civil War period,

* Garden City, N.Y.: Doubleday & Co., 1944.

many liberated American Negroes eagerly turned to music. Unschooled, unable to read, write, or even speak "good" English, they created their own idiom of song: the blues and chants of the fields, docks, warehouses, and railroad beds; the hymns and spirituals and incantations of the churches; the hollers and shouts and eight-bar group "singalongs" that even today are a rich and distinctive part of the American jazz repertoire. Gradually, too, they came into possession of musical instruments, which led to street bands and a marvelously new way of playing and singing the old marches and ballads and waltzes and mazurkas and quadrilles.

> "*The birth of jazz was now imminent. The music was no longer folk song and not yet jazz. It was something strange and indefinable; it was a cry of lament and joy piercing through the fabulous red-light district, Storyville. Among the unbelievably numerous bars of Basin Street, inside the legendary hot spots in which gambling, alcohol and vice flourished, there came into the world an as yet unbaptized music.*" *

New Orleans wasn't alone. In the immensity of the South, along the beautiful, unspoiled Gulf east into Florida and west through Texas, sweating plantation and farm workers, chain-gang crews, big-muscled men building railroads, and many an itinerant, floating musician and singer picked up the new and wonderfully natural music and helped disseminate and popularize it.

The First Bands

The earliest jazz bands featured no saxophones, no violins, no piano. A trombone, a bass—tuba or double contrabass—clarinet, drums, banjo, and at least one cornet generally comprised the full instrumentation.

Bands played much of their repertoire while marching. Research by Barry Ulanov† has convinced him that one of the earliest of these street bands was led by a cornetist, Claiborne Williams, who called his group the St. Joseph Brass Band. It played in parades, of course, but frequently it worked Negro dances, where sophisticated cotillion music in the old French style was favored. Ulanov concludes that the 1880s was the period for Williams, the same time that the band of John Robichaux, a drummer, also enjoyed popularity in New Orleans.

---

* *Ibid.*, p. 21.
† See Ulanov's *A History of Jazz in America* (New York: The Viking Press, Inc., 1952).

Lorenzo and Louis Tio, brothers, were exceptionally gifted clarinetists regularly featured in the Excelsior Band. Both Picou and cornetist Manuel Perez performed with this group in their teen days.

Frank Dusen formed the mighty Eagle Band in 1911, an organization that boasted a youngster named Sidney Bechet, together with Big Eye Nelson, Lorenzo Tio, Jr., son of the old Excelsior Band clarinetist, and, at various times, cornet-trumpet virtuosi Freddie Keppard, Bunk Johnson, and Tom (Mutt) Carey.

Perhaps better remembered today than the Eagle outfit is the Olympia Band. Keppard also played in this group, and became its leader because of his superb cornet playing and shrewd business skills. Keppard died in Chicago during the 1933 World's Fair, an alcoholic. Unlike so many of his colleagues, he recorded several masters, but on the primitive equipment the Keppard horn and his latter-day Jazz Cardinals are hardly impressive.

The Olympia Band, however, certainly did impress. A well-rehearsed, beautifully uniformed aggregation, all who heard it class it as the best of its kind. For the Olympia to play one's funeral was, as musicians say, the absolute end.

Picou's clarinet also helped make the Olympia a favorite. On *High Society*, an old, old march that had been played in France and Walloon Belgium a hundred years earlier, little Alphonse's fantastic piccolo improvisations on the clarinet solo became so renowned that even today, more than fifty years later, almost every clarinetist follows Picou's classic melodic pattern. Ulanov also confirms that Joseph Petit played valve trombone and simultaneously managed the Olympia saloon "on Elks Place across Canal Street from the railroad terminal." John Vean, known as Ratty, and Louis Cottrell, called Old Man, were the band's two drummers. Zue Robertson later replaced Petit with a slide trombone.

The Olympia, in retrospect, undoubtedly came closer to playing jazz than any of the other combinations of the 1890-1910 period. The one band that everybody agrees probably later topped the Olympia jazzwise was a sort of all-star assemblage founded in 1908 with George Bacquet, a classically trained clarinetist who won renown, too, as a teacher. It was, of course, the Original Creole Band, the first group to "export" jazz from Louisiana to the Pacific coast—Los Angeles—in 1913. It may have been also the first jazz orchestra to feature a string bass, played by William Johnson. Keppard skipped in and out of the band, never quite willing to abandon his lucrative connections in his hometown. Young Jimmie Noone wound up in the clarinet chair with the Creoles. In 1914, they returned East to play Chicago and Cincinnati. But at no time was their music billed as jazz.

Moteger's Tuxedo Brass Band, the Eureka, the Onward Band, and the constantly traveling Mahara Minstrel Band with young William Christopher Handy, fresh out of Memphis, playing *bravura* trumpet and soulful violin solos all had their followers in the Crescent City.

There were also dozens of majestic riverboats plying the Mississippi, most of them using New Orleans and St. Louis as their southern and northern bases. On various big graceful craft, a young Kentucky musician named Fate Marable was learning the ropes, gaining experience and perfecting his piano-calliope technique. Although he never recorded, Marable played a big part in the success of numerous young second-generation musicians.

Nor must we overlook the still-prevalent tradition of funeral parade music, which has been traced back to the eighteenth century when slaves under the French, in the South, were allowed to bury their dead with bands. Accompanying the body to the cemetery, the band played indigo dirges. *Just a Closer Walk with Thee* and untitled blues were given reverent renditions throughout the long march immediately ahead of the horse-drawn hearse. But once the services had concluded, and the phalanx of mourners was well out of earshot of the cemetery officials, the band would kick up the tempo with a military-like drum roll and stomp its way back to town, attracting hundreds of spectators along the route.

They still do it today. Only in New Orleans!

The Original Jazzmen

Most of the elderly Louisiana musicians who have been interrogated time and time again in the last twenty years insist that Charles (Buddy) Bolden, first of the dynamic trumpet kings, was the musician—and barber —who accomplished the most in behalf of the early jazz. Oldest of all jazz legends is the hoary but probably accurate appraisal of Bolden's incredibly powerful lip, and his eye-popping valve technique. Jelly Roll Morton's oft-quoted "I Invented Jazz" article in the August 1938 *Down Beat* spread the Bolden reputation throughout the world some 31 years after poor Buddy had been committed to a mental institution.

> "*On still or quiet nights, while Bolden played Lincoln Park, he could be heard on the outskirts of [New Orleans] in the Carrollton Avenue section, from twelve to fourteen miles away. When he decided to fill the park, that's when he exerted his powerful ability.*"

To win the approbation of Morton, Bolden must have been indeed an extraordinary performer.

Bolden, who is said to have recorded several cylindrical discs with his horn and band—discs that have never been found—was a nervous, overly aggressive man who booked his own jobs, planted his own publicity, wrote and edited his own little scandal sheet, *The Cricket*, and cut hair in his leisure. He became insane in 1907 and died in the East Louisiana State Hospital in November 1931. It was Bolden who first popularized *The Bucket's Got a Hole in It* and *Make Me a Pallet on the Floor*, along with his classic *Funky Butt* blues novelty:

> Funky butt, funky butt
> Take it away

Willie (Bunk) Johnson went unnoticed and uncredited for his pioneer trumpet work for more than a quarter century before the writer-historian William Russell learned of his early stature from Louis Armstrong. There followed recording sessions, engagements in New York, Boston, and San Francisco, publicity throughout the world, and the inevitable plunge back to obscurity in Louisiana. The Bunk Johnson revival, launched when the toothless old musician was working in the muddy New Iberia rice fields in 1938, is unquestionably one of the saddest incidents in jazz history. And yet all of us who witnessed the embarrassing emergence of a senile, forgotten old man might well have asked one another: just how good can any musician be who is starting a career all over again at 60?

Louis (Big Eye) Nelson played fine guitar, clarinet, and accordion. He and Manuel Perez, a proficient cornetist; George Bacquet, clarinet; Pete Bocage, cornet and violin; and trombonist Frank Dusen were among the first of the Southern musicians to play jazz professionally.

In 1964, in Hollywood, old Johnny St. Cyr was still plucking his banjo, at 75, on record dates and at Disneyland on weekends. A full half-century ago he had played with Piron and with the Tuxedo and other Crescent City bands. He is the same St. Cyr (pronounced by musician colleagues "Sincere") who won some sort of immortality for merely being on the 1926 Armstrong Hot Five records.

George Lewis, ten years younger than St. Cyr, has played professionally since 1916. He cannot read music, but has toured England at least twice with his own combo since his rediscovery à la Bunk Johnson in 1942. His clarinet style, self-taught, impresses a great many musicians and New Orleans *aficionados* as being particularly crude, with both technique and intonation on a kindergarten level. But perhaps he was more polished thirty and forty years ago—at his peak—when no company cared to record him.

Edward (Kid) Ory is another, sixteen years older than Armstrong, who sat in with Bolden and moved up from being a cigar-box banjo strummer to win an international reputation for his skill with the slide trombone, and as a leader. He mastered the bass, drums, guitar, banjo, trumpet, clarinet, piano, saxophone, and valve trombone. By 1911, young Ory had moved into New Orleans from his home bailiwick of La Place, Louisiana, and organized his first band, an outfit in which Mutt Carey and even Oliver and Armstrong played briefly. He followed the Creole Band to California, in 1919, and later in Chicago he was featured with all the topflight jazz orchestras. He, too, was a member of the Armstrong's Hot Five. During World War II, living permanently in Los Angeles, Ory enjoyed truly incredible popularity with a series of Standard Oil broadcasts, appearances with Orson Welles, and gigs in Bunk Johnson's futile comeback.

Ory composed the hardy *Muskrat Ramble* and, like Lewis, toured England and the continent at least twice in the late '50s. He is unquestionably the most famous of all New Orleans trombone players. He lives today, still playing occasionally, in San Anselmo, California, a remarkable man—and musician—at 78.

A warm, personable, cigar-puffing friend of Ory's, Arthur (Bud) Scott, enjoyed talking of New Orleans on record sessions in Hollywood at the time when Ory's resurgence was getting big headlines. Scott, a guitarist and banjoist, played in the revived Ory combo and was delighted to reminisce of his youthful days in New Orleans with Bolden, Robichaux ("a sweet, society outfit that never played jazz or rags"), and Keppard. Leonard Feather has traced Scott as the man who yelled, "Oh, play that thing!" on the King Oliver *Dippermouth Blues* 1923 record, a cry that has become one of the most revered traditions in jazz whenever *Dippermouth* is recorded or played "live." * Scott said something during a happy *History of Jazz* session in June 1944 that has somehow stuck:

> "*There were a lot of bad bands and bad music in New Orleans, too. The city was so musical that it seemed like just everybody tried to be a musician. The amateur spasm bands were terrible, and so were a lot of the marching groups. Of course we didn't call jazz 'jazz' in those days. That word came later.*"

Scott died five years after his memorable *Crawfish Blues* session in Hollywood.

Henry (Kid) Rena, 1900-1949, was another in the long and illustrious

---

* Leonard Feather, *The Encyclopedia of Jazz* (New York: Horizon Press Inc., 1960), p. 412.

line of trumpet players who helped make jazz the art it has become. He worked under Ory, and led his own band sporadically after 1924.

One year older, Louis (Kid Shots) Madison died one year earlier than his friend Rena. Madison also played trumpet (cornet as a youngster). Kid Shots blew with the Tuxedo unit, Celestin, Dusen, and, during the dark years of the Depression, a WPA brass band.

Tom (Mutt) Carey, previously mentioned as a member of Dusen's Eagle Band, deserves more. Born in New Orleans in 1892, he died in 1948 in San Francisco while featured with Ory. Starting as a drummer, Carey switched to cornet–trumpet and played in his brother's (Jack Carey's) band. Off and on, through the decades, Mutt worked as a musician—and as a mailman, pullman porter, and salesman—and was at last swept back into a certain amount of prominence with Ory in 1944. Like Chris Kelly, Carey was at his best using mutes. Some even today rate him alongside Oliver and Armstrong for sheer musicianship.

Kelly, Rena, Madison, and Carey were all superior trumpeters. Let's look at three bass men who have somehow gone unrecognized in connection with the old days of honestly-inspired jazz origination:

Wellman Braud began at 12, with a violin, in St. James, Louisiana. Later he migrated to the "district" and snared a job at Tom Anderson's saloon, going over to bass about 1918 after leaving New Orleans and, like so many musicians, moving north to Chicago. Eventually he landed with Duke Ellington, and in 1956 he toured Europe with Ory. Braud today is virtually retired, and living in Brooklyn, but still open for an occasional gig at 73.

George (Pops) Foster is a year younger, and enjoys his twilight days in San Francisco at a cool but alert 72. A kid cello player, Foster swept into New Orleans from his home, a farm north of the city, in 1902. He preferred the river to Storyville and, as every jazz filbert knows, wound up as string bassist with the "big" Armstrong orchestra of 1935-40, followed by tours of Europe with Milton Mezzrow, Jimmy Archey, and Sammy Price. Recently he worked long engagements with Earl (Fatha') Hines. His position in the field will always be secure. No man ever slapped a bass like the bespectacled, good-natured Pops!

Ed Garland is the third distinguished bassist who came out of New Orleans. Born in 1895, he was only 49 when he joined Bud Scott, Zutty Singleton, Barney Bigard, and other hand-picked musicians in recording for Capitol's *History of Jazz* album series in 1944. Still active in Los Angeles, Garland recalls his days with the Excelsior, Eagle, Imperial, and Security bands vividly. He deserted New Orleans in 1914. Little Ed, who appears to weigh all of 130 pounds and is often, on a record date, hidden by his big bull fiddle, prefers the West Coast today, but will hit the road when necessary. His work with Keppard, Oliver, Ory, and Hines is testimony to his skill and his understanding of authentic Louisiana-styled jazz. Old friends call him "Montudie."

John Lindsay (1894-1950), bass and trombone; Honore Dutrey (1890-1937), trombone; Buddy Petit (1887-1931), cornet; Tommy Ladnier (1900-1939), trumpet—a particular favorite of the French critic, Hugues Panassié; and Jim Robinson, the only Southern musician I ever heard of who served in World War I, and who is still active after a long career as a trombonist with Rena, the Tuxedo band and George Lewis are still other capable performers who are even now well remembered by Louisiana musicians. Each drove a peg in the jazz flooring.

KING JOE

Son of a plantation cook, Joe Oliver moved into the lively river city of New Orleans as a youngster, lost an eye in a street accident, picked up on slide trombone briefly and then abandoned it in favor of a cornet, and worked in the nondescript Melrose Brass Band before organizing a unit of his own.

Like Buddy Bolden before him, Oliver was an incredibly powerful soloist, with large, full, muscular lips and an embouchure that gave his horn a fiercely penetrating, brassy sound. In 1911 at the 101 Ranch, where he was paid $1.25 a night as a leader fee, young Joe got his start despite his physical handicap. Danny Barker, the New Orleans guitarist, once said to me, "He played so good that nobody noticed he was one-eyed."

From the Franklin Street musicians' oasis, Joe moved to a Bienville Street cabaret operated by the Abadee brothers. Neither was a philanthropist. Sharing leader billing with Richard M. Jones, the flashy pianist who sang, wrote songs, and enjoyed his role as a personality kid, Oliver was raised to a $12.50 weekly salary and given all the tips he could split with Jones and his musicians.

It was, time proved, an intolerable arrangement, but the Oliver-Jones alliance lasted long enough for Oliver to enhance his reputation in the free-wheeling "district" and acquire a better job—at $25 a week and tips —at Pete Lala's Cafe. Oliver followed the immensely popular Bolden into Lala's and hardly missed a beat as he provided a swinging brand of music that the musicians, house girls, and influential patrons all applauded wildly. Oliver, by 1917, and reputedly because of Kid Ory's special enthusiasm, became "King." He was one of several, including Bolden, Freddie Keppard, and Louis Armstrong, who were privileged to use the royal title.

Mutt Carey, a superb cornetist himself, has been quoted many times on Oliver's way of playing. Carey described it as "freakish" because of Oliver's reliance on mutes, cups, glasses, and even buckets. It was by using these artificial devices that King Joe obtained his unique sounds. Carey, who outlived Oliver ten years, was in no way belittling his friend's abilities. He always ended his remarks by grinning and adding, "I used all them gimmicks too. I was just as freakish."

And another quote, from the trombonist Preston Jackson:

> *"Oliver used to practice very hard. I remember he once told me it took him ten years to get a tone on his instrument. He used a half-cocked mute, and how he could make it talk! He played the variation style too; running chords, I mean. His ear was wonderful—that helped a lot."* *

AT THE PIANO

As a solo instrument, the piano was particularly popular in the drinking and pleasure palaces of New Orleans' Storyville. In the ornately-furnished parlors of Lulu White's Mahogany Hall and the luxurious mansions of Antonia P. Gonzalez, Josie Arlington, and Gypsy Shaeffer, men like Tony Jackson entertained with the popular songs of the moment, singing forcefully while playing a piano in the modish ragtime manner. Jackson, who could play in any key even though he was unable to read music, was rivalled only by the illustrious Jelly Roll Morton as New Orleans' number one solo entertainer.

Nobody ever argued about Jackson's talents. Nor do they today.

He could sing—something like Nat Cole, only better, said Clarence Williams years later—and his piano technique was by far the most advanced in the South. He was effeminate and homely, but when he sat down at the piano, as the ads say, his fingerbusters made all the other pianists want to take up drums. Tony composed *Pretty Baby* and years later became almost as popular in Chicago as he had been in Louisiana. He died in Chicago in 1921.

Kid Ross, Sammy Davis (not related to the dancing singer of a half century later), Alfred Wilson, and Albert Cahill were other outstanding solo pianists of the period. Yet it was Jackson, according to Morton, who was the greatest. Jelly loved to recall scenes of Jackson's triumph:

* Nat Shapiro and Nat Hentoff, *Hear Me Talkin' to Ya* (New York: Holt, Rinehart & Winston, 1955), pp. 41-42.

> "*When Tony walked in, all the other pianists would get up from the piano stool. . . . At Gypsy Schaeffer's, when Tony started playing and singing, they would open up the big champagne bottles and start pouring. He was the best.*"

Morton, about whom entire books have been written, came along a few years after Jackson. They later worked together, forming a showmanly act that clicked consistently before they split up and took separate routes. Jelly Roll, a hustling promoter, was never successful in getting Jackson's talent on records, however.

Morton—Ferdinand Joseph La Menthe—was born in Gulfport, Louisiana, in 1885. At seven he was playing mandolin. At ten, he could attract a crowd with his ragtime piano solos. An extrovert's extrovert, Jelly Roll Morton matured early, acquired a reputation quickly not only as a topflight musician, but also as a wit, braggart, business man, promoter, and flashy dresser.

There were still other versatile piano men of the original New Orleans cradle, men who made other contributions to the jazz art.

Richard M. Jones, pianist and composer, played in the Eureka Brass Band in 1902 and gained wide renown for his doubles: pipe organ, piano, cornet, alto horn, and other instruments came easy for him. *Trouble in Mind*, *Your Red Wagon*, and *Riverside Blues* are all his songs, and Lou Levy, who now publishes them in New York, reports that they earn more income today than they did in the '20s. Jones, who died in Chicago in 1945, worked with Clarence Williams and, like him, supervised hundreds of recording sessions. A few records under his own name are still prized by collectors of early jazz discs.

Clarence (Blue Five) Williams, a pianist and composer born in 1893 and now residing in Brooklyn, grew up in the "district" in his teens and gigged all over Louisiana and Texas with the first jazzmen. His interests were different from those of his associates. A gifted composer, Williams also possessed a marked liking for business details, and while others were writing successful songs and selling them outright for as much as $50 and as little as a bottle of wine, Williams studiously learned the U.S. copyright laws and launched his own music publishing firm. He had the maestro A. J. Piron as his partner in the first Negro music company in the South. Later, he composed *Gulf Coast Blues*, *Sugar Blues*, and *Royal Garden Blues*, and accompanied great singers like Bessie Smith, Sippie Wallace, and his wife, Eva Taylor. He was probably the first Negro artists and repertoire man in the world, and helped Armstrong, Bechet, and numerous others succeed as record artists. How different is his story from those of the other pioneer Louisiana jazzmen!

THOSE HALCYON DAYS

But was there ever a place like New Orleans?

It was a period to remember fondly. The musicians had their own hangouts, after-hours in the early morning, where they drank and played for kicks, and met their women. Sometimes they would eat a little something. Pete Lala's Cafe and the 101 Ranch were favored clubs. Here were the world's first jam sessions, cutting contests (not with knives, but with horns), and surely the first bars to accommodate jazzmen. It was a city, even then, of excellent restaurants. La Louisiane, at 725 Iberville, was opened in 1881; the chef Antoine Alciatore founded Antoine's in 1876. Successful musicians had everything they wanted.

It was an optimistic, promising era with World War I still in the future and the Spanish-American War all but forgotten. The year 1912 is as representative as any:

New Mexico and Arizona joined the Union, bringing the number of states to 48.

Airplanes were being made a little better, and they stayed in the air a little longer.

Motor cars were crowding horses off the city streets.

Big Jim Thorpe was the greatest athlete in the world.

George M. Cohan, Fred Stone, Eddie Foy, David Warfield, and David Belasco were America's favorite showmen, but ribald burlesque shows produced by the Minsky brothers in New York set the box-office records.

The Girl Scouts of America was founded.

And the year's biggest song hits included *When I Lost You*, *Moonlight Bay*, *The Sweetheart of Sigma Chi*, the inevitable *My Melancholy Baby*, and the first international hit with authentic, deep-South jazz roots, W. C. Handy's *Memphis Blues*, which had no lyrics and was copyrighted as a simple little piano solo.

In New York, the most luxurious restaurants featured the same old boring piano-violin duets, long popular in Europe, which offered semiclassical, pseudoclassical, and hackneyed popular music with meals. In New Orleans, in those *sans souci* days just before World War I, a gloriously different mood and music were evident. The blues, ragtime, hollers, slave songs, polkas, spirituals, quadrilles, mazurkas, and waltzes had all jelled into a single, daring, almost explosive music. All had somehow fused into jazz.

> *"Those were happy days, man, happy days. Buy a keg of beer for one dollar and a bag full of food for another and have a* cowein . . . *there were 2,000 registered girls and must have been 10,000 unregistered. And all crazy about clarinet blowers."*

That's an oft-printed quote from Picou. But Clarence Williams, still a creative artist, also recalls that "a small glass of beer cost a silver dollar in the more elegant establishments like Lulu White's, where one had to look white or Spanish to be admitted." * Countess Willie Piazza's hospitable house at 317 North Basin Street was no less palatial; only the wealthy were welcomed as clients.

If her place was perhaps not so ornate, Antonia Gonzalez had a natural trump card to snare her share of business in the Tenderloin. She put on her most glamorous gown and entertained between tricks with spectacular trumpet solos. Many a fine musician played the bordellos, but Spencer Williams (unrelated to Clarence, but a close friend and associate) is probably the only musician who was reared in one. The nephew of Lulu White, Spencer moved in to Lulu's Mahogany Hall when his mother died. As he recalls it:

> *"I became her adopted son, and every night I'd go to sleep hearing the piano playing lively ragtime tunes. It would still be playing when I awoke in the morning. . . .*
> *The saloons in those days never closed their doors. Little boys and grownups walked along the streets whistling jazz tunes."* †

Spencer Williams later composed *Mahogany Hall Stomp*, which was recorded and popularized in jazz circles by Louis Armstrong. His credits, before he moved to Europe permanently in the 1930s, also included *I Ain't Got Nobody, Royal Garden Blues, I Found a New Baby,* and other classic jazz songs.

Lizzie Miles was the outstanding blues singer of the early period, and although she sang with a half-dozen bands as far back as 1910, she was still active at 68 when she died, in March 1963, at her Tonti Street home in the Vieux Carré after returning from a Sunday mass.

Lizzie had a gimmick. On the most-requested standards like *Bill Bailey, Salty Dog,* and *Up a Lazy River,* she would break out in her powerful

* Shapiro and Hentoff, *Hear Me Talkin' to Ya,* p. 11.
† *Ibid.,* p. 7.

contralto in French—or a patois which melodically combined French with common Creole English. Whatever it was, it was unerringly effective. Recording her in 1950 at Station WDSU was a pleasure, and afterward, almost to the time of her passing, Lizzie persisted in mailing regularly to my Hollywood office generous collections of religious literature. Between takes on a session, she stirred her chicory coffee and reminisced of years long gone, and of her singing with tent shows, in the Alabama Minstrel troupe, and on the Negro vaudeville "wheel" in the South, and how she "owned" Paris briefly in her bright, beaded, spangled gowns. On records in the '20s she was accompanied by giants, not obscure sidemen. Morton, Oliver and Clarence Williams were "right pleased," she said, to record behind her persuasive, dramatic voice.

But now Lizzie is gone and the daily delivery of mail to my desk is perhaps a bit less exciting. Better fem blues shouters may have come along later but they didn't come out of New Orleans. Liz was the Queen.

3

Hello,

LOUIS

If ever there lived a man with less than half a chance to become a law-abiding millionaire, Daniel Louis Armstrong is the man.

His early days in the streets of New Orleans were just that—a life in the streets, like a stray mongrel. On New Year's Eve of 1913, when Louis was only 13, he "borrowed" a .38 revolver, shot it off at the corner of Perdido and Rampart Streets, and was immediately arrested by an elderly detective.

"I didn't even get to celebrate the arrival of the new year a couple of hours later," Louis chortles now. They put him in the Waifs' Home, and in his 1936 autobiography *Swing That Music* he recalls how he got his nickname:

> *"After a short while I had got so used to the Home that I forgot all about the streets. When the other kids started calling me nicknames I knew everything was all right. I have a pretty big mouth,*

ILLUSTRATION: Louis Armstrong. (Photograph by Charlie Mihn.)

20

*so they hit on that, and began calling me Gatemouth or Satchel-
mouth, and that Satchelmouth has stuck to me all my life, except
that now it's been made into Satchmo'—Satchmo' Armstrong."* *

He writes of his first horn, presented him by Peter Davis, the man in
charge of music at the Home, and how he was made leader of the band
within a few weeks.

*"I had a different uniform from the other boys. If they'd have blue
coats with white trousers, I would have a cream-colored coat and
blue trousers, all different. . . . I improved so much with this band
that Mr. Davis began to be proud of us. He began to take us to out-
ings and to street parades. We were glad to get a chance to see the
streets of the city again."* †

After some 18 months, Louis was released to his home in James Alley,
at Liberty and Perdido in the back-of-town section, where he resided
with his father, Willie, a turpentine worker; his mother, Mary-Ann; and
his younger sister, Beatrice, whom he has always fondly called "Mamma
Lucy."

Little Louis had no choice. Despite his love of music, he was forced to
get a job. First, he sold newspapers. Then he worked at a New Orleans
dairy—the Cloverland. He was 17 before he resumed playing his little
cornet. He writes:

*"Everybody was playing cornet then, but King Oliver, Papa Joe to
me, was way out in front of them all as the very best. . . . He was so
powerful he used to blow a cornet out of tune every two or three
months. I was constantly hanging around him. I looked towards him
as though he were some kind of god, or something similar. He was
my inspiration."* ‡

Joe Lindsay, a drummer, formed a six-piece kid jazz combo with
Armstrong in 1918. They emulated the Kid Ory–Joe Oliver band note
for note. Louis' break came almost immediately, although not as he had
hoped it might. Oliver made his decision to go to Chicago to work with
Bill Johnson and what was left of the Original Creoles. And Ory, wisely,
gave Oliver's chair to Armstrong.

* Louis Armstrong, *Swing That Music* (New York: Longmans, Green & Co., Inc.,
1936), p. 6. Reprinted by permission of David McKay Co., Inc.
 † *Ibid.*, pp. 17-18.
 ‡ *Ibid.*, pp. 25-26.

It proved a pleasant association. For eighteen months Ory's band played at Pete Lala's. They worked numerous private parties as well, and college dances at Tulane University. Louis married Daisy Parker, but it was a mismatch from the start, Louis writes, and he thinks his domestic difficulties may have affected his musicianship for a brief period.*

Young Louis was offered the opportunity of playing with Fate Marable's orchestra on the steamer, Dixie Belle, the largest and best of the Mississippi river paddle-wheel boats. In the spring of 1920, Armstrong boarded the immense craft at its berth at the foot of Canal street, accompanied by his mother and "Mamma Lucy." Daisy did not show up. For seven months, and nearly 2,000 miles, Louis plied the river. His reputation spread. Marable regarded him as a brilliant sideman. "It was a mess of traveling," Armstrong said later, "for a lonesome kid who had always been afraid to leave home before."

Armstrong broke in a brand new horn on that trip. One of the older musicians, David Jones, taught him to perfect his reading of music. The river job was a happy one for Louis. So much so, that he signed up again, and in the spring of 1921 made the long trek to St. Paul, arriving just before Labor Day. After that second trip, however, he tired of the water and upon his return to New Orleans he quit Marable, divorced his wife Daisy, and worked with the Tuxedo Marching Band "between bookings."

One day the following July (1922) after a long and tiring march in the humid, heavy summer air, Louis was handed a telegram. It was from Papa Joe Oliver. Oliver wanted Louis to join him in Chicago. It took some eight seconds for Armstrong to accept. As Armstrong told me years later, in Hollywood:

"*I arrived at the old LaSalle street station at night. The Gardens was at Thirty-first and Gordon Streets out on the South Side. I was nervous, and wondering how I'd make out. Joe had a lot of my old pals with him, Baby Dodds, Honore Dutrey, Johnny Dodds, clarinet, and Bill Johnson on bass, along with a piano and second trumpet whose names I've forgotten. I moved in with the Olivers, and the thing I recollect first aside from how fine that band was is my meeting up with the pianist over at the Dreamland Cafe with Ollie Powers' outfit. Her name was Lillian Hardin. She became my second wife at Chicago's City Hall on February 5, 1924.*"

On his first record session, in Richmond, Indiana, for the Gennett firm in April 1923, the 22-year-old Louis enjoyed one of his greatest thrills

* *Ibid.*, pp. 37-38.

when engineers placed him twenty feet back of the other musicians—including iron-lipped King Oliver, because the equipment would have been damaged had he been nearer.

About a year later, he quit Oliver with reluctance. Lil Hardin Armstrong had long been urging her husband to move out on his own. Yet Louis quit his second horn chair to take the first chair with Powers at the Dreamland with little confidence. The job lasted only a few weeks. Louis left Powers—and Chicago—to accept an offer from the great Fletcher Henderson in New York.

Henderson, a dapper college man who had studied chemistry and who might have become a prominent scientist, had seen Armstrong perform in New Orleans five years previously. "I never forgot that kid," he told me later. "Louis was even better than Oliver and let no man tell you differently." Known as "Smack" to fellow musicians, Henderson was probably the first Negro to orchestrate jazz for full-sized orchestras. He was a capable pianist as well. And his younger brother Horace Henderson likewise excelled as an arranger and pianist.

Louis joined the Hendersons at the old Roseland ballroom, just off Times Square at Fifty-first and Broadway. Nobody in Manhattan, Henderson excepted, had heard of him. None cared. And although he didn't get back to Chicago, and his wife Lil, for a full year, Louis admits nothing much happened in those fifty-odd weeks. "I met a lot of nice musicians," he says now. "Red Nichols, Miff Mole, and Sam Lanin I most remember, of those who came around to see us."

Louis did meet up with his Louisiana buddy, Clarence Williams, and through him earned a pot of extra money making records with Williams' Blue Five, and freshly-styled accompaniments to Virginia Liston, Josephine Beatty, Margaret Johnson, and Sippie Wallace, as well as to Eva Taylor, Maggie Jones, Clara Smith, Bessie Smith, Ma Rainey, Trixie Smith, Coot Grant, and "Kid" Wesley Wilson.

Bessie Smith was, in the opinion of most musicians, the most moving, most effective, and most talented blues singer who ever lived. Ma Rainey was close. Armstrong's soulful playing behind these great stars of the Negro entertainment world helped establish his name even more.

On this same trip he recorded frequently with the sophisticated Henderson band, one of the most memorable ever to be assembled, with men like Coleman Hawkins, Don Redman and Buster Bailey in the reed section; Charlie Green on trombone; Kaiser Marshall, drums; Charles Dixon, banjo; and Elmer Chambers and Howard Scott, trumpets. They appeared, not always under Henderson's name, on the Columbia, Vocalion and Perfect labels and are still sought by serious collectors.

But Armstrong, temporarily at least, had had enough of Gotham. He gave "Smack" his notice and checked out of his tiny Harlem hotel room

In Chicago, he returned to the Dreamland, where his wife was now th
leader of an eight-piece unit. Louis gradually attracted more attention
His playing improved. So did his confidence, and his showmanship. By
1926, he moved over to the popular Vendome theater to play under Prof
Erskine Tate's baton, and doubled at night in Carrol Dickerson's orchestra
at the hectic Sunset Cabaret.

Cook County, Illinois, forcefully resisted the Volstead Act that had
dimmed New Orleans' bright lights. Prohibition was unwanted and, to a
degree, unnoticed. Hoodlums from a dozen gangs made immense profit
dealing in illegal liquor. Hundreds of "speakeasies" operated openly
Chicago seemed to flourish, as did Kansas City later, in the gangster
period. The by-product was an artificial prosperity for musicians, singer
and performers of every kind. It was the incredibly lawless and infamous
Al Capone period.

The billing above the Sunset's entrance, in lettering a yard high, could
be seen for a block:

LOUIS ARMSTRONG
World's Greatest Trumpet Player

Joe Glaser was the Sunset's aggressive, persuasive, baseball-crazy
proprietor. He loved the games at nearby Comiskey Park, home of the
White Sox, but he loved the trumpet style and income possibilities of
Armstrong even more. He became his manager.

When Dickerson ran out his contract, Armstrong took over the Sun-
set Band. It was at this time, too, with the help of Thomas G. Rockwell,
that Louis recorded his immortal Hot Five and Hot Seven records for
Okeh. On November 12, 1925, with Kid Ory, who had moved North
from a near-dead New Orleans, on trombone; Johnny Dodds, clarinet;
Johnny St. Cyr, banjo; and Louis' wife Lil on piano, the quintet made
My Heart, Yes I'm in the Barrel, and *Gut Bucket Blues. Come Back
Sweet Papa, Georgia Grind, Cornet Chop Suey, Heebie Jeebies, Muskrat
Ramble, Oriental Strut,* and *You're Next* were all cut on sessions the
following February.

In June and November 1926, the Hot Five returned to etch *Don't
Forget to Mess Around, I'm Gonna Gitcha, Dropping Shucks, Who's It,
The King of the Zulus, Lonesome Blues, Big Fat Ma and Skinny Pa,
Sweet Little Papa, Jazz Lips, Skid-Dat-De-Dat, Big Butter and Egg Man,
Sunset Cafe Stomp, You Made Me Love You, Irish Black Bottom,* and
Leave Mine Alone, with John Thomas replacing Ory as trombonist on the
last three titles. All were big sellers. Musicians tried to acquire copies of
every title.

Little Louis, now a big boy, was in like Coolidge. He had become, indeed, the greatest trumpet player in the world.

It was the time of the "Charleston" dance craze. And it was, in other ways, a period to remember. Let's look back for a moment at 1926.

Nearly 2,000 violators of the Volstead Act died of poison liquor.

Floyd Bennett and Lt. Cdr. Richard E. Byrd flew over the North Pole for the first time.

Screen idol Rudolph Valentino died.

Gertrude (Trudy) Ederle became the first woman to swim the English Channel.

NBC inaugurated a radio network.

Gene Tunney dethroned Jack Dempsey by decision in Philadelphia.

The "Black Bottom" was introduced, and became as popular a dance, almost, as the "Charleston."

Ernest Hemingway's *The Sun Also Rises* and Thorne Smith's *Topper* were best-selling books.

Billy Mitchell was court-martialed.

Needle beer sold at $38 a case, champagne at $95, Scotch at $48 and rye, $85. And the U.S.A. observed its 150th birthday anniversary with a Sesquicentennial Exposition at Philadelphia.

The hit songs were *Among My Souvenirs, Chloe, At Sundown, Back in Your Own Back Yard, Let a Smile Be Your Umbrella, My Heart Stood Still, Me and My Shadow,* and *My Blue Heaven.*

It was also a Louis Armstrong year.

Louis was 26, in his physical prime, well-established throughout the Middle West—the corn belt—and unquestionably the greatest trumpet player alive. He had stamina, power, chops (lips) that every jazzman envied and technique that topped even that of his idol, King Joe Oliver, and the Boldens and Keppards before him. Chicago was his oyster, and his records had made him known west to San Francisco and east up to Boston. He was a particular favorite in the Deep South, where his discs were bought in great quantities.

When Dickerson and his band moved out of the Sunset, Glaser made Louis leader of the house orchestra, with two pianos featured. Armstrong still doubled in the Vendome pit under Tate's baton.

Closing at the Sunset in 1928, Louis worked briefly at the Metropolitan

Theater with Clarence Jones, the singer, and then returned to the Dickerson fold at the Savoy dance hall. It was a fine band, with Louis' old pal the genial Zutty Singleton, on drums; Mancy Carr, banjo; Gene Anderson piano; Pete Briggs, tuba; Jimmy Strong, sax and clarinet; Freddy Robinson, trombone; and Homer Hobson at the piano.

The bird was outgrowing the nest, however. As the weeks and months flew by, Armstrong became the attraction. Dickerson meant little in the face of Louis' spectacular horn pyrotechnics. In 1929, after about a year at the Savoy, he and the musicians decided to head for New York in four motor cars. Each man carried twenty dollars.

Louis and the troupe traveled leisurely, taking in places they had never seen before. Dayton, Detroit, Cleveland, Buffalo, and Niagara Falls were all on their itinerary, and after Dickerson's car was demolished in a highway crash they crowded into the other three and rolled into Manhattan, broke but triumphant.

Zutty distinctly remembers that all the time they were riding east, mile after mile in the rain, hot sun, and occasional fog, they heard little from Armstrong. "He was always curled up in the back seat asleep," Zutty says.

Rockwell, a soft-spoken Irish booker with a strong liking for jazz and Negro musicians, was the first man Armstrong contacted in Gotham. He booked Louis and the Dickerson band, under Armstrong's name, at Connie's Inn, run by Connie Immerman in the heart of Harlem. Along with the old, original Cotton Club, and Small's, Connie's Inn was one of the most popular and expensive clubs in the world. Whites as well as residents of Harlem jammed it every night, eagerly paying a $10 cover charge and exorbitant prices for drinks and food of dubious quality.

It was at Connie's Inn, with Louis playing and singing a new specialty number in the smash "Hot Chocolates" show, that he introduced and popularized *Ain't Misbehavin'*, composed by his friends, Harry Brooks and young pianist Thomas (Fats) Waller. Coast-to-coast radio broadcasts every night sent Armstrong's glorious trumpet and humorous vocal style to millions of listeners. He continued recording as well. Fronting the Dickerson orchestra on July 19, 1929, he waxed (and in those days, sound actually was captured on thick, round wax cakes) *Ain't Misbehavin'*, *Black and Blue*, *That Rhythm Man*, and *Sweet Savannah Sue* for Okeh, again thanks to Rockwell's interest.

He followed them by an odd session a month later with Tommy and Jimmy Dorsey's pickup combo, backing Seger Ellis' *Ain't Misbehavin'* and *True Blue Lou*. And again, with his Connie's Inn crew, he made *Some of These Days* and *When You're Smiling* (instrumentally), *Some of These Days* and *When You're Smiling* (vocally), *After You've Gone*, and two titles that were never issued, to my knowledge, *Little By Little* and *Oh Look What You've Done to Me.*

But even the "Hot Chocolates" show finally ended its run and, with no immediate job definite, the band broke up and most of Louis' sidemen returned to Chicago. Joe Glaser helped set up a new arrangement—fronting Luis Russell's orchestra on a long and tiring Southern tour. Russell, a Panamanian pianist, proved an excellent Armstrong partner. They later played Sebastian's Cotton Club in Culver City, so close to the immense Metro-Goldwyn-Mayer motion picture factory that Louis could "toss my soiled handkerchiefs over on top of Wally Beery's dressing room."

Armstrong hung around Hollywood (a place that loosely includes not only Culver City but Burbank, Van Nuys, Glendale, Pasadena, Encino, Tarzana, Sherman Oaks, North Hollywood, and the sprawling city of Los Angeles itself) about a year, fronting the Russell band, before he trained back to Chicago in 1931 and organized another, this one his own, hand-picked by him and Glaser.

From Chicago, and then New Orleans, Louis, by now enjoying a pride and confidence he had never had, played St. Louis five weeks, then the old Lafayette Theater in New York, and a second run, with Les Hite's orchestra, at the Cotton Club in California. From there he bought a Buick, drove it to Chicago, settled some business with Lil Armstrong, and shoved off for England.

Although Louis intended the trip as a vacation, Glaser quickly booked him into the London Palladium, a top theater renowned for its superior lighting and production features, in June of 1932.

It was a dreary, bleak, and despondent period as the Depression reached its depths. But Londoners nonetheless packed the Palladium for two weeks. And then Louis toured England and Scotland with Bruts Gonella, Lou Davis, Buddy Featherstonehaugh, and other first-rank British musicians assisting him. His appeal was based on his records. In those days, the British Broadcasting Corporation, government-operated, aired mostly classical music, talk, and news. English musicians and pop music fans could hear what they wanted only on discs. Also, they had something unknown in the U.S.A., Hot Clubs, comprised of jazz fanatics and professional and amateur musicians. To the British, American jazz had developed into a singularly unique art.

The French were no less enthusiastic. Louis gives his own view:

"Europe, you know, had gone pretty crazy over American jazz towards the end of the war when the Original Dixieland Jazz Band

arrived in London and even made records there. Then came Big Jim Europe, and other early American bands, and later Duke Ellington, Cab Calloway, and famous jazz combinations. Right from the first, English and European jazz critics had taken this music seriously, a lot more seriously than we did at home, and wrote a good deal about it —we just liked it without thinking so much about it. And it is right to say they heard the very best of our bands and records and did not have to listen to so much of the tin-panny kind of trash music that has made a lot of our home folks sick of any kind of jazz—and I don't blame them much, either." **

Louis visited Paris briefly, returned home the very day in November that Franklin Delano Roosevelt was first elected President, toured six months, and returned to England in July 1933. A jaunt through the Continent followed, with Armstrong proving a gracious and fantastically popular goodwill ambassador in a dozen countries.

When he once again sailed into New York harbor in January 1935, Louis Armstrong was the king of all kings of jazz. Long forgotten were his New Orleans elders, the beloved Joe Oliver, now living in poverty; Freddie Keppard, dead of alcohol; and Buddy Bolden, deceased after many years in an insane asylum.

Another new crop of jazzmen had arisen. The saccharine-styled dance orchestras that had dominated the popular music scene—records and airwaves—were fast being displaced by Glen Gray and the Casa Loma orchestra out of Canada; the Paul Whiteman unit with Jack and Charlie Teagarden, Mildred Bailey, and Johnny Mercer; the new and jazz-oriented crew led jointly by the battling Dorsey brothers; and the most exciting, most rhythmic band of all, Benny Goodman's history-making aggregation at Billy Rose's Music Hall in New York.

Louis had frequently talked about "swinging" music in his career. Now "swing" was a shining, exciting big new thing in jazz. Armstrong got off the boat and found that his New Orleans style of music was now palatable not only to all-colored audiences and musicians, but to college students, housewives, and business men in all forty-eight states.

Again taking over the Luis Russell orchestra, Armstrong returned to Hollywood, appeared in *Pennies from Heaven* with Bing Crosby (does anyone remember his *Skeleton in the Closet* production number?) and began tours lasting into years with his big band—Russell's—which featured Jay Higginbotham's trombone, Charlie Holmes' alto, and the generally out-of-tune clarinet of Bingie Madison. For Decca, which had revolutionized the record industry about this time by launching a new

* Armstrong, *Swing That Music*, p. 102.

company selling discs at three for a dollar—the idea of the astute brothers Jack and David Kapp—the Armstrong ensemble recorded hundreds of now-famous masters.

Joe Glaser, as Louis' manager, gradually succeeded in changing his client's public image from a jazz trumpet soloist who played freak high notes and yelled "Yeah, man, yeah," to a versatile, all-around entertainer, musician, singer, and actor who, by the late 1950s had worked up to an amazing plateau that found him co-starring with Bing Crosby, Grace Kelly, and Frank Sinatra in the extremely successful motion picture, *High Society*.

He also abandoned his big band, preferring to tour with a less-expensive, easier-to-travel combo since 1947, following his appearance in a disappointing, ineptly-made movie, *New Orleans*, in which the talents of Armstrong, Billie Holiday, and others were wasted. The late Jack Teagarden, Barney Bigard, Arvell Shaw, Dick Cary, and the late Big Sid Catlett, who had drummed in the big Armstrong orchestra, comprised the first combo, and later Billy Kyle, Joe Darensbourg, and Trummie Young proved able replacements.

The late 1950s saw the jovial, always-smiling Louis becoming an international ambassador of truly extraordinary stature. He toured Europe many times, and was as successful in Japan as in Stockholm.

With the years, Armstrong has purveyed, with enviable showmanship, American jazz on every continent. Nor does he have to work for a living. In June 1963, I contacted Manager Glaser to contract for Louis to come into a recording studio to make just one number for the series of long-playing albums known as *The Jazz Story*.

"What will you pay him for one tune?" Glaser asked sharply over the transcontinental telephone.

"Oh, maybe $1,000 for thirty or forty minutes of his time," I answered. "More if his usual fee is higher."

The other end of the line was silent for several seconds. Then came Glaser's brusque retort:

"Louis and I have been partners for 35 years. He became a millionaire many years ago and so did I. To tell you the truth, Dave, I wouldn't telephone and get him out of bed for a thousand bucks.

"You think the Angels will ever beat the Yankees out of a pennant?"

I don't know about the future of the American League, but I do know I have two excellent Armstrong masters in the five-volume, all-inclusive package, *The Jazz Story*. Even at 64, King Louis is worth more than $1,000 an hour.

4

Chicago and the Golden Era

What causes a city to change, lose its special pre-eminence, and modify its whole way of life? For New Orleans the answer is fairly simple: It begins with World War I and ends with prohibition. World War I resulted in a campaign to clean up the boisterous, segregated Storyville area (named after a city alderman, Sidney Story, when it opened in 1897) which covered thirty-eight city blocks bounded by Perdido and Gravier streets and Franklin and Locust streets. Zutty Singleton, one of the most gregarious and gracious of jazzmen, who grew up there, has recounted to me how it happened:

> "In 1917, in the middle of our war with Germany, the Navy Department established a base by the Mississippi River right close to the 'district' and the big brass in Washington demanded that the city permanently close the Storyville area. There was some argument, as I recall, but on November 12 everybody moved out.
> It was a sight none of us will ever forget, that last night with all

ILLUSTRATION: Frank Teschemacher, the Chicago clarinetist, killed in a motor car crash at the peak of the Golden Era.

the bands playing, and the rag pianists going hour after hour, only stopping a moment to drink up. The madames of the big, fancy, high-priced establishments rode out in their carriages to other parts of the city and to other towns and places along the Gulf. There were parades and fireworks and last goodbyes like we'd never seen before —you might have thought the Germans had arrived.

Men and women walked out of the 'district' carrying everything they owned, chairs, clothes, mattresses, little children in hand, why it was an all-night procession.

I guess New Orleans was never quite the same after that. At least it never was to me."

Closing of the area meant the end of jobs for musicians, singers and hundreds of other workers. But it was even more. It was the coda for a fantastic era, and the termination of New Orleans as the world's hotbed of jazz.

THE EXODUS

Chicago loomed, to the north, as the next-best site for jazz and jazzmen.

Joe Oliver wrapped his horn carefully, packed his bags and took the train to Illinois in early 1918, only months after the close of the bawdy "district." He arrived at the old, red-bricked Dearborn station and was met by Bill Johnson, the bassist with the Original Creole Band, which had been touring for a half-dozen years. The Creoles were tired of the road; the war had severely curtailed transportation for civilians, anyway. Johnson got a job on Chicago's South Side at a place known as the Royal Gardens.

"Now the King's in town," Johnson greeted one-eyed Joe, and Oliver not only cheerfully worked the Royal Gardens from 8:00 until 1:00 every night, but he swiftly shifted over to the Dreamland Cafe to continue until 6:00 a.m. In the groups were Johnson, bass; young Jimmie Noone on clarinet; Eddie Vincon, trombone; Lottie Taylor, piano; and Paul Barbarin, drums. At Dreamland, Oliver was delighted to work with other old friends from home: Sidney Bechet, who expertly doubled soprano saxophone and clarinet, and the sterling bassist Wellman Braud, among others.

Other musicians from New Orleans had gone to the Windy City well ahead of Oliver. Jack Laine had fronted the only white jazz orchestra in New Orleans in the early 1900s. Now, a new band came on strong in the white section of the city. Led by trombonist Tom Brown, it featured Gus Mueller (who later starred with Whiteman and was replaced by

Larry Shields) on clarinet; Billy Lambert, drums; Arnold Loyocano, bass and piano; and Ray Lopez, cornet; Brown's outfit took the unique new music to Chicago in the fall of 1914.

Paul Eduard Miller and George Hoefer, writing in the 1946 *Esquire Jazz Book** insist, however, that the Original Creole Band preceded Brown's unit to the Illinois city by a full year via their well-documented engagement at the big Grand Theater, followed by bookings at the Colonial Theater in the loop and a sixteen-week stand at the North American Restaurant at State and Monroe, also in the heart of the city's Loop.

But the Louisiana aggregation destined to make the most sensational changes in popular music—and cut the first jazz records in history—was to become known as the Original Dixieland Jazz Band, the ODJB, a raucous but entertaining combo that spread jazz not only to Chicago (December 1914) but to New York and London.

Nick LaRocca, cornet; Alcide (Yellow) Nunez, clarinet; Eddie Edwards, trombone; Harry Ragas, piano; and Anton Lada, drums; comprised the original ODJB, which broke up in two weeks despite its incredible success at Chicago's Casino Gardens. The usual "clash of temperaments" was given as the reason, and as historians Miller and Hoefer long ago established, Lada and Nunez sent to New Orleans for Charlie Panelli, trombone; Karl Karlberger, banjo; and Joe Calway, piano; and commenced a six-month job at the Athenia Cafe. This group became the Louisiana Five. The original man replaced Lada and Nunez with Larry Shields' clarinet and Johnny Stein, drummer, and began an engagement at Schiller's Cafe.

Miller and Hoefer have also traced a virtually unknown Louisiana trombonist, George Filhe, from New Orleans to Chicago in 1913. Filhe intended to work at his cigar-making trade, but instead wangled a playing job on the far South Side, Halsted at Sixty-third Street, at the Fountain Inn. His group, perhaps not so jazz-oriented as the Johnson-Oliver unit five years later, also worked the Arsonia Cafe and Tommy Thomas' cabaret.

Still another New Orleans combo made the scene. Led by the fine cornetist and cigar-maker Manuel Perez, it featured the brilliant clarinet artistry of Lorenzo Tio, the teacher, who was so good that he "fought off pupils with a sharp stick." Louis Cottrell, Frankie Haynie, and Ed Atkins rounded out the group's personnel. Years later, Perez returned home, retired from music, and flatly refused to discuss the subject with those who called on him seeking information.

And what became of old Jelly Roll, who could always make his rent

* New York: A. S. Barnes & Co., pp. 15-16.

money shooting pool (playing the role of a naïve hayseed), after he left New Orleans? Morton beat 'em all to Chicago, arriving there in 1910 and working the Elite Cafe in the overpopulated Black Belt of the city's South Side with his old pal, Tony Jackson. But two years in one location was too much for the nervous, big-talking pianist. He quit Chicago in 1912 and started bumming around the Middle West, staying for extended periods in Memphis and Kansas City—he liked their food and women, he said—and finally, pushing off for a long stay in California.

The professionals' mass exodus from New Orleans, by 1918, was alarmingly evident. Along the Mississippi, the Streckfus Line kept its fleet of luxurious riverboats constantly on the go, carrying passengers and freight profitably up through Natchez, Vicksburg, Memphis, Cairo, and Hannibal to St. Louis. Music was prominently featured.

Fate Marable enjoyed a reputation as the best of the river musicians. He was a shrewd judge of men for his orchestra, with an unexplainable knack of sensing that a sideman seeking a job was drunk, or a goldbricker, chick-chaser, or boat-jumper. Occasionally he interviewed a man who was none of these.

Marable, like Andy Kirk, Lionel Hampton, and Jonah Jones who followed him, was a Kentuckian. From about 1916-17 until World War II, he led his own orchestras up and down the river. He not only was an expert pianist and leader, but was highly regarded as a teacher of what was then "modern" jazz. Armstrong, Singleton, Johnny St. Cyr, the Dodds brothers—Johnny and Baby—Manuel Perez, and George Foster, all previously mentioned, worked as sidemen with Fate in their youth. So did Trumpeter Irving (Mouse) Randolph, later to become a bulwark in Cab Calloway's big band; Earl Bostic, the alto saxist who was among the first, in the 1940s, to popularize rhythm and blues records for youngsters; Gene (Honeybear) Sedric, tenor sax star with Fats Waller, who died in early 1963; Jimmy Blanton, the bassist with Duke Ellington who died of tuberculosis at 21; and Al Morgan, the eccentric bassist who for so many years led the Calloway band's rhythm section with Leroy Maxey. Blanton, regarded nearly a quarter of a century after his tragic death as perhaps the most skillful jazz bassist of all time, was a Marable sideman briefly in St. Louis before going with Ellington.

The mighty Streckfus Line regularly plied the Mississippi with its stately, picturesque boats. And yet, of the dozens of leaders employed over four decades only Marable and Tony Catalano, a trumpeter, who was still working on the paddlewheelers as late as 1940, are remembered today.

Musicians were rapidly vanishing from New Orleans, for those who left to work the boats never returned. Finally, in 1919, Congress passed the Volstead Act to enforce prohibition. It was an unpopular law every-where, but particularly in New Orleans. Cabarets, clubs, dance halls, ball-rooms, saloons, and cafes folded almost overnight, and as the remaining lights went out so did the rest of the musicians.

The illustrious New Orleans era was ended.

It took considerably more than the demise of New Orleans, however, to make Chicago the setting for a wondrous step in the evolution of jazz.

Night life in Chicago after World War I did not have to compete with the radio and talkies, Paul Eduard Miller recalls in the 1946 *Esquire Jazz Book*, and its cabarets put on shows lavishly produced and cast—some also featuring a jazz band, usually a large one. Chicagoans seeking enter-tainment frequented such spots, often operated by a syndicate made rich by the American propensity to violate prohibition. Being a direct, concise expression of the times, jazz appealed not only to the prohibition gang-sters, but to other Chicagoans who were caught up in a whirl of protest against a law they did not like. Biting and incisive, jazz personified this protest, this direct, raw approach to life, which offended the "solid" citizen and was looked upon as sinful by pulpiteers and preachers and as cheap and tawdry by small-minded classicists.

Tom Brown's band from New Orleans had played a brief engagement in 1914 at the Lamb's Cafe in Chicago. Brown's music, new to the ears of Cook County musicians, was described as "peppy" and called, with some derision, "jass."

But by the 1920s "jass" had become—once and for all—jazz. It had spread from New Orleans not only to Chicago but to the Eastern Sea-board—New York, Philadelphia, Boston—and to the Pacific Coast—San Francisco, Los Angeles, and San Diego. Yet it was Chicago that willingly served as the hub following the Louisiana exodus.

THE NORK

Oddly, the finest white band of the period was comprised of several visiting Louisiana musicians. Formed in the autumn of 1921 for an engage-ment at the Friar's Inn, just a block or so from the staid Chicago Public Library, the New Orleans Rhythm Kings provided what was, at that time, the most inventive and inspired white jazz in the United States. On that point every musician who heard the group is dogmatic. It was a band that compared well even with Joe Oliver's a few miles to the south at the Dreamland.

The NORK, as it is still known today, never played in New Orleans. Pianist Elmer Schoebel, of East St. Louis, was the executive spark-plug and the only member of the original unit who could read and score music. Leon Rapollo, clarinet; Paul Mares, cornet; Jack Pettis, saxophone; George Brunies (who later, at an astrologer's suggestion, changed his name to Brunis), trombone; Lew Black, banjo; Arnold Loyacano, bass; and Frank Snyder, drums; rounded out the personnel.

Before the group could get to the Gennett recording studios, Snyder left the band and was replaced by an aggressive Chicagoan, Benny Pollack. In September 1922, they made it to Gennett (over in Richmond, Indiana) and recorded *Oriental, Farewell Blues, Discontented Blues, Bugle Call Blues, Tiger Rag, Panama,* and *Eccentric.* The records created more than a stir. Musicians flocked to watch the NORK perform at the Friar's, and when Loyacano and then Steve Brown had to leave the group, they sent to New Orleans to get a man they regarded as the best young bass player in the South. He was Martin Abraham—Chink Martin—who was still making jazz records in New Orleans in the 1950s with Sharkey Bonano's combo and others, and he could read music as well as Schoebel could.

In the now-defunct British journal *Swing Music,* George Beall had this to say about the NORK:

> "*Most of the numbers recorded by the band were their own compositions, such as* Tin Roof Blues, Farewell Blues, Bugle Call Blues, Milenburg, That's a Plenty, *tunes which immediately became tremendously popular and have remained so down to this day. Several of these sold as many as 200,000 copies, most of which went into the hands of musicians or fans, where they have remained. For the age of these relics of a classic day, they are extraordinary. Many of them could compete as to genuine hot execution with a large proportion of later records by bands supposedly advanced in technique and ideas.* That's a Plenty *and* Tin Roof Blues, *recorded in 1922, is one of the best examples of the output of this group.*"

Beall points out that the influence of the NORK at the time was enormous, especially on young musicians in the Middle West. The band expired in 1925 in Indianapolis, the brilliant Rapollo, like Buddy Bolden earlier, committed to an asylum, where he died in 1943, unaware that America was at war. Brunies wound up with Ted Lewis, the Ohio showman and squawking clarinetist, whose persuasive "Is Everybody Happy?" vocal trademark sold millions of records to lovers of sentimental lyrics and to vaudeville patrons. Brunies, however, came back many years later to continue his career in jazz.

Youth Will Be Heard

Chicago, by now, was a beehive for kid musicians. Other fine bands were being organized. In 1923, perhaps inspired by the NORK, a group calling themselves the Wolverines landed a job on the North Side at the Cascades, a neighborhood ballroom on Sheridan Road. The band didn't last long, but it helped to provide a start for Leon Bix Beiderbecke, in from nearby Davenport with his cornet; Jimmy Hartwell, clarinet; Bob Conzelman, drums; Bobby Gillette, banjo; Al Gande, trombone; George Johnson, tenor sax; and Dick Voynow at the piano.

Simultaneously, a group of Austin High students on the city's West Side was enjoying the NORK Gennetts and attempting to launch still another little hot combo.

Calling themselves the Blue Friars, the Austin gang comprised Jimmy McPartland, trumpet; Richard McPartland, banjo; Jim Lannigan, piano; Lawrence (Bud) Freeman, drums; and Frank Teschemacher, the most gifted of the five, who played alto sax, mandolin, violin, and banjo, and (shortly after the group wangled a summer job at Lost Lake, just outside Chicago) clarinet.

Rehearsals and gigs around the West Side brought them into contact with other youthful musicians, including Benny Goodman, who was fresh from his Hull House charity music lessons and still wearing knicker-bockers and knee-high black stockings. Dave Tough—so expert as a drummer at 16 that Freeman quit his set (with the blinking electric light inside the bass drum) and took up C-Melody and later the tenor saxo-phone—was one who rode the elevated out from his Oak Park station to jam with the Austinites. Tough also brought along Floyd O'Brien, the trombonist. Dave North, a pianist who played so well that Jim Lannigan moved over to bass, succeeded not only in jazz but also with the Chicago Symphony, later, as an adult.

This was the time, bear in mind, when Louis Armstrong and Joe Oliver were the titans of the South Side. And of course Jelly Roll Morton was in and out, like a darting buzzfly.

Yet, in comparison to Eddie (Slick) Condon, who blew in from Good-land, Indiana, in 1922, even these musicians were relatively silent. For Condon was—and has remained for more than forty years—a combination pitchman and plectrum-plucker, confidence man and atomic blast. He went to work immediately at the modest Campbell Gardens, with men who were veritable mutes in his company: Earl Wiley, drums; George Lugg, trombone; Jimmy Lord, clarinet; and Harry LeGrande, piano. What a parlay Condon and Morton might have made together!

Francis Joseph Spanier, a prune-faced youngster who hung around Oliver and Armstrong so much that Louis fondly nicknamed him "Kid Muggsy," was a rabid White Sox fan, a classy ballplayer himself, and the best white trumpet player in town. But Spanier met his match in Bix Beiderbecke, who was three years older and who played in a vastly different style.

About the time Bix quit the Wolverines, Frank Trumbauer arrived in Chicago with Joe Kayser's orchestra for a stand at the Arcadia Ballroom. "Tram" and Bix teamed up almost immediately, wandering around the city after hours to seek jazz kicks. It was a history-making partnership, of which much more will be recounted later.

Chicago, Chicago, that toddlin' town . . . In July of 1924 the Mound City Blue Blowers led by a comb-tooter, William (Red) McKenzie, came to town. Gene Krupa was learning how to drum despite his studying to become a priest at St. Joseph's College. Big Joe Sullivan, the happy Irishman with the big fists, was mastering that piano. Boyce Brown, a brilliant student of many subjects, was learning the alto sax.

Joe Marsala was studying the clarinet, and driving a moving truck to finance his lessons. Art Hodes, like Sullivan, listened to records and learned the piano. And everywhere, it seemed, the little kid from the Hull House they called Benny popped up to play miraculous hot clarinet choruses on tunes with complicated, difficult changes.

Another excellent clarinetist in the jazz idiom was Don Murray, an Englewood High graduate, who was working regularly at Broadway and Balmoral in a speakeasy called Dinty Moore's with Bill Grimm, piano; Harry Gale, drums; Frank Leeman, banjo; and Vic Moore, drums.

All these were white musicians, most in their teens or early twenties, and all were ambitious, enthused, and eager to face whatever hardships lay ahead in order to make a living playing the new jazz. It was a gala period, which today is pegged by a number of historians and musicians as "The Golden Era."

Piano Town

Dr. John Steiner, for twenty years a record producer, writer and chemist, has many times pointed out that Chicago was a great "piano town," and rattles off names like Glover Compton, Jimmy Yancey, Clarence (Pinetop) Smith, "Cripple Clarence" Lofton, Romeo Nelson, Frank Melrose, Meade Lux Lewis, Jimmy Flowers, Alex Hill, Freddie Shayne, Jimmy Blythe, Albert Ammons, and—in more recent years—Don Ewell, Sammy Williams, Floyd Bean, Dorothy Donegan, and Jack Gardner, all of whom did, indeed, contribute to the Cook County jazz story in addition to Earl Hines, Cass Simpson, Charlie Elgar, Joe Sullivan, Art Hodes, Lil Hardin Armstrong, and the Morton-Jackson duo.

Cleo Brown, playing rhythmic boogie-woogie piano in the Pinetop Smith manner, Laura Rucker, and Gladys Palmer all sang and entertained from a piano bench. But today, when the talk turns to Chicago pianists, Earl Hines (who came out of Pittsburgh originally) gets the call as the city's most popular and most influential of all time.

Hines hit the Windy City in 1922 and worked with Lois Deppe, a singer. Musicians at once picked up on his unique "trumpet" style—featuring horn-like stabs at single notes with the right hand—and for several years Earl had more work than he could handle as he played with the Dickerson, Stewart and Noone bands. His records with Johnny Dodds, Armstrong, and Dickerson brought him to the attention of a legion of musicians, and in 1928 ("Right around Christmas time," he remembers) Hines launched his own big orchestra at the Grand Terrace on Chicago's South Side. He has been a leader ever since, and in San Francisco in May 1963, Hines, at a sprightly 58, recorded a dozen of his most renowned numbers for Capitol co-producers Stan Kenton and Lee Gillette with a vitality and digital skill that was almost miraculous.

THE WILD SIDE

Because one of Chicago's larger bordellos was called the Four Deuces, musicians named a ratty joint at 222 North State Street the Three Deuces. It was a convenient and cheap place to meet and jam between jobs, and when prohibition finally was abandoned, owner Sam Beers officially christened the Three Deuces with an exterior sign. It became a top hangout for musicians and singers, and eventually (in 1939) became known also as the Off-Beat Club.

Musicians in the middle 1920s frequently missed a beat when Al (Scarface) Capone or his brother Ralph or the handsome Dion O'Bannion and their henchmen paraded into a club and requested their favorite songs. The Capone headquarters was in nearby Cicero, in the suburbs, but the Capones as well as rival clans enjoyed night life and the excitement of loud, brilliant, slow and up-tempo jazz. Some of the speaks were owned outright by the hoods. Earl Hines said that his good friend Jimmie Noone as well as Lucky Millinder, Tiny Parham, and Boyd Atkins all were employed by the Capones at one time or another.

Jimmy McPartland remembers a night at Mike Fritzel's Friar's Inn (long after the NORK had departed) when a drunken bodyguard shot Jim Lannigan's bass fiddle full of holes. McPartland asked Fritzel to pay for the damage to Lannigan's instrument. Fritzel, accustomed to the tempers and mores of his mobster patrons, walked over, took a handful of bills from the hoodlum, returned to McPartland and counted out $850, which was a pretty fair payoff inasmuch as the bass had cost Lannigan only $225 to begin with. Lannigan bought a new and better instrument and sold the old one, too.

The Dodds boys have been mentioned briefly. Johnny was a remarkable clarinetist of the New Orleans caste. His brother Baby introduced a showmanly "shimmy" drum style that dancers applauded wildly and musicians approved because of his steady time. At a place called Kelly's Stables in Chicago in 1924, Johnny Dodds started an engagement that ran month after month. During his last illness in Chicago in 1940, he told me of his days at the Stables:

"We thought it was a bad job, with long hours, and the place itself was dirty. Everything inside it was painted black, and the stalls were still there from maybe twenty or thirty years before. It even smelled horsey. *But now, it don't seem so bad. We had a lot of fun in there in those days when we were young."*

Baby Dodds outlived his older brother 19 years, and strongly influenced young drummers Dave Tough, Gene Krupa, and George Wettling, who moved to Chicago from Topeka. Wettling became Dodds' greatest booster, and more than once suffered a parental swatting for sneaking out, late at night, to watch Baby and Johnny play at the Stables. It was Wettling, incidentally, who told this *Down Beat* reporter some twenty years afterward about the difficulty of playing in the Chicago speakeasies for gangster audiences:

"At the Triangle Club, the boss was shot in the stomach by mobsters one night, but we kept right on playing. After that, he walked sort of bent over."

COLLECTOR'S ITEMS

Chicago of the gangster period, the Golden Era, saw the first Vitaphone "talkie" movie from Warner Brothers opening in November 1926. Thirteen months later, the Negro weekly, the *Chicago Defender* commented on a new-fangled "Amplivox" in a South Side restaurant. It was a machine that reproduced Louis Armstrong's scatting vocal of *Heebie Jeebies.* Few musicians recognized the potential popularity of the primitive juke box. And even fewer anticipated the eventual sale of $600 million in records annually, and the millions in fees and royalties payable to musicians and singers for their services on records.

The same Tom Rockwell who helped Armstrong obtain a record contract with Okeh became attracted to the young clique of white Chicagoans and set up a record session, also for Okeh, which featured Red McKenzie and Eddie Condon as co-leaders; Jim Lannigan, bass; Jimmy McPartland, cornet; Gene Krupa, drums; Joe Sullivan, piano; Bud Freeman, tenor; and Frank Teschemacher, clarinet. On December 9, 1927, they recorded *Sugar* and *China Boy*, titles that sold extremely well and started the big-talking, banjo-strumming Condon on a long and lucrative career as a jazz leader, promoter, sideman, lecturer, and nitery impresario. A week later, the same men made *Nobody's Sweetheart* and *Liza*, with Milton (Mezz) Mezzrow allowed to sit in and gently tap a cymbal.

All four sides are still prized today by collectors, older musicians, and students of early jazz.

Jimmie Noone, a rotund, soft-spoken Louisianian who led his own group at the Nest, and in 1927 at the Apex Club with Hines as his pianist, took the solo clarinet a step farther than did Johnny Dodds. Benny Goodman has many times acknowledged his debt to Jimmie's fluid way of playing, and the Noone records of *Sweet Lorraine*, *I Know That You Know*, *Sweet Sue*, *King Joe*, and *Apex Blues*, etched for Vocalion in 1928, are additional titles to be considered for an all-time classic collection.

Noone rarely left Chicago. It was his adopted home. The group I enjoyed watching him front in 1939-40 on Chicago's South Side featured Darnell Howard, and later in Hollywood, in 1943, his mellow clarinet helped make my first disc session with the Capitol Jazzmen recording band an artistic triumph. But it was Jimmie's last record date. He died the following April while working at a modest little Hollywood Boulevard night club, the Streets of Paris, frequented by jitterbugging young service men who had never heard of him.

BOYCE

Another unpublicized but gifted Chicago musician was Boyce Brown, a gentle, extremely sensitive alto saxophonist who lived with his parents and spent many of his hours away from the bandstand writing sonnets. Almost blind, Brown was perhaps the most philosophic of numerous philosophic musicians I have encountered down through the years. To him, jazz was purely metaphysical, and he sincerely believed that the instrument he played actually absorbed part of himself and was more than an inanimate object.

Soft-spoken, well-read, highly literate and, in the opinion of many of his associates, a genius, Brown recorded rarely. With Paul Mares (the NORK trumpeter) and a band Mares led at Harry's New York Cabaret in 1934, Brown's alto was heard on *Reincarnation, Land of Dreams, Maple Leaf Rag,* and *Nagasaki,* all on Okeh. George Wettling, Santo Pecora, Jess Stacy, and Omer Simeon made up the Mares combo. A year later, in April of 1935, Brown cut four sides for Columbia with Joe and Marty Marsala, Zutty Singleton, Jabbo Smith, Charlie LaVere and Leonard Bibb, but they were never released. "They were not good performances," Brown told me later. "I failed to communicate with Agnes, but it was my fault, not hers."

Agnes was his alto saxophone.

The morning after my first interview with Brown, in 1939 in Chicago, his father arrived at *Down Beat*'s old Dearborn Street offices with a glossy 8 by 10 photograph of an alto saxophone, lying in its case without a mouthpiece and flanked on both sides by lighted candles. Boyce had typed on the attractive folder in which the macabre photo was mounted:

AGNES   LYING IN STATE   1928-1939

And on the inside of the folder to the left, he had pasted this mimeographed requiem and signed it with his first name only:

Her voice now is mute.

While life was breathed into Her, She revealed to me in audible measures many of my faults, and delicately intimate moods found expression through Her being;

Though She was wholly mine, I never was Her master—quite. Having fully enjoyed the completeness of Her unquestioning service, it is with no great sense of sorrow that I lay Her away;

As into the beautiful silence that precedes the touch of the Great Master.

Boyce Brown's finest recorded solo is in Decca's 1939 *Chicago Jazz* album, later issued in a long-play version, on the *China Boy* title with McPartland; his brother Dick McPartland, guitar; Floyd Bean, piano; Hank Isaacs, drums; Bud Jacobson, clarinet; and Lannigan, string bass. George M. Avakian, the internationally popular critic and producer of today, produced the session as a youngster fresh out of Yale. Avakian said of Brown's talents:

TRIBUTE TO ADOLPH.

HER voice now is mute.

While life was greatest that now has reveled to us is

...melodic measures many of a Smith.

And delicately intimate mood found expression through her body -- quite.

Though she was worthy else, I near was her superthings

master fully enjoys the completeness of her superthings

service,

It is with or great sense of sorrow that I lay her away,

As into the beautiful Silence that preceded the touch of

the great Master.

Doyle

"Brown shares a chorus with Jacobson and gives us a typical solo: perfectly executed, fast, full of notes, but completely logical and amazingly conceived. Boyce's personality is expressed in his music— a statement which has been worn thin, but here it is the cold truth. Boyce is unlike any musician you have ever met, and his is a completely individual and unorthodox style. Take warning that Boyce will need a lot of listening. His complexity makes a casual hearing worthless. Careful attention will be rewarded by an understanding of the subtleties of Boyce's ideas, which are distinctively his own." *

Perhaps a fragment, a spark, of the Charlie Parker genius was exhibited by Brown a full decade or more before the Bird flew his Kansas City coop and swooped down on the jazz world in New York. A number of excellent musicians think it may be true.

Hampered by his failing sight, the gentle Brown played the Liberty Inn on the near North Side with Earl Wiley and Pianist Clayton Ritchie for more than twelve years, then quietly joined the Servite Order and entered a monastery in 1953. Known there as Brother Matthew, he recorded a final album with an Eddie Condon pickup jazz group for ABC-Paramount in 1956, appeared amid spectacular publicity on a New York television show, enjoyed a feature story in *Time* magazine, then returned to the monastery and died of a heart attack in early 1959.

TOUGH AND TESCH

Dave Tough, the little man with the big mind, was another memorable Musician. As a youth he supplied the force behind the Austin High kids, showing an instinct for order, balance, continuity and intonation, although he was a drummer.

Tough was always ahead of his time, but like most gifted musicians, he was unaware of it. Great ideas poured out of him naturally. He added much to the expressive possibilities of drums, and established vital new ways to project his thoughts and keep time.

Little Dave, often ill after serving in Artie Shaw's Navy band in World War II, fell in a Newark street one night in 1948 and died of a skull fracture. Equally tragic, in retrospect, was the short life of his dear friend, Frank Teschemacher:

A violinist as a child in Kansas City, Frank was plagued with an eye ailment which, his mother told me in a day-long interview in 1939, made him shy and introverted. His clarinet style was unlike any other; his

* From Avakian's booklet for Decca's *Chicago Jazz* album (New York: Decca Records, Inc., 1940), p. 7.

modesty and musicianship endeared him to his fellow Austin High class-mates. It was my privilege to write three lengthy articles on Tesch, the first ones ever published, for consecutive issues of *Down Beat*. The eerie details of his death remain vivid.

He and Bill Davison were returning home in Davison's 1928 Packard. At the intersection of Wilson and Magnolia, Davison's car crashed into a Checker cab at high speed, throwing Tesch out on the pavement and fracturing his skull. Davison leaped out of the wreckage with a torn pant leg. The cab driver and his two passengers were not seriously hurt.

In an apartment nearby, a prominent Chicago musician named Bob Clitherow was playing jazz records with friends—they had been up most of the night enjoying his collection—when they heard the collision below. Clitherow ran down to find his friend Teschemacher mortally injured. Still spinning on the turntable up in his apartment, as he waited for the ambulance, was the McKenzie-Condon *Nobody's Sweetheart* disc featuring Tesch's hot clarinet.

A coroner's inquest absolved Davison of negligence, but Chicago musicians were so critical of him that he moved away.

FADEOUT

Death helped tarnish the Golden Era of jazz. And New York, fast accepting jazz as the high old good times of the flapper and coonskin coat era rolled merrily on, began to attract the nation's finest musicians.

Armstrong already had left to play at Connie's Inn. Then the whole young clique of McPartland, Condon, Krupa, Sullivan, McKenzie, Freeman, Lannigan, and Teschemacher had departed Chicago, too, to accept a job in New York with a popular singer-entertainer, Bee Palmer. As Sullivan recalled to me later:

> "We got there okay, but there was no job. Something had gone wrong. We went, instead, into the Palace Theater on Times Square to play for the Bennett-Sabin dance act. It didn't work out very well, and after a week we were unemployed again. I remember how Variety panned our band.
> Krupa's mother was dying, so he went right back to Chicago. The rest of us hooked on with Red Nichols. Most of us stayed around New York permanently after that, but Tesch went home after three months. He was homesick."

Marion Hardy brought his Alabamians into the Sunset in 1928, and Cabell Calloway of Pittsburgh was imported from the East to front the orchestra. Fletcher Henderson's smart New York aggregation played the Congress Hotel, where Benny Goodman was to enjoy incredible popularity nine years in the future. But dozens of little neighborhood clubs and cabarets were quick to feel the chill when, in October of 1929, *Variety* screamed its famous page one banner:

WALL STREET LAYS AN EGG

The plunge of the stock market brought inevitable, swift changes in the lives of everyone.

Chicago's Golden Era had come to an end. Jazz, still in its diapers, was to suffer a severe setback; yet, like Comiskey's erratic and beloved White Sox, it would bounce back vigorously.

5

BIX
and His
Friends

Leon Bix Beiderbecke was born three years after Louis Armstrong. He lived only 28 years. Yet, as a good many books, magazine articles, and newspaper features every year indicate, his brief appearance on this earth left an indelible mark. Bix introduced a biting, facile, bell-toned trumpet style that is still being emulated by older musicians today, and his skill as a pianist whose hands constantly probed the keyboard, seeking new harmonies and sound clusters, is recognized in jazz circles throughout the world more than thirty years after his death.

A handsome youngster whose parents planned a full college education for him, and who had every social advantage in his home town of Davenport, Iowa, Beiderbecke fled the expensive, "exclusive" Lake Forest Academy in the suburbs of Chicago to seek music—jazz—as a full-time occupation. He frequented the speakeasies and cabarets during the night and sat, more asleep than awake, in his daytime classes bored and determined to quit school.

THE WOLVERINES

Bix watched Joe Oliver and Louis Armstrong play their famous cornet duets at the Lincoln Gardens and later, at the Dreamland, he enjoyed Armstrong's high notes with Ollie Powers. He also admired the New Orleans Rhythm Kings at Friar's Inn. And when clarinetist Jimmy Hart-

ILLUSTRATION: The Wolverines with Bix. This rare 1923 photograph shows (seated, left to right) Bob Gillette, banjo; Vic Moore, drums; and Leon Bix Beiderbecke, cornet; and (standing, left to right) Dick Voynow, piano; George Johnson, saxophone; Min Leibrook, sousaphone; and Jimmy Hartwell, clarinet.

well was handed a chance to book a seven-piece "hot" band into the Stockton Club, 17 miles north of Cincinnati, he asked for help from Dick Voynow, a pianist and business head.

Voynow knew many of the Chicago musicians, and had no trouble obtaining Bix and three others for the engagement. George Johnson, a first-rate tenor saxophonist, joined the group in Stockton after gigging around New York with his Indiana friend, the singing lawyer, Hoagy Carmichael. The seven musicians called themselves the Wolverines. Through October, November, and December 1923 they played a happy, uneventful engagement. And then on New Year's Eve, with a capacity crowd dancing, imbibing and blowing tin horns, two rival gangs started a riot which kept the musicians playing—without a stop—for more than an hour. All that time they jammed *China Boy* in four different keys, each man fascinated by the sight of flying bottles and the sound of screaming women. The club was closed permanently because of the turmoil and it was two weeks before the Wolverines found another job, at Doyle's dance hall in Cincinnati.

By now, the Wolverines consisted of Bix, Min Leibrook, Vic Moore, Al Gande, Bob Gillette, Johnson, Voynow, and Hartwell. It was during the Doyle's stand that they drove to Richmond, Indiana, some 125 miles distant, to make their first records in March 1924. They made *Fidgety Feet* and *Jazz Me Blues*, then returned to Richmond two more times in 1924 to wax *Oh, Baby, Copenhagen, Riverboat Shuffle* (which Carmichael had composed as *Free Wheeling*), *Susie, I Need Some Pettin'*, *Royal Garden Blues*, and *Tiger Rag*. Carmichael became one of Bix's most devoted friends in the few brief years left of the cornetist's life.

After Bix died, George Johnson wrote in *Down Beat*:

> *"Although I played with Bix for more than a year and a half, I can honestly say that I never heard him make a mistake in playing. Knowing his style as thoroughly as we did, we could often detect, in one of his solos, that he had hit a note that he had not intended to hit, but by the time the phrase or passage was complete, he had angled and squirmed out of the difficulty in a run of notes that was so brilliant it would leave us almost breathless. Only his complete mastery, a mastery that was made up of unorthodox fingering, as unique as his ideas, could produce this result. Each chorus of his, every "break," could be depended upon to be new and different. Always exhilarating, his playing was so narcotic in its effect on susceptible listeners that I have seen some that were as truly doped by its effect that they had the manner of an opium addict blissfully happy after his pipe.*

*Others, like Carmichael, in the days when we played at Indiana
University dances, would be driven to tantrums of hysteria. . . .
Bix remained unimpressed, not in the least conscious that the playing
he enjoyed so much was the indication of genius."* *

After Gande left, the Wolverines continued gigging in and around
Indiana without a trombone. Their first records were issued, sold well
(all Gennetts must have been astonishingly successful!), and in early
September they nervously opened in New York at the Cinderella Ballroom, at 48th and Broadway, for a four-month run that climaxed the
unit's activity and led to its disbanding.

Great musicians stood in front of the bandstand, digging the Bix-
inspired jazz delightedly. Tommy and Jimmy Dorsey, Loring (Red)
Nichols, Milfred (Miff) Mole, Frankie Trumbauer, and numerous other
big name performers were constant visitors. Johnson relates how impressed the Wolverines were, in turn, with Ray Miller's orchestra playing just a few blocks away at the Arcadia Ballroom. While engaged at
the Cinderella the Wolverines recorded additional masters for Gennett,
in October 1924, including *Sensation*, *Lazy Daddy*, *Tia Juana*, and *Big
Boy*. On *Big Boy* Bix played a piano solo. George Brunies, their friend
from Chicago's NORK, sat in on trombone on *Sensation* and *Lazy Daddy*,
singing a raucous "vocal" on *Daddy*.

They were the last records the Wolverines made with Bix. He gave
notice he was leaving to join a band Trumbauer was forming, but with
his usual courtesy he obligingly remained several weeks to help Jimmy
McPartland take over his chair after a mad, nightmarish audition by Joe
(Sharkey) Bonano of New Orleans had proved disastrous—for Bonano.

McPartland, nervous in his first major league test, worked out well and
eventually led the Wolverines for a time. But it wasn't the same with
Beiderbecke absent. In 1925 the Wolverines disbanded, McPartland re-
turning to Chicago and a job with Al Haid. The others trained west, too.
But none ever hit the jackpot, the once in a lifetime brass ring, that the
Wolverine outfit provided.

EMMET

Even today there remains a clique of sincere New Orleans musicians
who are adamant in saying that a young white cornetist named Emmet
Hardy played Bix-style horn several years before Bix, and that the Iowa
youngster picked it up from Hardy while Emmet was playing the river-

* *Down Beat*, October 1938, pp. 6, 15; November 1938, p. 9; December 1938, p 8.
Reproduced by permission of *Down Beat* Magazine.

boats and occasionally stopping over in Davenport for excursion dances.

Three months younger than Beiderbecke, Hardy died in June 1925 of tuberculosis without ever having achieved the national recognition his Louisiana friends insist he deserved. Only 22 when he succumbed, Emmet was playing professionally at 15, using an oversized mouthpiece that he made himself in a New Orleans machine shop.

In 1923, he worked with the brilliant, erratic, marijuana-crazed Leon Rapollo of the New Orleans Rhythm Kings, playing the Orpheum Theater circuit with Bee Palmer. Bee loved good jazz and always tried to employ outstanding musicians, but she somehow couldn't keep them for long. Hardy and the wild-eyed Rapollo, soon to be committed to a mental institution for the remainder of his life, walked out on her in a salary dispute and joined the Carlisle Evans orchestra in Davenport. Evans led bands on the Streckfus riverboats for many years.

Tony Catalano, another river maestro, has often deposed that young Hardy taught young Beiderbecke the rudiments of music in Davenport. Numerous other reputable New Orleans musicians told me personally of the Hardy talents during a period in 1940 when I was researching a long Hardy feature for *Down Beat*, which I then edited. Some of their statements:

"I'm not the only musician who remembers how Beiderbecke hung around Emmet asking for advice. Bix developed into a fine musician, but you can't compare him with Hardy. Emmet taught Bix how to blow. Bix was a poor imitation of Hardy."—Ben Pollack

"Hardy in 1919 was playing the same stuff that Bix played with Whiteman ten years later. It's a hell of a note. Emmet never got any publicity and the guys who write about jazz have never given him a tumble. But that's only because he never made a record."—Paul Mares

"I can prove that Emmet 'carved' Armstrong one Sunday afternoon in 1921 on the Steckfus steamer, Sidney. *The two musicians played an hour without interruption and Louie set his own shiny cornet down, made a deep bow and said, 'Man, you're the king.' From that day on, Hardy was the favorite of every musician in the South."*—Arthur (Monk) Hazel

We checked this out with Armstrong later and he pondered Hazel's statement a moment before he answered.

"No sir, Pops, I just don't remember Hardy at all. The only white man I ever jammed with in those days was Bix himself. That was

*about 1924 in Chicago and we just played for our own kicks. No
sir, you got the wrong Louie, I think."*

Yet other upstanding, highly regarded musicians have insisted, with the
passing years, that Hardy was a giant of the cornet and deserves a prominent place in any written jazz history. Eddie Miller, Connee Boswell,
Ray Bauduc, Nappy Lamare, Santo Pecora, Arthur (Doc) Rando, George
Brunies, the Prima brothers, Sonny Lee, Earl Wiley, Steve Loyacano,
Jimmy Dorsey, and Bill Burton, among many others, have insisted that
Hardy be recognized. Other writers ignored him. But in the light of evidence supplied me in 1940 by so many prominent Southern musicians,
there seems little doubt that Emmet Louis Hardy was a jazzman and human being of exceptional merit.

From Goldkette to Whiteman

Beiderbecke worked with Charlie Straight in Chicago briefly before
going with Trumbauer. Charles (Pee-Wee) Russell also was in the band,
playing saxophone and the croaky, ungainly clarinet musicians love so
much. Tram, a leading saxophonist with his goose-necked C-Melody
sax, accepted an offer to work under Jean Goldkette's banner out of
Detroit, Goldkette at that time being in position to send out various
orchestras under his own name as Meyer Davis did in New York years
later. In Detroit, Tram and Bix joined a Goldkette unit in which Don
Murray was featured on clarinet and as an arranger, the same Murray
who had worked at Chicago's Dinty Moore's several years earlier. Russ
Morgan, not long out of the coal mines of Scranton, was another member,
and in those days Russ blew a sizzling 'bone. Bix thought he was marvellous.

The Goldkette crew also made records, all for Victor in 1926-27.
Eighteen titles were cut with men like Joe Venuti, the great jazz fiddler;
the two Dorseys; arranger Bill Challis; Eddie Lang, the first truly outstanding jazz guitarist; Steve Brown, the NORK bassist; Chauncey More-
house, drums; and pals Trumbauer and Murray. Only *Clementine*, in all
honesty, clearly reveals the gargantuan talent of little Bix. Evidently the
Goldkette band was vastly more impressive "live" than on records.

When Paul Whiteman watched the band in person one night in November 1927, he opened his checkbook and lured Bix, Tram, Lang,
Venuti, both Dorseys, Brown, and Trombonist Bill Rank, a Miff Mole
disciple, away from Goldkette.

To Goldkette's credit—and he rarely received any before he died in
1962—his was the first big white band to veer off from a straight and

boring dance book and attempt to present a far more exciting music. Until Whiteman broke the Goldkettes up with his big salaries, the Whiteman orchestra had achieved world-wide popularity and amassed a fortune for the rotund, good-natured violinist from Colorado, with inexcusably stodgy, unexciting arrangements.

Whiteman was universally billed and accepted as "The King of Jazz," a title that today, with a chance to compare Whiteman's music with that of Armstrong, Oliver and Fletcher Henderson of the 1923-27 period, seems no less than ludicrous. Perhaps Whiteman's conscience was pulsating; perhaps he was aware, after watching Goldkette's Detroit aggregation, how far off the mark his own orchestra was. But give Fatho' credit, too, for making an urgent attempt to improve his organization and justify, just a little bit, his pretentious "King of Jazz" monicker.

The Rhythm Boys were also featured with Whiteman at this time. Of the three singers, Bing Crosby, Harry Barris, and Al Rinker, only Bing is still active. Barris died in 1962 after composing great standard songs like *Wrap Your Troubles in Dreams, I Surrender, Dear,* and *It Must Be True,* all popularized by Crosby.

Most musicians agree that the best Bix-Whiteman records of this unforgettable era are *Louisiana,* with a Crosby vocal of rare good humor; *You Took Advantage of Me,* featuring a bouncing, hit-and-run "chase" chorus between Tram's old C-Melody and Bix's cornet; *From Monday On,* Bix playing a fantastic obbligato and leading a brass team which has Jimmy Dorsey on hot trumpet; *Changes,* with Dorsey on baritone sax and Beiderbecke, muted, blowing a white-hot solo in front of the Rhythm Boys; *San,* made with only ten musicians, and *Mississippi Mud,* with excellent hot solos by Bix, Izzy Friedman on clarinet, Tram, and Irene Taylor–Rhythm Boys singing. All except *Changes* were made in early 1928.

Beiderbecke, never a robust man physically, occasionally missed jobs because of illness. He also drank too much, and got little rest in his gruelling job as a major league musician. By mid-1928 the modest Bix was as famous as Armstrong, and regarded as a celebrity by thousands of musicians who flocked to buy his discs and see him work with Whiteman.

On the side, Bix recorded prolifically for a brief period. Five titles under Hoagy Carmichael's name on Victor are most remembered for the wild *Barnacle Bill,* with Benny Goodman, Bud Freeman, and Gene Krupa playing madly. Other Bix recordings were with the Chicago Loopers, the Sioux City Six and—the best of all in my opinion—those made under Trumbauer's name. It was with this orchestra that Bix made *Singin' the Blues,* his best-known cornet solo; *I'm Coming Virginia, Way Down*

Yonder in New Orleans, *Three Blind Mice*, and *Japanese Sandman*, all for Okeh.

His moving, moody, *In a Mist* piano solo was recorded September 9, 1927, and the last disc he cut was with Carmichael and a pickup group on September 15, 1930. Joe Venuti sang a hokey vocal on *Bessie Couldn't Help It* (Victor matrix 63655). It ended Beiderbecke's recording career, and no more than a half-dozen jazzmen have surpassed it for artistic achievement.

When Whiteman's troupe of singers and instrumentalists left New York for Hollywood in 1929 to appear in the Universal motion picture *King of Jazz*, they travelled in high style. Because they were doing a weekly network radio show for Old Gold cigarettes (with Gershwin's *Rhapsody in Blue* as a theme), the tobacco company, Universal Pictures, and Whiteman took over an entire train, painted the passenger cars gold, and slowly rolled to the West Coast with stops in almost every town and village.

END OF THE ROAD

On the Coast, Bix went down like a stumbling halfback, becoming so ill that Whiteman, Trumbauer, and others of his pals, Bing Crosby included, insisted he return to his home in Davenport and recuperate. He did, unwillingly.

Crosby had his troubles also; he was jailed on a drunken driving charge and out of action for 30 days during the filming of the picture. Whiteman gave Bing's big production number, *Song of the Dawn*, to John Boles.

The only song by the Rhythm Boys, *So the Bluebirds and the Blackbirds Got Together*, was cut and edited so drastically that one had to refrain from blinking in order to get a quick glance at Bing and his buddies Rinker and Barris. It was a miserable picture. Bix missed nothing by being home in Davenport.

Whiteman returned East eventually without the blazing, vibrant Beiderbecke cornet. When Bix regained some of his strength, he joined Glen Gray and the Casa Loma Band, a magnificent dance orchestra with ingenious arrangements requiring such odd instrumentation as oboe, bass clarinet, bass saxophone, flute and bass flute voiced with alto, tenor, and baritone saxophones. Its big-band jazz was perhaps stiff and below the standard of the contemporary Negro bands, but it required extraordinary musicianship and kept the dancers jumping. Clarence Hutchenrider played fine solo clarinet, Grady Watts blew solid, Dixie-tinted hot trumpet, and Walter (Pee-Wee) Hunt's jazz trombone and Billy Rausch's first 'bone were inspired. Bix liked the band's style and the Casa Loma musicians to a man, but their brassy, difficult book was simply too much for his lip and constitution. He quit after four or five nights, more discouraged than before.

In the spring and summer of 1930, Bix worked sporadically with Charlie Previn's orchestra, and frequently played college gigs. Young kids appreciated his music more than the business man–housewife crowd, just as they did when he was a kid with the Wolverines in Illinois and Indiana.

He never knocked the musicians he played with, even though virtually all of them were inferior to him professionally. A majority of the records he cut reflect this imbalance of skill pathetically.

He never married, but Trumbauer and those close to Bix knew of his one big romance and helped him keep it private. It is said that Dorothy Baker used the career of Bix as an inspiration, but not a basis, for her phenomenally successful 1938 novel, *Young Man with a Horn*, which Warner Brothers in the mid-1940s made into an unrealistic, three-handkerchief movie starring Doris Day.

Bix died preferring his little cornet to the modern, long-belled, brightly lacquered trumpet used by most musicians. The trumpet, he said, had a pee-wee tone.

Bix enjoyed composing, and in his last few months he completed *Flashes*, *In the Dark*, *Candlelights*, and others with the cheerful help of Bill Challis, his old friend from the Goldkette and Whiteman bands, who copied them carefully and placed them with the Robbins-Feist-Miller publishing combine.

More and more, he hung around Plunkett's Bar, or remained in his little hotel room, drinking and thinking. Only 28, he looked 40. Warren W. Scholl, one of the first American jazz historians to carefully research Beiderbecke's career—back in 1936 for *Down Beat* and for the Victor firm—tells of the darkening skies, the end of the road:

> "*Any number of unpleasant stories have been circulated about the manner in which Bix died. Some claimed he was shot in a brawl in uptown New York, others that he drank himself to death, etc., etc., but here is the accepted story as vouched for by Bix's old friend Trumbauer.*
>
> *Princeton University, over in New Jersey, was having a dance during the summer of 1931 and had hired a pickup band for the occasion, with the express understanding that Beiderbecke would appear in person with the group. A few days before the dance, Bix was compelled to take to bed with a severe cold and told the leader*

of the orchestra that he was ill and could not play the date. He suggested a substitute player whom he knew was available for the evening, but the dance committee at Princeton informed the leader that he must bring Bix with the group or he need not bother to bring any musicians at all—a stand that was conveyed to Bix.

Out of pure generosity Bix then consented to play, very much against the orders of doctors and intimate friends. He drove to Princeton in an open car while running a fever of more than 100 degrees. Between the extreme heat of the dance party and the cold ride back to Manhattan, Bix's cold developed into pneumonia and a few days later, on August 7, 1931, he succumbed in a Long Island hospital." *

Musicians held a funeral of sorts and returned his body to Davenport, where formal services were held by Bix's family. Burial was at Oak Dale Cemetery. A simple, undated headstone is the only marker on the grave of a young man who accomplishd more in 28 years than most jazzmen accomplish in sixty.

Whiteman, if not a gifted jazzman at heart, loved jazz and its practitioners, and far too many writers in the last quarter century have failed to credit him for being the generous, good-hearted leader and showman he was for so many decades. He kept Beiderbecke on full salary for the entire last year of Bix's life, and whenever he's had the chance since that dark August day in '31, Whiteman has lauded Bix in radio, newspaper, magazine, and television interviews.

Beiderbecke's name was not Leon Bismarck Beiderbecke, as many writers have repeatedly written. In 1939, *Down Beat*'s staff published a striking Les Zacheis photograph of Bix's granite headstone, and his legal name, in raised capital letters, plainly read LEON BIX BEIDERBECKE. The enterprising Pauline Rivelli of *Jazz* magazine in late 1962 confirmed *Down Beat*'s findings with a letter from Bix's brother, Charles B. Beiderbecke, who was still residing in Davenport.

"It was our father whose middle name was Bismarck," he graciously advised Miss Rivelli. "Leon's middle name was Bix." And that's that.

Tram—An Epilogue

Frank Trumbauer was never the same after Bix died. My first meeting with him at the Frog Hop Ballroom in St. Joseph, Missouri, in 1937 was a shocker—he was diffident and uncommunicative almost to the point of rudeness.

* From Scholl's booklet accompanying an RCA-Victor album of Bix reissues, 1936.

Later, in contacting him for personal, first-hand information and photographs on Bix, Eddie Lang, and other musicians with whom Tram worked in his younger days, he was more cooperative. Subsequent meetings found Trumbauer to be a reflective, cautious man who was slow to warm to new acquaintances. His records, we were to learn as the years went by, influenced untold hundreds of young musicians. The inimitable Benny Carter and Lester Young are among many who admired Tram's tone and astonishing technical proficiency.

In Trumbauer, Beiderbecke had found a serious companion who shared his interest in Debussy, Delius, Ravel, Stravinsky, and other modern composers. Musicians today know their classic works note for note, but forty years ago jazzmen, if asked, would have guessed they were ballplayers.

Fond of Whiteman, as were all musicians, Tram remained with his troupe through 1936—five years after Bix's death. He then went out with his own orchestra again, retired in 1940 to fly with the Civil Aeronautics Authority and to help in the nation's war effort. In 1945 he made an abortive attempt to work network shows in New York staff orchestras. Yet, at 55, the Carbondale saxophonist who could also play acceptable trumpet, piano and clarinet (and even sing on records) performed with consummate skill on his last record session, for Capitol, in New York.

Trumbauer died in Kansas City June 11, 1956. Jazz lost a titan and my father a sharp-shooting golf partner. Like Bix, Hardy, Tough, and far too many others, Tram went too soon. And so did happy Don Murray, who was found dead in the street; Bill Rank, the slippery trombonist; both Dorseys, fiery Tom and giggling, soft-spoken Jimmy, and Miff Mole and Goldkette as well.

The Beiderbecke era was a brief one. Louis Armstrong has proved himself a king over a period of fifty years. Duke Ellington's career has spanned forty. Little Bix of the bow tie and shy smile played professionally about eight. But he, too, will be remembered along with Armstrong and Ellington and Bird Parker into the twenty-first century. His one chorus of *Singin' the Blues* insures his immortality.

6

On to New York

New York was tardy in accepting jazz. But when the most populous city on the North American continent finally welcomed and became excited about the pulsating new music, employment opportunities for musicians boomed. Clubs, cabarets, theaters, and speakeasies scrambled to acquire talent and attract capacity patronage.

The Original Dixieland Jazz Band had moved into New York from New Orleans—via Chicago's Schiller Cafe—in December 1916. But at least two other New Orleans jazz groups had beaten them into Gotham: the Original Creoles in the fall of the same year (at Shubert's Winter Garden) and drummer Anton Lada's combo from New Orleans, the Louisiana Five. In Lada's group, which swept into New York in July 1915 for an engagement at Bustanobie's restaurant on Broadway at Thirty-Ninth, were Karl Karlberger, banjo; Charlie Panelli, trombone; and pianist Joe Calway and clarinetist Yellow Nunez, who had worked together previously in Chicago, at the Athenia Cafe.

The ODJB was the most successful of the three Crescent City imports, creating riots, almost, at Reisenweber's famous restaurant off Columbia

ILLUSTRATION: Fletcher Henderson (left) and Duke Ellington. (Photograph of Ellington by Charlie Mihn.)

56

Circle. Its agent, Max Hart, then booked the combo into London for another appearance that proved extremely successful. The ODJB recorded in New York and London, returned to Manhattan, was featured in the *Folies Bergère* and disbanded in 1924 as other—and better—jazz bands moved up into the golden circle.

Meanwhile, around Manhattan in general and in uptown Harlem in particular, Charlie Cherry, Jack the Bear, the Seminole, Luckey Roberts, James P. Johnson, Willie (The Lion) Smith, and Fats Waller roamed the streets and cafes as Morton and Jackson had roamed New Orleans before them, playing house parties, bordellos, speakeasies—anything, any place, for a buck or two, a pigfoot, or a bucket of beer. As far back as 1905, it is said Will Marion Cook employed saxophones for the first time in a pop orchestra at Proctor's Twenty-Third Street Theater, a great vaudeville palace second only to the Palace on Broadway at Times Square.

Willie Smith, a cigar-smoking, big-talking pianist who could hold his own with Jelly Roll in musicianship, boasting, humor, lying, drinking, eating, swearing, sleeping, and possibly everything but wielding a pool cue, served with distinction in World War II with the 350th Field Artillery and was decorated for heroism under fire. Proud of his heritage of being part Negro, part Jew, The Lion got his start across the Hudson in Newark. In 1964 he was still active, at 67, playing a refreshingly original piano style which mixes ragtime with ultra-modern harmonic ideas. He was always a tough man in a cutting contest.

James P. Johnson was born six years before Smith, also in New Jersey, at New Brunswick. By 1904, the *Encyclopedia of Jazz* relates, he was working for $9 a week in Manhattan. He cut piano rolls (a lucrative task for many early jazz pianists) and toured Europe with an all-Negro show, *Plantation Days*.

Luckey Roberts, born in 1895 in Philadelphia, experienced an even more unlikely career, working as an "actor" at 3 in *Uncle Tom's Cabin*, as an acrobat for a time, "society" bandleader, music publisher, owner-bartender of the Rendezvous Club in Harlem, jazz advisor to the Duke of Windsor, unofficial teacher of Johnson, Ellington and scores of other pianists, and possessor of one of the most unbelievable names in jazz history, Charles Luckeyeth. But for all of Luckey's activities, he will be remembered in the future for something else—being the composer of the pop tune *Moonlight Cocktails* (1941), which Glenn Miller's orchestra and the Modernaires transformed into an international evergreen via their still-played Bluebird record.

Fats Waller, a few years younger, died at 39 on the Santa Fe Chief as

it pulled into Kansas City's Union Station. He lived half as long as Johnson, Smith, and Roberts; yet he became by far the best known and most
popular of the four skilled pianists.

I first was attracted to Waller's talents in 1934-35. Shortly after midnight, every morning, a program aired from Cincinnati's WLW called
Green River featured an unctuous male reader of poetry against an organ
background. Revolting though it sounds, the organ was played by Waller;
his diversified, imaginative improvisations quickly made the listener unaware of the treacly-voiced narrator.

Waller was far more than a pianist, organist, and composer of outstanding pop tunes (*Honeysuckle Rose, My Fate Is in Your Hands, Ain't
Misbehavin', Keepin' Out of Mischief Now, Blue Turning Grey Over
You* and *Squeeze Me*, among others). His rare, unmatched sense of humor has never been replaced, and if anything is wrong with jazz and
jazzmen these days it is the profession's appalling absence of humor.
Waller recorded hundreds of drab pop tunes with his tongue in cheek,
burlesquing the lyrics, urging his sidemen (Bugs Hamilton and Gene
Sedric in particular) to blow spectacularly, and demonstrating his uncommon pianistics brilliantly. The finest record of *Jingle Bells* ever made
was by Waller, but he could become serious at times and play legitimate,
magnificent pipe organ on Negro spirituals, as he did on a visit to England in 1938.

Waller accompanied blues singers, played "flicker" music for early
movies in Harlem theaters, soloed in cabarets and joints, and was as much
in demand as a singer and entertainer as any man who ever lived in
Harlem. His records, almost all for Victor, were eagerly awaited by
musicians and the general public throughout his recording career.

He went out to Chicago and worked with Prof. Erskine Tate, Armstrong's old mentor, at the Vendome Theater. He went to France as far
back as 1932. He was a big, jovial, hard-drinking man with a wonderfully mobile, plastic-like face which enhanced his showmanship. Seated
at the Baldwin in the gaudy Panther Room of Chicago's Hotel Sherman
in 1939, broadcasting over a network coast-to-coast, Fats would lean into
the microphone and yell, "I wondah what the poor people are doin' tonight?" He had an enviable enthusiasm, constantly shouting to his musicians for all-out efforts. "Yas, Yas, Yas," Fats would bellow across the
Panther Room—and on his records—while his big left fist was stroking
a barrelhouse bass figure. He appeared in several motion pictures; Fats
died returning home after making *Stormy Weather* for MGM in Culver
City with Lena Horne, Benny Carter, and others of his friends.

Of Jack the Bear, the Seminole, and Charlie Cherry, little is known except that they played in various New York clubs forty years ago. And

as for white ragtime or jazz pianists, apparently Ben R. Harney, who was paid fat fees in 1896 for engagements at Keith's and Tony Pastor's, was the first to bring the Southern piano style into New York. He died in poverty in Philadelphia, March 1, 1938, and on the headstone of his grave, which went unmarked for three years, the line, "Creator of Ragtime" is inscribed under his name.

Eubie Blake, still appearing as a "guest artist" on network television shows as recently as 1963, at 80, came out of Baltimore and became a popular name in New York but more so as an entertainer teamed with Noble Sissle than as a pianist.

Scott Joplin, the greatest of all rag pianists, became a New Yorker in his late years only because the major music publishers were there. He rarely worked cabarets as a soloist, but his *Maple Leaf Rag, The Entertainer, Weeping Willow, Euphonic Sounds*, and *Wall Street Rag* were all played by other prominent pianists, and still are. Joplin died April 1, 1917, in the Manhattan State Hospital on the East River's Ward's Island. He had originally come out of Texarkana, Texas, and at the 1893 World's Fair in Chicago had worked with the billing, "King of the Ragtime Composers." That predates even the amazing Jelly Roll Morton!

Morton visited New York occasionally, but never for more than a brief check-in until the middle 1920s, when he recorded his renowned *Red Hot Peppers* discs.

SMACK

It was in 1920 that the dapper Smack arrived in New York.

His full name was James Fletcher Henderson, and New York had, at that time, never seen a man like him.

Smack (and no historian has yet revealed how he got such an odd nickname, not even his friend, advisor, and champion, John Hammond) had majored in mathematics and chemistry at Atlanta University, near his home town of Cuthbert, Georgia. Now, at 22, his cool, sophisticated, knowledgeable personality immediately appealed to New Yorkers, and while his first interest was to do postgraduate work at Columbia and eventually win his master's degree, he started working as a part-time employee for W. C. Handy—the same Handy of Memphis fame, who had made it big as a composer and music publisher.

The frantic, exhausting pace and big financial returns of Gotham music circles stimulated Henderson, and by late 1921 he had decided to abandon studies at Columbia, give up his job with Handy's publishing firm, and accept a pianist's spot with a promising new record company, the Black Swan firm in Harlem.

Black Swan was one of the first all-Negro disc companies, founded in New York in 1921 by Harry Pace. Precisely the same year, and about the same month, the songwriting Spikes brothers (*Someday Sweetheart*) were launching their Sunshine label in Los Angeles with six sides featuring the New Orleans jazz of Kid Ory.

Henderson was delighted to go to work for Pace and Black Swan, putting in long hours as a musical director selecting songs, accompanying singers, and acting as a versatile handyman for Pace, who had established a reputation as W. C. Handy's lyric writer and partner in a music publishing venture. When Pace suggested that Henderson go out on tour with Ethel Waters to help promote the sale of her slow-selling Black Swan discs, he accepted.

They were gone six months, opening in Philadelphia on the same bill with the gigantic boxer, Jack Johnson, the one-time heavyweight champion. In Henderson's little band were the great and always underrated Joe Smith, cornet, and Garvin Bushell, sax and clarinet. Smith was the modest little man who, on a rare occasion, would take a wooden spool, use it for a mouthpiece to obtain a certain indigo effect, and make an entire audience cry. He was especially effective, as a result of this sensitivity, accompanying blues singers. Several of Bessie Smith's records confirm his exceptional talent.

In New Orleans, Henderson ran across young Louis Armstrong blowing his pyrotechnics in a little Creole band with Zutty Singleton on drums. Louis declined Fletcher's offer to return with him to New York; but several years later Henderson was able to hire Armstrong as a result of that first New Orleans meeting.

Back in New York, Henderson and Don Redman, a West Virginia musical prodigy who had played trumpet at 3 and had studied at the Boston and Detroit Conservatories, teamed up at Black Swan for a series of dance orchestra recording dates which were so far ahead of their time they lost money for the label. Joe Smith, on trumpet, and Redman, playing advanced alto sax, were joined by Henderson at the piano; Coleman Hawkins on tenor sax; Charlie Dixon, banjo; Bob Escudero, tuba; and Kaiser Marshall, drums. This was 1922-23, after Smack had waxed three piano solos which are extremely rare today.

Hawkins was a suave, sophisticated musician who, like his boss and Redman, had acquired a college education—at Washburn out in Kansas —and had toured incessantly with the singer Mamie Smith and her Jazzhounds. He was quick to become a favored name among musicians for his booming, gusty jazz solos. Still active, and still playing magnificent saxophone, Hawkins merits an entire book to himself. More of his illustrious life in jazz will be recounted in subsequent chapters.

Outside the studio, the band worked its first night job at the Club Alabam, opening in the summer of 1923 with Elmer Chambers and Howard Scott, replacing Smith, on cornets; Ted Nixon, trombone; and a violinist, Allie Ross, hired as a front man and conductor. They stayed a year, then moved a few blocks across midtown Manhattan to the Roseland ballroom. It was here that Smack and his music rang the bell.

Ross was canned and Henderson led the band from the piano. Redman's skill as an arranger, coupled with the leader's creative ideas and scoring, gave the band the finest, most modern library in the world. The organization rehearsed and practiced and trained over and over, like the Green Bay Packers or the New York Yankees, until every move and every note was perfect.

To play the Henderson book, a musician had to be a cut above all the others. It required a high intelligence, immense technical proficiency, and an outstanding appearance to qualify. Yet, Horace Henderson, Fletcher's younger brother, who now resides in Los Angeles, remembers the autumn evening in 1924 when Armstrong joined the band at Roseland, wearing "a rube box-back coat and high top shoes of a sort of vile amber color." Buster Bailey of Memphis also joined about that time, on clarinet, and the band got better and better, Horace declares.

But Horace Henderson, six years younger than Smack, today reflects on the early Henderson orchestra and admits it played "a certain amount of junk—concert things à la Whiteman and some very bad vocal arrangements of current pop tunes just to comply with the dancers' requests."

Henderson, Redman, Hawkins, Armstrong, and troupe switched over to the Vocalion label during the Roseland run and left a generous output of masters, some of which are included in the recent Columbia *Thesaurus of Classic Jazz* album package, which offers sixty-four epochal Henderson performances on four long-playing discs (Album C4L-19).

When Armstrong returned to Chicago, Rex Stewart took his chair and provided more superb trumpet styling, sitting alongside Joe Smith, who rejoined the band with his subtle, blue horn. Tommy Ladnier also came in (Henderson, his brother says, always insisted on at least one top solo trumpet player and, through most of his career, two) along with trombonists Benny Morton and Jimmy Harrison (regarded by some musicians as the greatest Negro player of all time on the instrument) and, in 1928 as a successor to Redman, the genial Benny Carter.

Carter fitted the Henderson image perfectly. He, too, was a college man—having attended Wilberforce University with Horace Henderson—a slick dresser, a charming conversationalist, and a near-genius musically, playing alto sax, trumpet, piano, and other instruments easily, without training. His arrangements were even more progressive than Redman's and Henderson's, but Redman nevertheless deserves belated recognition for the help he gave Henderson in the '20s. Many a memorable score was from his pen, not Smack's, as was assumed. Don left to join a rising and formidable Detroit orchestra, McKinney's Cotton Pickers, who became just about as popular as Henderson's ensemble.

Horace—Little Smack—and Carter teamed like Ruth and Gehrig in giving the band a one-two punch with their advanced charts. Each section of the band played intricate figures with a precision and swing that astounded musicians and spawned imitators everywhere. Only Jean Goldkette and Duke Ellington, by 1927, were in the same class.

Frank Driggs, in his notes for the Columbia Henderson album already mentioned, offers another view of the group in the late 1920s when taxes were at their lowest, the Eighteenth Amendment was still in force, but poorly enforced, and prosperity ruled:

> "Ironically, in the very same year that the Henderson band rose to its musical peak, popularity and musical bookings began to decline. The reasons were manifold. There was, to begin with, the band's attitude toward the business end of music. Fletcher was a very kind-hearted man, a reasonably strict leader when musicianship was involved, but a relatively poor businessman who gave little thought to the financial future. In those halcyon days, few thought about anything but good times ahead. Fletcher was carefree, his men were strong individualists, and inevitably, things got out of hand. Musicians began arriving later and later for one-nighter dates, sometimes causing cancellations. Fletcher suffered a serious accident in 1928 when his Packard went off the road as he was trying to pass a car which wouldn't pull over. His left collarbone was broken, and he suffered a long gash on his forehead which resulted, years later, in complete paralysis of his left side."

There occurred a great number of personnel changes in the months to come, Bobby Stark and Cootie Williams joining on trumpet; Walter Johnson, drums; Clarence Holiday, Billie's guitar-strumming father; John Kirby, the bassist—the turnover was alarming.

Came the Depression, as the rowdy, gin-drinking decade ended. Driggs writes of the transition period sadly:

> "Although Henderson continued to direct exceptional bands with stellar musicians, others took the lead.
> In 1929, the Henderson band replaced Duke Ellington in a tour-

ing company of Vincent Youmans' Great Day, which ran for a few months on the road, and closed before reaching New York. Other road tours became more arduous, extending farther South and West. The Roseland management lost confidence in Fletcher, who seemed to care even less about business details after his automobile accident. He returned to Roseland briefly during the fall, then began a road tour in the spring of 1930, traveling as far as Oklahoma City, where he helped Andy Kirk get a summer job at Roseland and the Savoy. Unfortunately, the Henderson band didn't play enough blues for Missouri and Oklahoma tastes; the tour was a failure. Returning to New York in the fall, Henderson did get a decent booking in Connie's Inn . . . where he remained through May, 1931."

The marvelous Jimmy Harrison, an entertaining singer as well as a super-star trombonist, died that July of cancer.

Horace Henderson became more and more active, and was of much help to his brother in arranging, playing piano, hiring and firing musicians, and assisting with the business end. New sidemen included Edgar Sampson, saxophone and violin; Jay C. Higginbotham and Sandy Williams, trombones; and Hilton Jefferson, alto, who joined as others left. John Hammond, a crew-cut, white Yale student and jazz fanatic, tried to assist the Hendersons in this period—early 1932—by booking the band into theaters and getting it record sessions. He took no fee, nor did he later when he helped Count Basie, Benny Goodman, Teddy Wilson, and other talented musicians achieve success. But a promised engagement at the Cotton Club fell through, Hawkins gave notice and went to England, and bookings were scarce. Smack auditioned Lester Young for the tenor chair but failed to appreciate the Prez's astoundingly futuristic style, and sent him back to the Midwest. Leon (Chu) Berry also failed to make it. Smack settled on Big Ben Webster, who played "like Hawkins."

And so the mighty Henderson organization was disbanded in the bleak Depression winter of 1934.

At Hammond's insistence, Goodman soon requested a batch of arrangements from Fletcher for the new Goodman band, just signed for NBC's *Let's Dance* radio program and sponsored, if I remember rightly, by a biscuit firm. The Goodman job lasted 26 weeks, into 1935, and restored confidence and hope in Henderson and brother Horace, who also supplied Benny with several challenging charts, *Christopher Columbus* and *Blue Lou* among them.

It was, for Fletcher, the end and the start of an era. Jazz is studded with eras. This, however, was destined to become the most unforgettable jazz period yet. Not just in New York, Chicago or New Orleans, but everywhere.

THE DUKE

Duke Ellington entered the jazz picture later than Armstrong and Henderson, but just barely. A year younger than Henderson and a year older than Armstrong, Edward Kennedy Ellington was born in Washington, D.C., in 1899, and at 6 was studying piano. His family was, like Henderson's, well-fixed, and determined that their son receive a thorough education in the best possible schools.

Duke got his nickname from a high school buddy who was impressed with Ellington's sharp clothing and lordly manner. Duke thought for a while he would become an artist, and showed talent in drawing and painting, but never developed the skill beyond painting commercial signs in his teens while gigging about Washington with a semi-pro jazz band which featured the Ellington piano, Arthur Whetsol's trumpet, Sonny Greer's flashing drums, Elmer Snowden's thumpy banjo, and Toby Hardwick's alto, C-Melody and bass.

This motley, amateurish combo migrated to New York in 1922 and failed to connect. The urbane Duke learned hunger for the first time on that ill-advised assault on Harlem, where the ragtime pianists were cocks of the walk and where the educated Georgian, Henderson, was beginning to make his name known with Black Swan.

Home again in the capital, Ellington studied with Oliver (Doc) Parry, with whom he improved his pianistics and learned the rudiments of arranging. In 1923, Ellington tried New York a second time, worked with the Wilbur Sweatman and Snowden bands (Snowden had remained in New York and landed a modest job), and then, in company with Snowden, formed the Washingtonians for an engagement at an uptown New York cabaret known as Barron Wilkins'. Fats Waller, whom Duke had met on his first New York visit, is said to have persuaded Ellington to return to Manhattan.

The Washingtonians were no sensation, but they were good enough to move to midtown for a run at a basement club called the Hollywood. With Freddy Guy joining on banjo (Snowden had departed), the Duke of Ellington now got down to the serious business of composing, arranging, leading, playing piano, and creating new sounds, new moods, and new techniques in jazz and dance music.

For a brief period, Ellington trailed Henderson as a creative leader of an orchestra. But it wasn't for long. The Duke and his men watched the Hollywood become the Kentucky Club, and gradually acquired a following that included all the show business immortals of that time—Al Jolson, Paul Whiteman and his musicians and singers, Harry Richman, and the team of Clayton, Jackson, and Durante, the last partner being a funny-talking, big-nosed ragtime pianist who had worked all the joints in New York and Brooklyn before Ellington left the District of Columbia.

These years were memorable not only for the gradual development and extension of primitive, sophomoric Ellington attempts at jazz, but for the emphatic changes in Duke and his musicians personally. Charlie Irvis joined the band on trombone, and then Bubber Miley came in on trumpet. Both were native New Yorkers, both "got around" with the prettiest girls in the fanciest Harlem cabarets, both enjoyed the bottle and both played their horns with a natural, built-in ferocity. Smack Henderson wouldn't have hired either.

Now it was late 1924, and Whetsol's chair was occupied by the happy Miley and his array of mutes, plungers, and odd devices designed to make his golden trumpet more expressive. Whetsol had returned to Howard University to resume his medical studies.

Two years later, Irvis departed and was replaced by good-natured, humble Joe Nanton. He, too, became a wah-wah soloist, using a rubber plunger and a tricky embouchure to get savage, rhythmic, growlly trombone effects much like Miley's on trumpet.

Along about November 1925, Ellington recorded for the first time, for the Perfect label. He remembers nothing about the first session except the titles: *I'm Gonna Hang Around My Baby All the Time*, *Trombone Blues*, *Parlor Society Stomp*, and *Georgia Grind*. None is distinctive. Henderson's 1925 records are unquestionably better. "But we were always thrilled to get into a studio," Ellington relates, "for in those days a session was a most uncommon thing. Only a few bands and singers were given the chance."

Duke and his men also believe they recorded for Gennett, the Indiana label that recorded the New Orleans Rhythm Kings, Beiderbecke, and other early artists, but nobody remembers the tunes cut and nobody can come up with copies of the records. "It's just as well," Duke says today, slyly.

Within months, and with the intervention of Irving Mills, a song publisher, the Ellington band began making good records under a new contract Mills was successful in negotiating with Columbia. Little Harry Carney joined the reed section, although he was only 17 years old (and was still there in 1964 as anchor man, on the big baritone). And the aggressive Mills, sensing he had a hot potato on his hands as the Ellington troupe became more popular every month in Manhattan, also was able to get a radio microphone placed in the Kentucky for local broadcasts over WMCA and WHN with an assist from the late Ted Husing, who was one of Ellington's most vocal admirers.

Columbia waxed Duke's pretty theme, *East St. Louis Toodle-oo*, and an innocuous instrumental, *Hop Head*, on its first session and then switched the band over to its subsidiary label, Vocalion, for its next few sides. Trombonist Joe Nanton, a marvel with his plunger, and Miley, who played similarly on trumpet, dominated the *East St. Louis* performance on Columbia and a subsequent version on Vocalion. The latter remains today the oldest available Ellington record, thanks to the Decca-Brunswick album, *Ellington—Vol. 1*, which it was my privilege to produce from original masters some twenty years ago when Decca commissioned me to inaugurate a new line of jazz album reissues.

Let's check the band as of 1927. Ellington, at the piano, was surrounded by Fred Guy on banjo, Braud on string bass; Sonny Greer's drums; a reed section comprising Otto Hardwick, Rudy Jackson, and Harry Carney; and Trumpeters Miley and Louis Metcalfe, plus Nanton's tricky 'bone. By now, Ellingtonia was becoming the smart music of the East. It was on a level with the more cerebral Smack Henderson product. Barry Ulanov tells of this period in his fascinating biography, *Duke Ellington:*

"*After the Columbia-Vocalion dates, the needs, interests, and offers of the record companies in New York were by no means satisfied. From other companies, Melotone, Oriole, Cameo, came offers to do record sessions. The money was too good; it couldn't be turned down. But, on the other hand, there were contractual obligations to Columbia. These were easily overcome: for Melotone, Duke used the* noms-de-danse *of Georgia Syncopators and Earl Jackson and his Musical Champions; for Oriole, he led the Whoopee Makers; on another label, the band became the Lumberjacks.*" *

Henderson's band, and Louis Armstrong out in Chicago, faced the same problem and likewise coined fictitious names for other labels. It was Louis, I recall, who was summoned to the office of Okeh's Tom Rockwell one afternoon and admonished by Rockwell that legal action could be taken if Armstrong attempted such a deliberate contract breach.

"Listen to this record, Louis, and tell me who can play just the way you do for another company," Rockwell said, playing a competitor's disc. "Who is that blowing trumpet?"

Louis listened intently for a moment, then shook his head and lifted

* New York: Creative Age Press, Inc., 1946, p. 63.

the needle off the table. "I don't know who's blowing all that mellow horn," he answered solemnly, "but I won't do it no more."

After switching affiliations again, in October 1927, the Ellington band teamed with the popular singer, Adelaide Hall, on a couple of historic Victor sides (*Creole Love Song* became a classic) and began waxing another series of important, long-lived records which are still eagerly sought by avid collectors in all areas of the world. The band also moved from the old Kentucky Club uptown to the Cotton Club, a far more glamorous job with network radio broadcasts assured.

The Cotton Club at that time was in Harlem, on Lenox Avenue at 143rd Street, but its patronage was almost exclusively white. It was a valuable location for Duke: radio disseminated his music through the 48 states and Canada, the spot itself meant prestige, and it gave the men a chance to record in the afternoons and enjoy a stable home life.

Mills abruptly moved the band from Victor to Rockwell's Okeh label, and the renowned New Orleans clarinetist Barney Bigard joined. Johnny Hodges, a relative of the flashy little hunch-backed Baltimore drummer Chick Webb, also moved in to play alto sax solos. Hardwick had taken a leave of absence for a couple of weeks, but didn't return for some three years, so Hodges' position was secure.

Now, as the 1920s neared an end, the Ellingtons were big enough to go out on long road trips, playing weekly stands in all the key cities as bands did in those days, and until, in fact, the mid-1940s. In Hollywood, they appeared in *Check and Double Check* and introduced *Three Little Words*. Left-handed Freddy (Posey) Jenkins on trumpet and Charles (Cootie) Williams, the big-shouldered Mobile trumpeter, moved into the unit, and Ellington was just entering into a highly prolific period as a composer.

It was a period of vast, unexpected economic changes as well. The Depression drifted in like a monstrous dark cloud and much of the hilarity and big-spending of New York night life disappeared.

Duke's pretty, simple *Dreamy Blues* was recorded in October 1930; it became a money-making hit song under the title of *Mood Indigo* which Irving Mills published, adding his name to the composers' credits. And in 1931, while hungry fathers of big families stood in the snow selling apples, pathetically trying to eke out an honest living in a world of unemployed, the Ellington band's stature was such that it suffered hardly at all. Mills kept the group busy in clubs, theaters, and one-night stands.

Poor times they were, but the music was superb. Cab Calloway led the old Marion Hardy Alabamians at the Cotton Club, alternating with Ellington, and in theaters just as Duke had, but commanding considerably larger fees because of his zany, showmanly *Minnie the Moocher* songs and chants.

It was an eventful year, 1931:

Some 2,300 banks failed.

New York's Empire State Building (1,449 feet high) opened at a cost of $54 million.

The Federal government purchased the Virgin Islands from Denmark.

Women began wearing transparent mesh stockings.

The magazine *Ballyhoo*, which hilariously burlesqued national advertising layouts, was the biggest publishing success of the year.

Paper *Hit of the Week* records (music only on one side) went on sale in thousands of drug stores at fifteen cents each. Ellington was featured on a couple.

Wiley Post and Harold Gatty circled the world in record time in their white Lockheed Vega, the Winnie Mae.

Thomas A. Edison and Knute Rockne died.

Popular motion pictures included *Trader Horn, Skippy, The Smiling Lieutenant, Cimarron, Street Scene*, and Charlie Chaplin's *City Lights*.

The year's hit songs included *I Apologize, All of Me, Dancing in the Dark, Love Letters in the Sand*, and *Where the Blue of the Night*, the last used as a radio theme by Bing Crosby, who had become the most popular singer in the world on the Cremo Cigar program.

Ellington next looked to England and France. The prominent British bandleader, Jack Hylton, was the man behind Duke's first trip outside the U.S.A. Hylton met Ellington and his men (and Ivie Anderson, the new singer) at Southampton one week after the S.S. Olympic sailed from Manhattan June 2, 1933.

In London, despite unexpected racial discrimination and ignorance (newspapers persisted in referring to the musicians' home bailiwick as Haarlem, like the suburban Dutch community just outside Amsterdam) Ellington and his music "went down well," as the English say. The band played the Palladium for two weeks. Duke met and liked the Prince of Wales. He and Greer let the handsome prince play drums one evening at a gala private party the famous publisher, Lord Beaverbrook, gave in the Prince's honor.

During their brief stay in Paris, the band clicked big in three concerts.

Home again, Duke and his band were ready to face another era. Of course he and his men and Ivie didn't know it then.

THE COTTON PICKERS

New York in 1933 was still mired in the Depression and yet, through the grey clouds, streaks of sunshine were occasionally visible. Certainly, jazz did its part in brightening up the scene.

The top jazz orchestras were Ellington, Henderson and a rip-roaring, madly swinging ensemble out of Detroit, McKinney's Cotton Pickers, in which the genial, multi-talented Don Redman of Smack Henderson renown was now a dominant force.

McKinney's Cotton Pickers, not to be confused on records with the 1924 white Cotton Pickers under Phil Napoleon and Miff Mole, hit with their first Victor cutting of *Four or Five Times*, arranged by the clever Redman and boasting a young, hard-hitting lineup that included the trumpets of Rex Stewart and Joe Smith, who like Redman were alumni of Henderson; Quentin Jackson, trombone; Benny Carter and Hilton Jefferson, altos; Cuba Austin, drums; and Billy Taylor, bass, among others. This band recorded more than fifty titles between 1928 and 1933, almost all of them good to excellent by any standard.

And who was McKinney?

It takes a bit of digging to learn that he started out of Paducah, Kentucky, just as did the late Irvin S. Cobb and the hot clarinetist and arranger, Matty Matlock, as well as the rajah of riverboat musicians, Fate Marable. William McKinney played drums and first led a group around Springfield, Ohio. By 1926, McKinney had augmented his band and landed a job at Detroit's Arcadia Ballroom. Nearby, the rising, nationally famous Henderson orchestra was playing the Greystone ballroom. McKinney, as competent in business as Henderson was inept, hired Austin to take over the percussion and became the group's manager. His guidance, and persuasive powers, made the band a big name, a surefire box-office attraction which frequently produced highly artistic, first-rate jazz platters.

Redman, for sure, was the Cotton Pickers' spark-plug. McKinney lured him away from Henderson and let him double as a singer, and others like Prince Robinson and John Nesbitt, tenor; Sidney DeParis, trumpet; Eddie Cuffee, trombone; and George Thomas, a singing saxophonist who died at 22, all helped make McKinney's unit big. They invariably clicked in New York, and as far west as Dallas, Oklahoma City, and Kansas City.

Some of the unit's best records, all on Victor (and they should all be reissued on twelve-inch long-play) include Ben Bernie's old theme, *It's a Lonesome Old Town*, *To Whom It May Concern*, *Wrap Your Troubles in Dreams*, *Zonky*, *It's a Precious Little Thing Called Love*, *Rocky Road*,

I Found a New Baby, their best-selling *If I Could Be With You* and my
own favorite, *I Want a Little Girl*.

ALL AROUND THE TOWN

Cab Calloway's band pursued a more showmanly course than the Cotton Pickers, but all too many historians fail to credit Calloway with a
group that, at times, was certainly one of the four or five best big jazz
bands in the world.

Calloway featured Leroy Maxey on drums. Jealous of Sonny Greer's
expensive array of bells, gongs, chimes, cymbals and cowbells, Maxey
bought up every accessory he could find in every city the popular Calloway played. Finally, Maxey's drums required as much space onstage as
the entire combined trumpet and trombone sections (just as did Greer's
lavish set-up). Cab's reeds included Andrew Brown, Thornton Blue,
Arville Harris, and Walter (Fats) Thomas; with Doc Cheatham, Eddie
Swayzee and Lamarr Wright, trumpets; DePriest Wheeler and Harry
White, trombones; Morris White, guitar; Al Morgan, bass; and Big Bennie Payne, piano—the same Payne who for more than fifteen years since
World War II has accompanied Billy Daniels, with ribald assistance.

Phil Napoleon, a white trumpet player out of Boston—the first jazzman to be born in the Hub—led his own, Dixie-styled Memphis Five
from 1923 to 1928, a combo which introduced the remarkably inventive
Miff Mole and his trombone. Frank Signorelli, piano, and Jimmy Lytell,
clarinet, were also Memphis Five stalwarts along with Jack Roth, a drummer who had worked around New York with Jim Durante. Napoleon's
records were fairly successful, and he worked steadily in the New York
area, but eventually he entered commercial radio as a staff musician and
by 1934 his Memphis Five was remembered only by jazz collectors.

Rudy Vallee's Connecticut Yankees were the biggest sensations of the
Depression period around New York, broadcasting for Fleischman's Yeast
nationally and turning out records almost every week with Vallee's
syrupy, nasal vocals featured on every side. Vincent Lopez, his ricky-
tick piano and orchestra, held down the Hotel Pennsylvania and St. Regis
bandstands year after year; Guy Lombardo, via Cleveland and Chicago,
was ensconced in the Hotel Roosevelt with his schmalzy saxophones;
Fred Waring and his regiment of singers and musicians with Poley Mc-
Clintock at the drums were radio and theater favorites; and the finest,
most musical nonjazz dance orchestra of the period, that of Isham Jones,
became a fixture at the Hotel Lexington. The Lexington had not yet
discovered the hula.

Across town, in Brooklyn at the Hotel Bossert, Freddy Martin and his Mariners wore sailor suits and played peppy fox-trots and waltzes. Hal Kemp and the International Favorites, with Skinnay Ennis on drums and doubling as a breathless, whispering vocalist, also preferred the Hotel Pennsylvania's Manhattan Room, the same room that later became the Cafe Rouge and featured Glenn Miller's music.

Paul Whiteman's position already has been recounted in detail. He was no longer the Number One stage attraction, in 1934, that he was in the late 1920s.

Several of the Chicago jazzmen were, by now, employed in New York by an aggressive Utah trumpet player named Red Nichols. A devoted disciple of Beiderbecke (Nichols had watched Bix play with the Wolverines, Goldkette, Trumbauer, Whiteman, and on gigs around town shortly before Beiderbecke died), he made hundreds of records under a dozen or more phony names and was in a position to deal out work to many a Local 802 member. He led the pit band in various Broadway musical shows, *Girl Crazy*, and *Strike Up the Band* among them, and almost always during his New York residence was contracted for network radio shows. He conducted the studio orchestra on Bob Hope's first broadcasts.

Benny Goodman, Gene Krupa, Joe Sullivan, Dave Tough, Bud Freeman, Harry Goodman, and Eddie Condon, all from the Chicago gang, worked and waxed with Nichols as did Jimmy and Tommy Dorsey, Eddie Lang, Pee-Wee Russell, Art Schutt, Vic Berton, and trombonists Miff Mole, Jack Teagarden, and Glenn Miller. From May through September, Nichols would go out on the road to reap the financial results of his network airtime and records. Sometimes—at least when he came through Kansas City—his Famous Pennies were, more accurately, Unknown Collegians who were delighted to make a summer tour with a famous name maestro for union scale—and in some towns there was no union.

Red's beautiful horn solos, and the marvellous musicianship of his record sidemen, nevertheless gave Nichols a high position on the jazz totem pole down through the years. The best of these titles are still available in a Decca-Brunswick *Red Nichols Classics* album that I assembled from treasured old masters in 1942 and that later was transferred to long-play vinylite.

China Boy (with what many consider to be Red's most inspired solo, at bright tempo à la Bix), *Peg O' My Heart, The Sheik of Araby, Indiana* (Red attended Culver while Hoagy Carmichael was at Indiana University) and *I Want To Be Happy* are the more memorable titles, although the durable Nichols was still making excellent jazz discs in 1964 and blowing fancy, elegant, Bixish trumpet solos with his latter-day Hot Pennies in Los Angeles.

The great, open Southwest was, like New York in the late 1920s and early '30s, a kind of jazz incubator ready to give birth to another important and significant school of musicians. But make no mistake: New York had far outstripped New Orleans and Chicago as the hub of the jazz wheel by 1930. It was the Apple then and it is today. Everything the other side of the Hudson, musicians sneered, was strictly bush-league.

7

Jazz

in the

West

The West begins as one leaves St. Louis and the winding, murky Mississippi, although it isn't until one crosses Jackson County, Missouri, and moves into Kansas that the topography and people begin to *look* Western.

Jelly Roll Morton never played Topeka, Wichita, Oklahoma City, or Muskogee, but he was known and liked in both Kansas City and St. Louis.

Home of Augie Busch's massive show horses and ball-playing Cardinals, as well as vast Budweiser and Busch Bavarian vats, St. Louis has never been a good theatrical town. Showmen regard any week of the year there as despairingly as they do the dreaded seven days before Easter in Catholic Boston. But it is a city with assets: nice parks, two exceptional daily newspapers which are used as models of modern journalism in colleges the world over, and a million or more law-abiding residents, some of whom enjoy dancing.

It was at first a ragtime town, more so than other cities of the Midwest. It was the home of little Louis Chauvin, greatest of the early solo pianists, a young man who perished, like Beiderbecke, much too soon, and whose incredible technique is said to have eclipsed all other pianists of that era. Chauvin died at 25 in a Chicago hospital five months after he had left St. Louis. He weighed no more than 148 pounds, adored women

ILLUSTRATION: Bennie Moten's Kaycee Band. Shown in this 1930 photograph are (seated, left to right) William "Count" Basie, Booker Washington, Thamon Hayes, and Willie Mc Washington; and (standing, left to right) Vernon Page, Oran "Lips" Page, Ed Lewis, Jack Washington (leaning on chair), Harlan Leonard, Ed Durham, Woody Walder, Leroy "Buster" Berry, Jimmy Rushing, Bennie Moten, and Bus Moten (with baton).

73

and bourbon whisky, rarely considered his health and, some say, was an opium addict when the end came in 1908.

Chauvin wasn't alone. The same Scott Joplin who was to die in New York in 1917 also resided in the Mound City for several years (1900-1903) at 2658-A Morgan after living for a time in Sedalia, Missouri, where in 1899 he had composed *Maple Leaf Rag*.

Well before the World's Fair in St. Louis in 1904, Tom Turpin was an eastern Missouri legend. He operated the Rosebud Cafe, a tough, rough gambling–hotel–bar installation which became the "in" after-hours spot for the Greater St. Louis area. As one of the first rag pianists in Missouri, Turpin attracted musicians from everywhere, including New Orleans riverboat sidemen. Johnny and Bob Moore, brothers; Joe Jordan, a Cincinnatian; Sam Patterson, St. Louis born and perhaps the tragic Chauvin's closest pal; and a young man known only as "Klondike," who bragged of his experiences in the Alaska gold fields, but whose appearance indicated he had struck out, all played in the 1900-1918 period together.

It is said that shrewd Lulu White, of Mahogany Hall in New Orleans' Storyville, was so impressed with Chauvin and Patterson on her visit to the World's Fair that she offered them both long-term jobs in her high-priced house. Both declined. They had everything they wanted in St. Loo.

John Stillwell Stark & Son, publishers of Joplin's original rags, built the world's most complete ragtime catalog in St. Louis. Arthur Sizemore, Paul Pratt, Cad St. John, Ed Mellinger, Art Matthews, Charles Thompson, Sonny Anderson, and Arthur Marshall all played rag piano well; Charlie Creath, the St. Louis bandleader who played various saxophones, accordion, and trumpet (and whose personable sister Margie has long been married to Drummer Zutty Singleton) even remembers several excellent women ragtime players, Louella Anderson, Sweetie Bell, and the first female to join the union, Theodosia Hutchinson. Margie Singleton played piano in her brother's band at one time.

Ragtime died out as jazz bands swept into popularity, but there most certainly wouldn't have been any jazz had there not been ragtime pianists. St. Louis musicians deserve more recognition than they've been given.

The Charlie Creath band goes 'way 'way back, to 1914, and it remained active—and in demand—through 1930 in the Mond City vicinity. Dewey Jackson and the travelin' Fate Marable were frequent attractions, and in more recent years the Jeter-Pillars orchestra (led by Jimmy Jeter and Hayes Pillars) has ranked as the outstanding local jazz group. There was a period in the 1920s when the ebullient Frankie Trumbauer led a top-drawer band, but in 1927, when he and Beiderbecke rushed to Detroit to work with Goldkette, it meant the end of St. Louis as a Tram base. Jess Stacy, a pianist from Cape Girardeau, Missouri, who got his training on the riverboats with Carlisle Evans, and who enjoyed Beiderbecke's cornet on stopovers in Davenport, ended up in St. Louis for a lengthy stay before moving on to Chicago and the piano chair in Benny Goodman's band in 1935.

Charles Ellsworth Russell, the Pee-Wee of the clarinet, was born in St. Louis in 1906, attended school in Oklahoma and slowly worked his way up the ladder to international prominence via Herbert Berger, whose nickname, of course, was Ham; then with Beiderbecke and the Chicago gang in the 1920s and finally on into the '60s as a free-lance, always-employed jazzman. Pee-Wee is a character among characters, playing with a zonky, croaking sound that somehow mesmerizes listeners, musicians especially.

Willie Austin, a slide 'bone player, was active in and around St. Louis in the early '20s, as was the trumpet player Eddie Allen, who recorded with Clarence Williams. Oliver Cobb, a trumpet player of the Armstrong mould, attracted attention until his death by drowning. It was his orchestra, taken over by Eddie Johnson, a pianist, that was to become known in 1932 as the Crackerjacks. Ern (Chick) Franklin and Harold (Shorty) Baker sparked the group in the early 1930s. The Crackerjacks went under the baton of Pianist Chick Finney about 1936 and are still remembered in the Mound City. So are Eddie Randall, in whose group trumpeter Miles Davis got his start, and George Hudson, an alumnus of Jeter-Pillars.

Surely the most unorthodox of musicians to hail from St. Louis is Jack Bland, a banjo-guitar player who formed the Mound City Blue Blowers with Dick Slavin, who "played" a ten-cent kazoo, and Red McKenzie, singing and blowing a tissue-covered nickel pocket comb.

The MCBB created such unbelievable effects, and jazzy syncopations, that in 1924 they recorded a hit single for the purple Brunswick label, *Arkansas Blues* and *The Blue Blues*, thanks to the efforts of Isham Jones. He was Brunswick's big attraction at the time, leading his first orchestra in Chicago. Later, in New York, the whacky triumvirate of Bland, Slavin, and McKenzie were joined by Eddie Lang, the finest jazz guitarist in the world at that time. All musicians and collectors of rare jazz wax value highly the MCBB 1929-31 versions of *Hello Lola, One Hour, Georgia on My Mind* and *I Can't Believe That You're in Love with Me* with an augmented lineup that also featured Coleman Hawkins, Glenn Miller, Gene Krupa, Eddie Condon, Muggsy Spanier, Jimmy Dorsey, Al Morgan, Pee-Wee Russell, and others, on Okeh and Victor.

In more recent years St. Louis has produced a disproportionate number of other reputable musicians. Feather's *Encyclopedia* alphabetically lists Chuck Berry, the late Jimmy Blanton, Milt Buckner, Teddy Buckner, Buddy Childers, Wallace Eckhardt, Jimmy (*Night Train*) Forrest, Sam Gardner, Bob Gordon, Jimmy Gourley, Wendell Marshall, Louis Metcalfe, the late Velma Middleton, Oliver Nelson, Lennie Niehaus, Singleton Palmer, Irving (Mouse) Randolph, the late Gene (Honeybear) Sedric, Arvel Shaw, Floyd Smith, Don Stovall, Clark Terry, Cal Tjader, Ernie Wilkins, and Juice Wilson.

Across the state, some 260 miles west, located on cliffs above the intersection of the Kaw and Missouri rivers, Kansas City loomed as a hotbed of jazz. The census of 1870 credited the city—in Missouri, not Kansas—with 32,000 citizens, some of them blanketed Osage Indians. Some 5,000 others were foreign-born, with Irish predominating.

The first bands to appear in the Jackson County metropolis were just that—*military bands*. Arthur Pryor played the 1914 Fraternal Order of Eagles convention and composed a striking new tune, the *Heart of America March*, in honor of the event. John Philip Sousa immediately chose it as the official Camp Funston song, and played it with his world-renowned band for years afterward.

Thomas J. Pendergast, a poor scholar but an outstanding baseball player at St. Mary's College across the Kaw in Kansas, moved up within the city's rugged first ward to become not only a leading local political figure, but a power throughout the entire "Show Me" state. It was because of Pendergast that Kansas City, and to a lesser extent its little sister community across the intercity viaduct, Kansas City, Kansas, became a citadel of jazz in the '20s.

As in St. Louis, Chicago, and New Orleans, solo pianists playing jerky, syncopated ragtime started the jazz ball rolling. James Sylvester Scott was perhaps the first. A Negro, he was born in Neosho, Missouri, far to the south of Kansas City, and then resided in Ottawa, Kansas, and Carthage, Missouri, before he moved to Kansas City in 1914. Until his death in 1938, Scott made the Pendergast city—Tom's Town—his home.

Scott's most noted rag tunes include *Broadway Rag, Evergreen Rag, Dixie Dimples*, and *Prosperity Rag*. In his later years, he led a band in the Negro section of segregated Kansas City, but it was never an outstanding group.

The white Charles L. Johnson also became a territory favorite as a rag pianist at the time Scott was composing and playing in Kansas City. By far his best known rag title was *Dill Pickles*, which is still heard today, but his other credits include *Sweet and Low, If I Only Had a Sweetheart*, and *In the Hills of Old Kentucky*. Johnson, like Scott, became a dance band pianist who played competent jazz and ragtime solos in theater, hotel, and ballroom bands for more than a quarter of a century. He was admitted to the American Society of Composers, Authors and Publishers in 1941, at the age of 65. *Dill Pickles* assures Johnson a share of fame in any history of Middle West jazz.

Euday L. Bowman was a Texan, from Fort Worth, who migrated northeast to work the lush cabarets and saloons of the booming Heart of America city. His *Twelfth Street Rag* is the biggest-selling, most popular rag of all time. Stockmen, especially, applauded his playing and made him a favorite entertainer in the early, formative days of Kaycee jazz. Bowman also composed *Petticoat Lane, Shamrock Rag*, and *Eleventh Street Rag*. The latter failed to make it.

Lucien Denni came to Kansas City all the way from Nancy, France, where he played semi-pop piano. He became a name in Kansas City chiefly with theater audiences. His *You're Just a Flower From an Old Bouquet* became a smash national hit, as did his raggier *Oceana Roll*, but Denni was not a rhythm pianist of the Scott-Johnson-Bowman school. He was much too classy. He died in California in 1947.

Musicians of Local 627, led for a quarter of a century by William Shaw, even now recall five other ragtime pianists who left their mark. Charlie Watts and Thomas (Scrap) Harris apparently never composed any rags or tunes that became nationally popular, but they were so expert on the keys that many of the community's musicians followed them around the Negro residential and business districts on the Missouri side. They were somewhat like James P. Johnson and Willie Smith in New York. Pianists looked up to them.

In the public schools, Major N. Clark Smith at Lincoln High taught music to a number of eager youngsters. Harlan Leonard, Walter Page, Jimmy Smith, Eli Logan, and Lamarr Wright were just a few of his hundreds of pupils.

Charles N. Daniels, writing under the name of Neil Moret, moved to Kansas City from his birthplace, Leavenworth, Kansas, as a child, and began composing pop songs at 17 after studying piano and harmony several years. His *Chloe, Moonlight, Sweet and Lovely*, and *Put Your Little Arms around Me* were more in the vaudeville field than the ragtime-jazz idiom. He, too, moved on to California, where he died in 1943.

Bennie Moten was born in 1894; George E. Lee entered this world in 1896. With an incredible similarity, the two musicians worked side by side, in competition, until the early '30s. Moten at 12 was playing horn in Lacy Blackburn's children's band, and because his mother had taught him piano, he formed his own jazz combo in 1922 with Dude Lankford, a drummer, and Bailey Handcock, a singer. Lee, who got his start later than Moten because of his war service, also launched a trio in 1922 with his

sister Julia Lee at the piano and Bruce Redd on drums. The two trios
worked on Eighteenth Street at rival cabarets. Lee played piano and
baritone saxophone.

By the *Black Bottom* dance craze period, before the market collapse on
the infamous Black Thursday of October 1929, Moten and Lee were leading the two best bands in the Kansas City area. Boss Pendergast had
become a power. Prohibition was in effect from California to Vermont,
but the tiny spot on the map labeled Jackson County prospered merrily
as if the Volstead Act were only a rumor. More and more speakeasies
were opening, more and more bookies operated publicly; vice and graft
and corruption in the city's government increased while a small handful
of citizens expressed alarm.

Moon-faced Tom Pendergast, who went to bed every night promptly
at 9 o'clock and allowed his cronies and henchmen to run his bars and
make collections from the various Pendergast enterprises, weighed 200
pounds, stood three inches shorter than six feet and bore a startling facial
appearance. He quickly outstripped his older brothers Jim, John, and
Mike as a vote-getter, friend of the poor, and organizer of the city's
precincts. In a city election on November 3, 1925, he won political
control for thirteen years, by fewer than 200 votes. A few days after the
election, he appointed a slim Iowan named Henry F. McElroy as city
manager. Together, they opened the gates for a fantastic period of corruption—and jazz growth—that continued almost until the start of World
War II in Europe.

Kansas City, Kansas, gave birth to Jesse Stone, a clever and ambitious
arranger, composer, and musician who rated along with Moten and Lee
over on the Jayhawk side; Paul Banks also led a popular jazz group there.
Budd and Keg Johnson, Eddie Durham, Booker Pittman, Ben Smith,
Chauncey Downs, and later, Bassist Eugene Ramey and a pudgy little kid
named Charlie Parker were other jazzmen coming out of the Kansas side.
Musicians from the two cities, of course, worked in both. Jack Washington, the saxophonist, recalls his "back and forth" trips—long before he
anchored Count Basie's reed section—with a grimace. "On bitter cold
nights," he says, "I hated both Missouri *and* Kansas."

The city became more and more corrupt and musicians from the entire
Southwest, attracted by the lush employment opportunities, arrived to
play the joints. The fancy Hotel Muehlebach's Plantation Grill had its
own attractions, the Carlton Coon–Joe Sanders "Nighthawks" orchestra
among them. The late Ted Weems, out of Texas, also was a frequent
Muehlebach attraction long before Perry Como hooked on as vocalist.
The rival Baltimore Hotel a block away didn't play as many name
orchestras but, strangely, Jack Teagarden was one of several titans who

occasionally appeared with orchestras there. The Bellerive Hotel's Terrace Room came later with Hal Kemp, Ben Pollack, Glen Gray and Casa Loma Orchestra, and Bernie Cummins. Unfortunately for those of us living there, it was one of Pollack's less illustrious bands. And Casa Loma was just beginning its semi-jazz stylings in '31.

While the roster of Local 627 swelled with the happy influx of musicians, the rise of crime became a matter of national interest. In Kansas City in 1928, exactly 89 persons were murdered, and only three murderers were sentenced to be hanged. In all of England that same year (and keep in mind the population was eighty times as great as Kansas City's) only seventeen persons were murdered. Of these murderers, thirteen were hanged, four received life sentences and two cases remained unsolved.

In 1927, figures show, Kansas City under Pendergast domination outdid Chicago with a murder rate of sixteen for each 100,000 population; Chicago's rate was 13.3 murders. Yet in 1930, looking over the last four years of rule by the McElroy-Pendergast combination, the conservative, sometimes holier-than-thou *Kansas City Star* said editorially: "For the last four years, with all its faults and failures, Kansas City probably has had the most efficient city government in its history."

Efficient, no. Exciting, yes. And the music went 'round and 'round with Bennie Moten and George Lee, the old rivals, leading the baying pack. But they were not without competition.

Perhaps the two best were Alphonso Trent and Walter Page. A big, strong bassist who had studied at Kansas University after his graduation from Kansas City's Lincoln High, Page organized in Oklahoma City with Oran (Lips) Page, Buster Smith, Singer Jimmy Rushing, Eddie Durham, and Bill Basie, who had been stranded after a panic tour with the Gonzale White road show. The band was known as the Blue Devils.

Basie had become a Count, of course, and Lips Page, who was a half-brother of big Walter, wound up in New York as a name trumpeter with Artie Shaw, and others. Durham established himself as a Jimmie Lunceford arranger and trombonist who, oddly, doubled guitar. Smith, the little professor, was possibly the most advanced and inventive musician of the group, and without any question led Charlie Parker into Bird's futuristic groove. But he never achieved wide recognition.

Trent, a pianist, was an urbane college man who had left his birthplace in Fort Smith, Arkansas, and clicked in Dallas with WFAA broadcasts and a long run at the Adolphus Hotel. Stars of the caliber of Leroy (Stuff) Smith, Snub Mosely, Lee Hilliard, Peanuts Holland, and Hayes Pillars, the saxophonist who years later joined saxist Jimmy Jeter and became the dance and jazz band king of St. Louis with the Jeter-Pillars orchestra, were all Trent sidemen. Dan Minor, Harry Edison, Henry

Bridges, and the immortal Charlie Christian, who revolutionized the jazz guitar, and helped "invent" bop jazz, also worked for Trent in the '20s and '30s. But for all the excellent music he produced, Trent never became a household word like Armstrong and Ellington. It was perhaps too much of a musicians' band. And it never made the appealing records that Bennie Moten's combo recorded so consistently.

George Morrison was an older man, from Fayette, Missouri, the home of Central Methodist College. A violinist, he played no jazz himself, but was enough of a virtuoso to play concerts in Europe and form an outstanding dance band in Denver immediately after World War I. Andy Kirk, just a kid out of Kentucky, played tuba with him briefly. Jimmie Lunceford played saxophone. The late actress, Hattie McDaniel, who won an Oscar for her emoting in David Selznick's *Gone With the Wind*, worked happily as Morrison's singer. Kirk has often told me how well she sang the blues and pop tunes alike.

Kirk, who now manages the Theresa Hotel in New York's Harlem, moved from Morrison to trumpeter T. Terrence Holder's orchestra in Oklahoma, then took over the band called the Clouds of Joy in 1928 and started an enviable career that kept him active until 1948. John and Mary Lou Williams, Benny Thigpen, the magnificent tenor saxist Dick Wilson, who died of tuberculosis in 1941, and a host of other sterling jazzmen happily worked with the gracious Kirk through the years.

Musicians also lauded the band of Jasper (JAP) Allen, Kansas City-born and another of the Lincoln High students. For a brief time it looked as if Allen might become another Moten, but despite the fine playing of Alton (Slim) Moore on trombone and Booker Pittman, alto, Allen disbanded in 1931. The late Clyde Hart played piano and did the arranging, most of his charts resembling those played by the hot and heavily-publicized McKinney's Cotton Pickers. Maybe that's why the band folded.

George E. Lee enjoyed one hit record side, *If I Could Be With You*, which reportedly outsold McKinney's version throughout Kansas and Missouri, but the passing years proved that his piano-pounding, big-voiced sister, Julia Lee, was a superior musician. When the Lee band eventually folded, Julia worked as a single and with her Boy Friends, usually a trio, and became by far the best known entertainer in the Greater Kansas City area. She even enjoyed hit records (*Gotta Gimme Whatcha Got, King-Size Papa, Snatch and Grab It*) in the 1940s, and in working with Julia many years as her producer I acquired most of the information on Kansas City jazz published in *Down Beat, Jazz Cavalcade*, and here.

Bennie Moten, for all the color and vitality of so many jazz bands of his time, remained the king of the hill until well into the '30s. Page and his Blue Devils eventually joined him, giving Moten a roster, through the years, of men like Basie, Rushing, Lips Page, Walter Page, LaForest Dent, Ed Lewis, Lamarr Wright, Paul Webster, Tiny Taylor, Bus Moten (his nephew, who played accordion and piano), Eddie Durham, Buster Smith, Ben Webster, Eddie Barefield, Woodie Walder, Leroy Berry, Dan Minor, Willie McWashington, Joe Keys, Jack Washington, Harlan Leonard, Thamon Hayes, Sam Tall, Willie Hall and Abe Bolar. As with Henderson and Ellington in the East, to have worked regularly with Moten was the highest recommendation a musician could carry.

This was the Moten whose theme, *It's Hard to Laugh or Smile*, hit the air over Kansas City's KMBC and WDAF from the Winnwood Beach ballroom in North Kansas City, or from Frank Duncan's Fairyland Park on the far South Side. To those of us living there, Moten was our own major league entry, and his records always got big receptions.

Along the little music shops in Kaycee's Harlem, from Independence Avenue south through Twelfth Street to Eighteenth Street and beyond—in the area bisected by the rambling Paseo Boulevard—photos of Bennie and his men hung high on the walls and patrons sat in booths spinning his new releases. Jenkins' in the heart of downtown Kansas City also found Moten to be a brisk seller, and we who followed the new record releases then as today's kids keep tab on the Beatles found the Moten Victors fine listening, prejudiced as we were with a home town talent.

Some of the better titles were *Missouri Wobble, South* (the band's all-time biggest seller); *Kansas City Squabble, Rite Tite, Boot It, Rit-Tit Day, Moten's Swing, Tony, Lafayette*, and Jimmy Rushing's shouting vocal of *I Wanna Be Around My Baby All the Time*. Bennie's death on a table while undergoing a tonsilectomy April 2, 1935, has been recounted many times. Kaycee was never the same after his death.

The jazz fan, or musician, who spent time in Pendergast's friendly bastion in this period of the late 1920s and early '30s experienced a time that was distinguished not only by extraordinary sounds, but sights and smells as well.

The odor of Kansas City is in no way like that of, say, New Orleans, which has its own variety from blooming magnolias to caramel pralines to perfumed B-girls. On a warm night, Kaycee suffers from unbearable humidity and a vast blanket of heavy air hanging, like a big balloon, over its expansive, active stockyards. It is a rich, heavy, unavoidable and meaty smell matched only by that emanating on similar summer nights from Chicago's South Side cattleyards. There is, as well, a cabaret atmosphere that is evidently unique—in no other city in the fifty states, or in Europe, the Orient, or South America, have I encountered quite the same odd contribution to the atmosphere of jazz. Perhaps it is the tall Armour & Co. lard can, three feet high or more, filled with hot boiling shrimps or fresh water crayfish—crawdads, in Missouri—which are served, gratis, to bar imbibers not so much as a reward for their patronage but, alas, to induce an unquenchable thirst and the sale of additional drinks across the mahogany. Selected customers at tables also are favored with a plate of the pink, heaven-scented, blisteringly hot hardshells. Did Escoffier ever prepare so tantalizing a dish? Those of us who frequented Pendergast-era niteries believe not. Few shrimps or crayfish, unfortunately, may be found in bubbling lard cans today. Like needled Muehlebach beer, they were perhaps a delicacy not destined for universal popularity.

Chili con carne originated in Texas, but in Kansas City the making and serving of it was developed into a high art. There were countless chili parlors which served nothing else. All musicians ate chili in awesome-sized servings, the better to line their stomachs with heavy grease. Then they could safely drink amazing quantities of liquor while working. Charlie Parker was an avid chili gourmet until he died.

Ribs? Only the finest barbecue in the whole, hog-lovin' world, Mary Lou Williams used to say. They were short, blessed with choice, lean pork and served in sauces that Mildred Bailey, Duke Ellington, and other connoisseurs favored so greatly they would telegraph orders to be shipped on the midnight TWA flight out of state. Blackened to a crisp over Boone County hickory, Kaycee's succulent ribs are even now renowned among musicians, even though it is the less impressive steaks that get the publicity and exploitation.

We will add, in this brief account of choice gastronomical memories, one other unorthodox favorite of Jackson County's musicians. It was in great demand at one time. We refer to nutmeg.

Mixed with milk, or a soft drink, nutmeg in quantity becomes a cheap substitute for alcohol. Like the kid glue-sniffers of the '60s musicians imbibed fantastic quantities of the spice. To inquiring dancers, or the boss, they would explain they used the 'meg to flavor their toast, or breakfast rolls, or whatever came to mind, during intermissions. On some band-stands in some of the city's nicest clubs, forty or fifty empty nutmeg containers were not an uncommon sight by midnight. Jay McShann and Bird Parker were users, but the formula had been popular twenty years before they came along.

So much for food and potables. We will only add that years later, the gentlemanly Jimmie Lunceford, a popular visitor to Kansas City hundreds of times in his career as a leader, ate a double order of chili can carne in a small Oregon restaurant while on tour and died almost immediately. That he was poisoned by tainted food was established beyond question. Jimmie never drank liquor. Yet his death has, strangely, always been listed in music publications as caused by a heart attack.

The passing of Moten changed the jazz picture, but did not lessen its momentum or influence in the Heart of America city.

Bill Basie, a Waller-styled pianist, had left Moten before Bennie's tragic surgery. His twelve-piece band at the crowded, ill-ventilated Reno Club developed by chance almost, not by plan. Walter Page, at one time Basie's boss in the Blue Devils, was on string bass; the trumpets comprised Joe Keys, Dee (Prince) Stewart, and Carl (Tatti) Smith. George Hunt was the sole and soulful trombonist. Saxes included Lester Young, in from Andy Kirk, on tenor; Buster Smith and Jack Washington, altos; Slim Freeman, tenor; Clifford McTier, guitar; Willie McWashington, drums, and Vocalists Alice Dixon and Jimmy Rushing. From the first, underpaid as they were, but imbued with a startling spirit and humor, the Basies were a standout. Smith wrote clean, hard-swinging arrangements for as little as $3 (and was never paid for some of them) which utilized reed voicings and brass punctuations more Henderson than Ellington in concept, and yet purely Basie-Reno as subsequent records confirmed. Few would have predicted Basie's thirty-year jazz reign at that time. Even Basie had no such ambitions.

Tommy Douglas, the most inventive of the three Douglas brothers in Kansas City, was born in nearby Kansas and educated at the Boston Conservatory. He led his own band, off and on, in the Kansas City area as early as 1931, playing alto, tenor, and baritone saxophone and writing strong, jazz-oriented arrangements somewhat like those of the little professor, Buster Smith. At the Amos and Andy Club, with Jo Jones on drums before Jo went east with Basie, Douglas displayed a band somewhat like Basie's. His own saxophone solos, at the time, were regarded as ultra-modern, and while he is alleged to have influenced the young Parker in the wine-nutmeg-roses period of the early 1930s, Bird himself told me that Smith was more his idol.

It was, in retrospect, a town of sin and saxophonists. Ben Webster, Lester Young, Dick Wilson, Jimmie Keith, Henry Bridges, Jack Washington, Harlan Leonard, Buster Smith, the brothers Tommy, Bill, and Buck Douglas, Joe Thomas, John Williams, Booker Pittman, Ed Inge, Eddie Barefield, Don Stovall, Lem Johnson, Freddie Culliver, Bob Mabane, John Jackson, Walter Knight, Herman and Woodie Walder, Budd Johnson, Franz Bruce, and, when they were in town, Coleman Hawkins and Leon (Chu) Berry all clashed with their axes. What a place for reed salesmen! Parker was younger. Not until 1935-36 did the Bird soar into view and slowly orbit his way into outer space.

Musicians sometimes tangled in blowing contests which ranked with the lions and gladiators of Rome. Basie, Kirk, Mary Lou Williams, Buck Clayton—all fondly recall the sessions in which the brass set a riff behind the reeds for hour upon hour with seven or eight contending soloists wailing and weaving brilliant improvisations purely for their own pleasure.

Nor did a Young or a Webster always emerge the winner. Dick Wilson of the Clouds of Joy band, certainly the most handsome, frequently upset the bigger names with his musicianship. Young, a taciturn and inhibited man off the stand, often became an incredibly bold and forceful soloist in competition with a Webster or a Herschel Evans, who later joined Young in the early Basie band at Chicago's Grand Terrace. Miss Williams, who held her own at the piano against Basie or anyone else in town, recalls how she once dropped by an after-hours club, enjoyed a saxophone session for an hour, went home to shower, change clothes and have a sandwich, then returned to watch the same musicians still jamming out the same tune. "And they never repeated a phrase," she says. The late Lips Page was the best of the trumpet players when it came to creating background riffs.

The Cherry Blossom and the Subway (and later, Lucille's Paradise) were favored meeting places of musicians, and from 2:00 a.m. around the clock until noon it was every man for himself. With prohibition ended, potables were easily available to go with the blackened shortribs and chili.

Along the rocking Twelfth Street East of downtown Kaycee was the Sunset Club, a modest nitery operated by the late Piney Brown. Here, stolid Pete Johnson rocked the keyboard with his fierce and emotional boogie-woogie piano. Sam (Baby) Lovett, a New Orleans emigrant, pounded the drums. Behind the bar, a massive man, Joe Turner, tending bar, shouted the blues and urged Johnson to "roll 'em, boy, let 'em jump for joy." He and Jimmy Rushing, who worked as a strolling singer at the old Cherry Blossom, were the town's best singers, although a little guy named "Little Buck" was also highly favored by many. Like Andy Kirk's Pha Terrell, he emphasized pop ballads of the day in a high tenor rather than the earthy, rollicking indigo numbers of Turner and Rushing.

No matter how loud the jazz, musicians suffered no police interference. Patrol car officers frequently were to be seen inside the Sunset, in fact, enjoying the blues of Johnson, Turner, and Lovett. Pendergast saw no harm in cabarets; his beer and whisky companies supplied potables to hundreds of clubs, just as his cement company paved all the highways and byways of Missouri. Then too, the bookie joints grossed twice as much operating round the clock as from standard eight- and twelve-hour shifts, a lesson well-learned and still practiced today by Las Vegas gamblers.

Have we missed some of the better Kansas City musicians? Jesse Price succeeded Lovett as the city's favorite—and flashiest—drummer. There were A. G. Godley, Eddie Mallory (later Ethel Waters' conductor), and the late Eddie Tompkins, who became a topflight trumpeter with Lunceford only to die in 1942 when struck by a rifle bullet in army camp maneuvers. Another exceptional group of youngsters of Bird Parker's age were on the way up, too. In 1936, the booming Kaycee era was far from ended.

To the south, Gene Coy's Aces were as popular around Amarillo as was Bennie Moten in Missouri. A transplanted New Orleans bassist who worked as a teen-ager with Punch Miller and Buddy Petit, the late Nat Towles, migrated to Texas, Oklahoma, New Mexico, and Missouri with a band of his own, winning the respect of all the Southwestern musicians. Later, in Omaha in the mid-1930s, Towles featured young men who were to become first rank jazzmen, Buddy Tate, Sir Charles Thompson, Henry Coker, and the late Freddy Beckett among them. Neil Hefti is said to have sold his first arrangements, as an amateur, to Towles, who died in 1962 in Berkeley, California, of heart disease.

Milton Larkins' band in Houston featured Eddie (Clean Head) Vinson on vocals and alto sax, as well as Illinois Jacquet, Arnett Cobb, and Bill Davis. Boots and his Buddies (Cliff Douglas) were San Antonio's best. Don Albert, a trumpet player; Edgar Battle; Troy Floyd, in whose band Herschel Evans and George (Buddy) Tate got their start; Ernie Fields; Charlie Christian; Jim Daddy Walker; and the colored Sweethearts of Rhythm, fronted by slender Anna Mae Winburn, were all talented and popular Texas-Oklahoma musicians of the same period.

To the west, San Francisco was slow in welcoming jazzmen, but Los Angeles had heard the Original Creole Band of New Orleans as far back as 1913. One of them, Dink Johnson, remained on the Coast while the others returned home. Mutt Carey reconsidered, returned to Los Angeles and remained there until his death in the late '40s.

The indefatigable Jelly Roll Morton hit California in 1917, sent word to New Orleans that he had a well-paying job at Baron Long's roadhouse in Watts, a South Los Angeles suburb, then welcomed Wade Whaley, Frank Dusen, and Buddy Petit, who were dressed so unfashionably at the station that Morton and Johnson hid them inside their big MacFarland sedan and drove directly to a tailor's shop. There they outfitted the three rubes with new, double-breasted suits and junked their tattered, country box-back jackets.

Kid Ory, as recounted earlier, made the first jazz records in Los Angeles for the Spikes brothers in 1921 with drummer Dink Johnson on clarinet; Carey on cornet; Ben Borders, drums; Ed Garland, bass; and Fred Washington, piano. Roberta Dudley and Ruth Lee, singers, also recorded with Ory at that time.

Merritt and Henny Brunies of New Orleans were probably the first white jazzmen to play on the West Coast, also in '21. Merritt played trumpet, Henny the trombone (as did their brother George Brunis* in New Orleans) and Billy Lambert was on drums at the Dome in Ocean Park. Jake Flores, a trombonist in Paul Whiteman's original orchestra at the time, says the Brunies brothers were sensational. "They played real jazz, not the stuff Whiteman was playing, and all the musicians were crazy about them. We had never heard that kind of music in California."

Ted Lewis, who had left the Earl Fuller orchestra in the East, fronted a commendable jazz band in California at that time, Flores adds. The late Abe Lyman employed jazzmen as well. Miff Mole was his star trombone soloist at brother Mike Lyman's Sunset Inn long before he recorded with Red Nichols in New York. Gus Arnheim was Lyman's pianist, and Roy Fox, who became a name maestro in London society circles later, played trumpet. Then, too, Ben Pollack played in Venice, another Los Angeles suburb, with Benny Goodman and Glenn Miller in his lineup.

Wingy Manone, a wandering, one-armed trumpet minstrel from Louisiana, saw an immense banner atop an Albuquerque ballroom while waiting for a change of trains, and was intrigued with its message:

DOC ROSS

And His Recording Orchestra

Featuring Jack Teagarden and His Euphonium

Manone, who had met Ross previously, wandered into the ballroom and learned that Teagarden also doubled on sliphorn. As he described it to me in 1944:

> *"The minute I heard Jack blow, I knew that here was a man with a future. I wired my band in Winslow that I quit; I asked my musicians to keep on going and get a new leader. And right there, on the spot, I became a member of Ross' orchestra. That's how I discovered Jack Teagarden."*

* It is the *Brunies* family. But about 1940, George (the trombonist, and the most renowned brother) changed his name to *Brunis* on advice of an astrologer. He has been *Brunis* ever since.

A year later, Wingy and Jack were in New York, where Pollack (through Wingy and Gil Rodin) hired him for his swinging Park Central Hotel band. Manone also recalls that Paul Dedroit, a drummer, had another fine California band at that time.

Whiteman and Art Hickman made the most noise, however. Neither had much jazz to offer. Hickman featured Bert Ralton in a novel act. He smoked two cigarets while playing a C-Melody saxophone solo. Arnheim later made it big with a band in which Bing Crosby, for a time, and Stan Kenton were featured. Jimmy Grier, Anson Weeks, Tom Gerun, who employed Woody Herman and Tony Martin; Williams & Walsh, Phil Harris, Henry Halstead, Everett Hoagland, Paul Pendarvis—all these were commercial, beautifully wardrobed orchestras that unfailingly served up innocuous dance music.

Los Angeles later produced Les Hite's band, an exceptional one that was long featured at Sebastian's Cotton Club in Culver City with Lionel Hampton on drums and vibraphone.

Compared with Louisiana, Illinois, Missouri, and New York, the Golden Bear state was anything but prolific jazzwise. Curtis Moseby led his Blue Blowers for a time but dropped them to become a night club operator. What other groups there were, it appears, left little permanent imprint in jazz history. Buck Clayton's 1933 group was on a par with Hite's, but the late Teddy Weatherford, a pianist, killed the Kansas trumpet player's future in California by hiring the entire group to play an engagement with him in Shanghai. Buck took Bumps Myers, Eddie Beal, Teddy Buckner, Baby Lewis, and Caughey Roberts to China. On their return, more than a year later, Clayton and Roberts joined Basie in Kansas City —and that was the end of the fine Clayton orchestra, although it is still happily remembered in China, some say.

Thus did the first Western period of jazz conclude. Musicians swiftly moved up as the oldsters retired and died off. An impish, 14-year-old saxophonist who had trouble reading music, Bird Parker; an amiable Muskogee pianist, Jay McShann; a veteran sax player with Moten, Harlan Leonard, and numerous others in the West were eager to dive into the pool off the high board in 1934.

Out West, the best was yet to come.

8

The Singers

Mamie Smith, a struggling thirty-year-old blues shouter of Cincinnati, recorded *Crazy Blues* in 1920 for the Okeh label and made history: it was the first jazz vocal ever recorded; it was the second Negro performance to be preserved on records (the first was by the inimitable Bert Williams); it made the unknown Miss Smith the favorite of all Negro singers of her time.

At a time when a record was an expensive, luxurious novelty, *Crazy Blues* sold 7,500 copies the first week, at a dollar a copy. Ten million American Negroes had never heard "their" music, or a member of their race, on record before. Miss Smith was a sensation everywhere. She purchased a palatial home, wore $2,000 beaded gowns and played theaters throughout 1920-21 with crowds consistently lined up for as far as two blocks; she even had her own Jazz Hounds orchestra to travel with her throughout the nation. One of its members, Coleman Hawkins, was only 15 when he joined her troupe. He's still around, a giant among saxophonists. And Mamie is long forgotten.

THE FIRST LADIES

There were other superb femme singers, and other Smiths, none of them related. Mamie was known as "Queen of the Blues." Bessie Smith was the

ILLUSTRATION: Mildred Bailey (left) and Billie Holiday. (Photograph of Billie Holiday by Charlie Mihn.)

acknowledged "Empress of the Blues" and the favorite of all musicians. Trixie Smith had no such pretentious title, but she was also liked on discs.

Gertrude (Ma) Rainey came out of Georgia, and became perhaps the nation's favorite blues singer as Mamie Smith's flame diminished in the mid-1920s. It was in one of Ma's touring troupes that Bessie Smith got a start. It was ironic, moreover, that Bessie subsequently topped her benefactress as a song-seller on records.

Ma was the oldest of the early jazz singers. Born in Columbus in 1886, she worked with the Rabbit Foot Minstrels, in which her husband, William (Pa) Rainey, was a featured entertainer. Not until 1923 did she record. Then, for Paramount with Lovie Austin's Serenaders, Ma waxed such classic shouts as *Boll Weevil Blues, Moonshine Blues, Barrelhouse Blues*, and the unique *Ma Rainey's Mystery Record* with Tommy Ladnier on trumpet, Jimmy O'Bryant on clarinet, and Lovie Austin at the piano. Her career continued until 1933, when she retired and returned to Georgia. She died in 1939.

Bessie, from Clarksburg, Mississippi, was eight years younger than Ma, and possessed a more compelling voice. She toured with the Raineys throughout the Theatre Owners Booking Association or T.O.B.A., circuit (Negroes wryly called it "Tough on Black Acts" time) and started her series of unforgettable recording sessions in early 1923 with *Gulf Coast Blues, Down Hearted Blues, Keeps On a Rainin,'* and *Tain't Nobody's Business If I Do*. Even more so than Ma Rainey, she was greeted with the idolatry of America's Negro citizenry and it is said that her first discs sold more than 2,000,000 copies the first year.

Bessie employed only the best available jazzmen on her records. Clarence Williams served as her coach and pianist, but he was showman enough to team her immensely powerful voice with Henderson, Armstrong, Redman, Hawkins, Joe Smith, Charlie Green, Buster Bailey, James P. Johnson, Charlie Dixon, Tommy Ladnier, Porter Grainger, and Louis Bacon on the hundreds of selections she recorded so magnificently through 1931. But as it has to so many jazz artists, the end came tragically to Bessie, in 1937, in a motor car accident outside Clarksdale, Mississippi. Some say she was refused medical treatment at a hospital, and died while enroute to another many miles distant. *The Death of Bessie Smith*, in fact, was the title of a bitter play presented in 1962 in New York and Los Angeles. But by then only a few musicians and singers remembered Bessie, and her marvellous singing style.

Columbia Records has issued a number of Bessie's most memorable original records in long-playing albums called *The Bessie Smith Story*, which include the last four titles she made at the insistence and under the supervision of John Hammond in New York in the fall of 1933. Accompanied by Frankie Newton, Chu Berry, Jack Teagarden, Buck Washington, Billy Taylor, Bobby Johnson, and a youthful Benny Goodman, Bessie is at her best shouting *Do Your Duty*, *Take Me For a Buggy Ride*, *I'm Down in the Dumps*, and my own all-time favorite, *Gimme a Pigfoot and a Bottle o' Beer*.

While Lizzie Miles was a hit in Paris, Alberta Hunter of Memphis was the first American blues singer to ring the bell in London. She did it in 1926, when she was 29 years old, introducing *St. Louis Blues* to a tumultuous reception. In London, at the Drury Lane, she played the role of "Queenie" in the first touring production of *Show Boat* with Paul Robeson.

A far more sophisticated performer than Bessie, Lizzie, Ma, Trixie, and Mamie, Miss Hunter was the first to sing *A Good Man Is Hard to Find* (which she personally taught to Sophie Tucker) and, at the old Panama Cafe on Chicago's South Side, *Someday Sweetheart*. Before World War II, she sang in twenty-five countries on four continents. During the war, under auspices of the USO, she performed in both the European and South Pacific theaters. More recently, she has worked as a nurse at a New York hospital. Few singers have enjoyed such productive lives.

Julia Lee has previously been noted as the singing sister of George E. Lee, the Kansas City maestro. At four, she was singing with her father's string trio. At ten, she was playing piano. In her teens she sang at private parties, house rent socials and the usual amateur functions, usually playing the piano in a semi-Waller groove and emphasizing humorous lyrics. In 1939, a big name in Kansas City as a result of her many years at Milton Morris' friendly Troost Avenue taproom, Julia played the Three Deuces in Chicago for Carl Cons and Sam Beers, proprietors. But rarely did she leave Jackson County after that engagement ended.

In 1944, she made her first records, in Kansas City for Capitol. Many were best sellers, even though she was 42 before she launched her career on discs. As Julia's producer for seven years, it was a labor of love for me to select songs, assemble musicians and try to catch her good-natured piano and vocal talents on records. In Hollywood we backed her with Benny Carter, Vic Dickenson, Red Norvo, Jesse Price, Red Nichols, Red Callender, Dave Cavanaugh, and her Kaycee steady, Baby Lovett on drums.

Julia's death in December 1958 left the world of jazz with one less great singing entertainer. At times she was Wallerish, at times Mortonish, but her delightful rhythm piano and husky vocals could always quickly be identified as Julia Lee's. How much more effective might she have been had she recorded as a young woman!

The early recording artist Ethel Waters also made *Oh, Daddy* and

Down Home Blues for Black Swan in New York with Cordy Williams' Jazz Masters in the fall of 1921, shortly before Fletcher Henderson joined the company and became Ethel's musical advisor-conductor. No great shakes as a blues singer, Miss Waters was more of a straight pop vocalist like Lena Horne and Dinah Shore today. Her style, however, attracted millions of white fans and she moved into a vastly different world from that of Rainey, Bessie, Julia Lee, and her contemporaries. She was featured in the 1929 film, *On With the Show*, first of the "super" Hollywood musicals. Her records, perhaps not so pure aesthetically as others', nevertheless were appreciated by musicians. Songs like *Am I Blue, Cabin in the Sky, Happiness Is a Thing Called Joe*, and *Stormy Weather* are strongly identified with Miss Waters, who in her forty years of show business also wrote a best-selling book, *His Eye Is on the Sparrow*, and starred in a number of Broadway plays and Hollywood filmusicals. She has lived in Southern California in her sunset years, anxious to perform but infrequently called.

Florence Mills was said to be the most beautiful and most feminine of all the Negro singers. She apparently did not record; yet older musicians have never forgotten her—and her voice—and Duke Ellington is said to have composed *Sophisticated Lady* in her memory. A star of Broadway and numerous Harlem shows, she died young. In more than one way the career of the late Helen Morgan was similar to Miss Mills' tragic life.

Miss Waters recorded *Porgy* and *I Can't Give You Anything But Love* with the Ellington band in 1932, a record that is difficult to come by now, more than thirty years later. Ellington also recorded with Adelaide Hall, a favorite in Harlem and England, and Alberta Jones before he signed a showgirl, Ivie Anderson, as his permanent oriole in the early 1930s.

The list of singers is long. Ida Cox recorded as far back as 1925 and as recently as 1960. Gladys Bryant, Faye Barnes, Katie Crippen, Maude DeForrest, Rosa Henderson, Edna Hicks, Maggie Jones, Emma Lewis, Viola McCoy, Julia Moody, Josie Miles, Hazel Meyers, Mary Straine, Isabelle Washington, Inez Wallace, Hannah Sylvester, Bessie Brown, and Lena Wilson are all listed in Charles Delaunay's *Hot Discography* as having recorded with the popular Henderson band in the '20s. Louis Armstrong recorded magnificent accompaniments to such singers as Maggie Jones, Bessie Smith, Ma Rainey, Trixie Smith, Virginia Liston, Margaret Johnson, Sippie Wallace, Alberta Hunter (who used the name of Josephine Beatty to evade contractual commitments), Bertha (Chippie) Hill, Blanche Calloway (Cab's sister), Eva Taylor, Hociel Thomas, Lillie Delk Christian, Victoria Spivey, and still another Smith Girl—unrelated to Bessie, Trixie, and Mamie—Clara Smith, who also recorded with Henderson.

There were others: Rosetta Crawford, Sara Martin, Virginia Liston, Viola Bartlett, Edmonia Henderson, Roberta Dudley and Ruth Lee of Los Angeles, Anna Bell, Lil Johnson, Monette Moore (who was shoutin' blues lyrics at Walt Disney's Disneyland in California at the time of her death in 1962, some forty years after she first recorded in Chicago with Pianist Jimmy Blythe); Lottie Beaman, Sodarisa Miller (and there's a rare one), Ethel Ridley, Louise Vant, Mary Johnson, Alice Moore, Julia Jones, Hattie McDaniel (the actress), Ann Cook, Helen McDonald, Helen Baxter, Mae Scott, Lavinia Turner, Thelma La Vizzo, Irene Scruggs, Annie Turner, Ada Brown, Mary Bradford, Lela Bolden—the list runs on and on, truly incredible when one considers the few record companies in the '20s compared to the more than 700 labels active today. There must have been a king-sized market for female blues singers in the turbulent '20s.

Jazz and blues singing was born in the deep South, and was the natural expression of Negro plantation workers, domestics, laborers, and perhaps most of all, churchgoers. The pure gospel music of the Southern Baptists closely resembled secular music a hundred years ago and it still does today.

Each year brought a more sophisticated wordage in the songs sung by the first jazz singers. Simple complaints: "My man's done gone," repeated again and again, gradually gave way to more complicated, ingenious lyrical expressions: "A good man is hard to find." Humor began to be a requisite for all singers by 1925, and much of it was cleverly double-entendre as so many of Bessie Smith's discs attest. But through all the sly innuendos of *Nobody in Town Can Bake a Jelly Roll, If You Don't I Know Who Will, You've Been a Good Ole Wagon, Trombone Cholly, Put it Right Here, Kitchen Man,* and *Need a Little Sugar in My Bowl,* a wealth of honest human emotion was displayed, far more so than was evident in the puerile popular songs of the moment. The same is true today.

The Men: Leadbelly, Jelly, and Others

Choosing songs and producing, from the control booth, records by the immortal Huddie (Leadbelly) Ledbetter in Hollywood in 1944 proved a privilege such as few artists and repertoire men enjoy in a lifetime. Alert, sensitive, and determined to make the best discs of his career, Leadbelly insisted on Paul Mason Howard's soft and unobtrusive zither accompaniment. It was a wise pairing. Leadbelly's big twelve-string guitar, Howard's zither, and the voice of Leadbelly combined for a fresh and distinctive sound. Capitol reissued twelve of these records in the spring of 1963;

boosted by artificial reverb and new equalization, they sound even better than when originally issued.

Leadbelly was almost certainly one of the first great jazz and blues singers. Although born in Louisiana, at Mooringsport, he was reared in Texas, and in 1900 (he was then twelve) he played not only guitar, but raggy piano and accordion as well. Huddie learned hundreds, perhaps thousands, of worksongs, shouts, hollers, stomps, blues and rags in his lifetime, some of it spent in prisons and jails on charges of murder, attempted homicide, and assault, on all three of which counts he was convicted.

Many of Leadbelly's songs were recorded for the U. S. Library of Congress, as were hundreds of Jelly Roll Morton's.

Morton, too, was a singer of sorts. More accurately, he was an actor who recited lyrics to his own subtle piano accompaniment, but with amazing effectiveness. His narration of the moody Mamie Desdume lyrics in *Mamie's Blues* is just one sample of his dramatic skill. Jelly was three years older than Leadbelly. Their paths must have crossed many times in the early days.

In August 1940, in New York's humid Harlem, I enjoyed my first and last interview with Morton. He wore a green business suit, striped in yellow, and he confidently chewed a cigar as he awaited the arrival of his "chauffeur." He may have had no more than a dollar in his pockets, but his manner reflected prosperity, sophistication, and compelling interest in world affairs. It was at the time of the Germans' horrendous blitz of London.

"Hitler can't last," he predicted dourly. "It's against the laws of God to do what he's doing."

Morton, in the grand manner, presented his business card—the largest I had ever seen—and drove off to what he called a "vital business appointment."

George Hoefer, *Down Beat*'s veteran columnist, remembers that same summer and how Morton appeared in person on the Blue network's popular *Chamber Music Society of Lower Basin Street* program in Radio City. Jelly started playing and singing on the coast-to-coast Sunday afternoon show and when time was up refused to heed the producer's frantic arm-signals. The engineer did everything but cut off the microphone, but Morton continued his act until the announcer moved in and took the show off the air. The girl singer never did get on with the two songs she had rehearsed with Paul Laval's orchestra all week. She was Dinah Shore.

The fast-talking, pool-playing entertainer, who carried a diamond in one of his front teeth in his earlier days, moved out to Los Angeles a few months later, but was no more successful in finding work than in Harlem. On July 10, 1941, the man who repeatedly claimed he had "invented" jazz, died of asthma and heart disease in Los Angeles. His old friends from New Orleans assisted his widow in having Roman Catholic services performed at St. Patrick's church and burial in Calvary cemetery. Kid Ory, Mutt Carey, Fred Washington, Ed Garland, Paul Howard, and Frank Withers served as pallbearers.

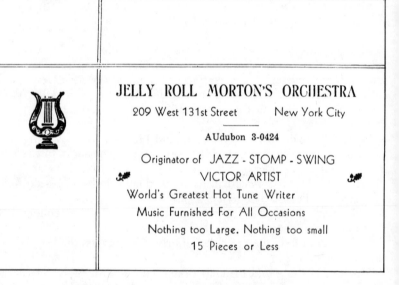

JELLY ROLL MORTON'S ORCHESTRA

209 West 131st Street   New York City

AUdubon 3-0424

Originator of JAZZ - STOMP - SWING

VICTOR ARTIST

World's Greatest Hot Tune Writer

Music Furnished For All Occasions

Nothing too Large. Nothing too small

15 Pieces or Less

Thus, the incredible saga of Jelly Roll Morton came to an end far from his beloved New Orleans and the excitement of the "district." Morton may have been an egotist and a braggart, but he could back up many of his claims. Many of his original compositions have become international standards. A legion of musicians were influenced by his pioneer piano and vocal contributions to jazz. The world is poorer for his passing.

Louis Armstrong was, of course, a cornet-trumpet soloist first of all, but his singing was instrumental in making him a record favorite throughout the world. His first recorded vocal is said to be on *Gut Bucket Blues* (with his Hot Five), recorded November 12, 1925, in Chicago. The first jazz "scat" singing came less than three months later when Louis, recording a light novelty called *Heebie Jeebies*, dropped his sheet of lyrics on the floor during a "take" and quickly improvised a rhythmic, chant-like vocal in which no words were used. Cab Calloway, Leo Watson, George (Bon Bon) Tunnell, and numerous others later scatted jazz with varying success.

Jimmy Rushing in Oklahoma and Joe Turner, the shouting bartender of Kansas City, came along as singers, and one also remembers the fly, sly vocalistics of little Don Redman. His *I Heard, Four or Five Times, Gee Baby Ain't I Good to You* and *The Way I Feel Today*, most of them with McKinney's Cotton Pickers, are still playable today.

Lonnie Johnson played guitar, somewhat like Leadbelly, and sang blues so well that men like Duke Ellington invited him on record dates as vocal soloist. Lonnie, unfortunately, never made it with the public. But there are few more entertaining baritones around just to sit and watch and enjoy informally, as so many of us have enjoyed Johnson for several decades.

Red McKenzie's singing with the Mound City Blue Blowers was mentioned in the preceding chapter. His singing and comb-playing were far more popular with musicians than with record buyers.

Williard (Big Bill) Broonzy, a Mississippian, recorded sporadically over a thirty-year period. Son of a slave who lived to be 102, Bill sang the blues as well, and as distinctively, as any man. But despite appearances in New York's Carnegie Hall, Broonzy, like Johnson and McKenzie, remained a virtual unknown to the American public and won wide acceptance only in Great Britain shortly before he died of cancer in Chicago in 1958.

Samuel B. Charters and other students of blues, and blues singers, rate Blind Lemon Jefferson as an extraordinary talent. A Texan, Lemon worked with Leadbelly in the Lone Star State and recorded as far back as 1925 for the old Paramount label. He died in 1930, but is still talked about and is said to have influenced a number of later singers. Charters, in his book *The Country Blues*,* described Jefferson as "fat, dirty, dissolute, but his singing was perhaps the most exciting country blues singing of the 1920s."

There were other blind singers, including Blind Arthur, also recorded on Paramount; Blind Blake; Blind Gary, who made fourteen sides for Melotone; Blind Mack, on Vocalion; Blind Norris, Decca; Blind Percy, Paramount; Blind Willie, Vocalion; and Blind Lemon's Buddy, King Solomon Hall.

Also prominent were Ora Alexander and Texas Alexander; Amos—that's all, just Amos—on Bluebird; Andy Boy, also on Bluebird at the

* New York: Holt, Rinehart & Winston, 1959.

same time, 1936; Shelley Armstrong, who was accompanied by the legendary Scrapper Blackwell; Kokomo Arnold, who popularized *Milk Cow Blues* and was a prime Chicago favorite; Billy Banks; Lee Brown, the Decca ace of the late 1930s; Barefoot Bill; Amos Easton, the renowned "Bumblebee Slim," who waxed hundreds of titles on at least five labels; and Leroy Carr, a prolific artist who also enjoyed Scrapper Blackwell's guitar accompaniment.

There were others: Bo Carter, who introduced *Ants in My Pants* in 1931; Dusky Dailey; Charles (Cow-Cow) Davenport, whose piano was more exciting than his singing; Walter Davis, the Victor-Bluebird king from 1930 to 1945; Little Bill Gaither, who sang under the name of Leroy's Buddy; Blind Boy Fuller, who teamed with Sonny Terry on numerous records; Sleepy John Estes; Robert Hicks, who used the name of Barbecue Bob on his many Columbia records; and Peg Leg Howell, also a Columbia artist.

These were the singers who prevailed, in blues and jazz circles, long before the "modern" era. None played the New York Paramount Theater, none was ever starred in a Hollywood musical, none ever broadcast over a network or faced the ugly red eyes of television cameras. Yet their talents helped mold the styles that evolved, through the decades, into Ella Fitzgerald and Ray Charles.

Going Modern: Mildred . . .

Mildred Bailey was one of the first of the great orchestra singers to bridge the gap between popular and jazz audiences. Featured with Paul Whiteman's troupe (in which her husband, Kenneth "Red" Norvo, was xylophone soloist), she introduced a completely unique manner, one that incorporated honest blues and jazz phrasing with commercial singing such as Mildred's contemporaries, Ruth Etting and Kate Smith, were offering in the early 1930s.

Mildred, part Indian, had a sound as far from Bessie Smith's as one could get. Her voice was high, light, and almost delicate like a child's, but despite her lack of powerful physical equipment she had intelligence, background, musicianship, and heart in excess. Her first solo records in 1929, with the late Eddie Lang's guitar and orchestra, established her immediately as a favorite of musicians, and her subsequent cuttings until her death in 1951 invariably met with raves. She sang under her own name, with Benny Goodman's pickup bands, with Norvo's superb dance orchestra, with Whiteman (her brother Al Rinker was one of the Rhythm Boys), with the Dorsey Brothers' band and with studio groups in which she hand-picked musicians like Teddy Wilson, Buck Clayton, Bunny Berigan, Mary Lou Williams, Lester Young, and dozens of others of highest rank to accompany her inimitable, swinging style.

Following five years with Whiteman's organization, Mildred and Norvo formed their own band and for several years turned out records of extremely high jazz quality. Poor health, due partly to extreme over-weight, forced La Belle Bailey to retire early. She was but 43 when she died. No white singer has ever replaced her. Wherever she went, she was made welcome. In clubs in Los Angeles, Chicago, Kansas City, and New York's Harlem I more than once accompanied her in making a regal entrance, then watched her devour two or three orders of short ribs, and loudly yell her pleasure at the entertainment offered. She must have been the first of the truly, all-knowing hip chicks, blessed with an unerring ear and astonishing good taste in jazz. At one time, she and Billie Holiday vied for Number One honors in all the musicians' polls, and though Mildred deplored her rival's personal habits—including the addiction to narcotics—I watched Mildred cry uncontrollably as she applauded the incomparable dramatic ability of Lady Day in a West Fifty-Second Street night club.

Mildred was good company. She had a wild, unbridled sense of humor matched only by her voracious appetite. She had horrible, frightening periods of depression as well, and many a musician withered before her profanity when dark moods beset her. But Mildred Bailey was the first of the white queens of jazz singing, and today remains the best. Excellent examples of her ability are offered in the 1962 Columbia package of three long-play discs featuring forty-eight of her best-remembered vocals (C3L-22).

. . . LADY DAY . . .

Billie Holiday, the Lady Day of jazz, was by any standard Mildred's equal as a singer. A Baltimorean, she was the illegitimate daughter of Fletcher Henderson's guitarist, Clarence Holiday. A childhood spent in poverty in New York gave her a bitter, cynical outlook and she never quite believed it when told she was an extraordinary talent.

Unlike Mildred—who was eight years older—Billie was an almost illegally attractive woman physically. The fresh white gardenia in her hair was her trademark, and her underplaying of each word in a song added to her moody, soulful presentation on a night club floor. She sang of lynchings in the deep South in *Strange Fruit*, she sang of raw sex in *Them There Eyes* and *You Go to My Head* and perhaps several hundred other love songs, and she sang of her Savior in *God Bless the Child* and

other semi-sacred works dear to her heart. Shortly after she had left the
Artie Shaw and Count Basie bands, disgusted with the jazz world and life
itself, she sat for four hours one morning in the basement of Chicago's
Three Deuces—entirely sober and without narcotics—pouring out the
story of her life to me for a *Down Beat* feature that was published in
1939. I quote from that story:

> "Billie says she isn't satisfied now. She wants to get somewhere.
> Maybe on the stage. She wants to make money—lots of it. She wants
> to buy a big home for her mother. She doesn't expect any happiness
> —she is used to hard knocks, tough breaks. And she admits she is
> envious of Maxine Sullivan and other colored singers who have
> gotten so much farther ahead than she. Someday, she thinks, she'll
> get a real break. But she's not very optimistic about it. Billie Holiday
> is convinced the future will be as unglamorous and unprofitable as
> her past." *

The pessimistic Lady Day was not entirely accurate in her prediction.
Only 24 then, she lived to be 44, and to be hailed throughout the world
as an impeccable singer who earned a fantastic income for personal
appearances, including two treks to Europe in 1954 and 1958. She had a
part in the disappointing Jules Levey motion picture, *New Orleans*, of
1946, in which she sang beautifully, and her many records with Teddy
Wilson and other first rate jazzmen attest to her genius. In his *Encyclopedia of Jazz*, Leonard Feather sums it up as well as anyone:

> "During her last few years the many tragedies in her personal life,
> marked by endless and hopeless battles with narcotic addiction, took
> a heavy toll on Billie's voice, but almost until the end enough of the
> original quality remained to enable her at times to recapture at least
> a shred of the glory of her early years. She made her final appearance
> at a benefit concert at the Phoenix Theater in Manhattan in June '59
> and a few days later was taken to a hospital where, because of the
> U. S. laws that treat narcotic addiction as a crime, she was arrested
> on her death bed.
>   Though the subject of what is and what is not jazz singing had
> led to many differences of opinion among experts, Billie Holiday's
> voice had in it elements that were indisputably the essence of jazz.
> Hers was one of the incomparable voices that jazz produced in the
> '30s. Some observers likened her to Bessie Smith, and she admitted

* "I'll Never Sing with a Dance Band," *Down Beat* (November 1, 1939), p. 4.
Reproduced by permission of *Down Beat* Magazine.

*to a great admiration of Louis Armstrong, but her debt to any earlier
artist was minimal." ***

Again it is Columbia that has taken many of Lady Day's most memorable old single records and presented them in an album of three long-play records (C3L-21) entitled *Billie Holiday: The Golden Years.* In choice of masters, it excels the Bailey collection. And in the notes, Ralph J. Gleason, the erudite San Francisco jazz expert, makes this ironic comment: "It is sad beyond words that Billie never knew how many people loved her."

In her bank account, when she died, was seventy cents.

Bessie Smith, Mildred Bailey, Billie Holiday—Olympians all, from a talent standpoint. There is one more as well.

. . . ELLA

Ella Fitzgerald was born an orphan, but her life became roses when the little drummer, Chick Webb, spotted her singing at an amateur contest in a Harlem theater and became her guardian and music mentor in the last few years of his life.

Three years younger than Holiday, eleven years younger than Bailey, and twenty-four years younger than Bessie Smith, Ella came out of Newport News and caught on with musicians, at least those in the East, with her first record (Webb's *Love and Kisses* on Decca) in 1935. Her purity of sound, exceptional ear, and love of singing (all still evident today) placed her high on the lists of musicians' favorites throughout the '30s. When Webb, a hunchback, died in late 1939 she took over his band for a time, but eventually was forced to work as a single when the wartime draft sent thousands of musicians into the armed forces.

Ella has worked solo ever since. She is said to enjoy years with an income of more than $150,000 annually. She is a frequent guest on network television shows, hosts like Perry Como, Dinah Shore, Andy Williams, Ed Sullivan, and Jack Paar paying as much as $10,000 for two songs. And through it all—close to thirty years of singing professionally—Ella has retained her natural graciousness, sweetness, and love of people. She never acquired any of the corrosive habits that have downed some of her singer and musician colleagues. She is a devoted mother and a smiling perpetual optimist who has without question accomplished more for jazz than any other woman in history, and more than most men. Her early records on Decca and her more recent performances in Verve albums are uniformly excellent if, at times, somewhat monotonous for their absolute

---

* Feather, *Encyclopedia of Jazz,* pp. 257-258.

vocal perfection. Ella lacks the pathos and dramatics of Holiday but she has assets even the immortal Lady Day lacked. What more can be said of the best jazz singer in the world today?

It is when one looks below the modern triumvirate of Bailey, Holiday, and Fitzgerald that judgments suddenly become difficult.

More Songstresses

No two musicians will agree on singers' abilities. If one argues that Detroit's Della Reese is one of the greats, another will counter that she sings no jazz at all and is purely a pop vocalist with an irritating, unnatural style that she has carefully devised to attract attention. The dissenting opinion aside, to my ears Miss Reese is indeed a fresh and welcome addition to the expanding ranks of jazz and blues singers today. Her experience as a gospel performer with Mahalia Jackson (greatest of the religious singers, but well outside the jazz idiom despite her successful collaboration with Duke Ellington in Columbia's *Black, Brown and Beige* suite), and her recent albums indicate that Della—born as recently as 1932—is most certainly an outstanding jazz songstress. Her 1961 *Special Delivery* presentation with Mercer Ellington's music on RCA-Victor is proof enough.

Nancy Wilson is another young one with a bright future. From Columbus, Ohio, she leaped into the light in a happy teaming with the Cannonball Adderley Quintet in a 1962 Capitol album. *Down Beat*'s readers elected her second only to Fitzgerald in its '62 poll, giving her almost twice as many tallies as the third place winner, Peggy Lee.

Peggy, at her best, is a remarkably versatile jazz singer who can swing like a house-rent hostess, shouting the jumps and delicately hovering over ballads with equal skill and affection. If she is not always at her best, then neither are other singers—Fitzgerald excepted. Try Peg's *Mink Jazz* Capitol album for a representative selection of her efforts in a highly competitive and difficult field.

Anita O'Day has been established since 1939, when she stormed out of Kitty Davis' cocktail lounge to accept a job at Chicago's hangout for jazzmen and record fanatics, the Three Deuces. It was during Anita's first engagement at the Deuces, incidentally, that I held that memorable *Down Beat* interview with Billie Holiday, long after Anita and the waiters had departed. Anita had never heard of Billie until the Deuces gig was begun.

Uninhibited, ever-hip, and consistently in high good humor, Anita made hit records with the Stan Kenton and Gene Krupa orchestras in the

1940s and since becoming a single, has recorded hundreds of titles in a romping, ebullient jazz groove on Verve. She has numerous imitators, including June Christy and Chris Connor.

Dinah Washington, a Lionel Hampton discovery during World War II, was as distinguished a singer as anyone but was considered to be more of a rhythm and blues performer than a jazz thrush. Under certain circumstances, in a ballroom filled with jazz fans, Dinah could carve all the other fem chanters into oblivion with her raw, righteous, down-to-earth bent notes and power. Like Ray Charles, she often transported audiences into hysteria. She died in December 1963.

Kay Starr might also rank higher these days if more care was paid in preparing her records. She now works only the gambling houses of Las Vegas, Reno, and Lake Tahoe in the Far West, and her recent discs indicate she has little interest in retaining musicians and jazz cultists among her followers. At her best, like Peggy Lee, Kay is a thrilling singer who can move audiences into a frenzy with her compelling manner at the mike. Fiddles and vocal groups have led her astray.

Also enjoying their special followings in the jazz world are Carmen McRae, another singer who knows the value of dramatics; Sarah Vaughan, boomed as the "next Fitzgerald" during World War II when she worked as Earl Hines' vocalist, but who somehow fell short of becoming a true great; Nina Simone, a more recent entry; and Gloria Lynne, another youngster.

Annie Ross of the unbelievable range, who helped the Lambert–Hendricks–Ross trio score with their ingenious Count Basie vocal arrangements, quit the group recently and returned to her home in Great Britain, but she still retains a following here. Her *Twisted* record solo is a minor jazz classic.

Abbey Lincoln, Betty Carter, Gloria Smyth, Mabel (Big Maybelle) Smith, Dakota Staton, Carol Sloane, Teddi King, Etta Jones, Vi Redd—who also plays Bird-like alto saxophone—Anne Gable, Sheila Jordan, Teri Thornton, Aretha Franklin, Barbara Dane—who re-creates ancient but still honorable Bessie Smith blues with her incongruous but attractive deep contralto voice—Nancy Harrow, Helen Merrill, Ernestine Anderson, Billie Poole, Lorez Alexandria, Meg Welles, Rita Reyes, Marian Montgomery, Odetta, Pat Thomas, Ketty Lester, Kitty Doswell, Ethel Ennis, Etta James—a compelling young singer in the Mahalia Jackson tradition—and Jeanne Lee are additional femmes who record and work clubs (what few are left) as jazz singers.

Leaping from the earliest of singers to the contemporary stars necessarily omits a number of top-drawer artists who merit more than a listing.

Helen Humes was a popular blues singer long before Count Basie signed her for his band in 1938, and she remains a popular singer in the '60s, in her fourth decade as a professional.

Ivie Anderson, an Ellington stalwart for eleven memory-making years, made records that are still extraordinary today. *I Got It Bad and That Ain't Good* is perhaps her most famous discing, though Ellington fanatics can easily name a dozen others of jazz interest. Ivie died in 1949. Ellington has hired scores of girls since and never found one to approach her.

Maxine Sullivan, whose easy, lightly swinging style was the envy of Billie Holiday when the Sullivan vocal of *Annie Laurie* proved a big 1938-39 record hit, is remembered as a talented jazz singer with a personal style. Connee Boswell likewise was held in high regard for many years after the illustrious Boswell Sisters trio disbanded. Helen Ward and Martha Tilton with Benny Goodman recorded several good jazz vocals. Nellie Lutcher whipped a Steinway like Earl Hines and sang hot, even on slow love ballads. Had she recorded back in the '30s she, like Julia Lee, almost certainly would have moved up to a class with Bailey and Holiday. But it wasn't until the spring of 1947 that the amiable Lake Charles, Louisiana, gal was lured into a waxing studio in Hollywood.

Sister Rosetta Tharpe sang sacreds and pops with an urgency and virility that all jazz connoisseurs enjoyed, and her backwoods guitar added a flavor no other singer possessed. Cleo Brown, who accompanied herself at the piano like Nellie Lutcher and Julia Lee, made her mark with a series of five Decca records including *Pinetop's Boogie-Woogie*.

Lee Wiley of Oklahoma, part Indian like Mildred Bailey and Kay Starr, is still active with her showmanly slit skirts, gorgeous legs, and bouncing vibrato. On Commodore (with Muggsy Spanier) and RCA-Victor albums, Lee still sings circles around many of the younger girls even though she will be fifty on October 9, 1965.

Savannah Churchill, Una Mae Carlisle, Ella Mae Morse, Georgia Gibbs, Liza Morrow, Frances Wayne, Joya Sherrill, Betty Roche, and the late June Richmond, who died in Europe, all made jazz records of varying degrees of excellence. The late Lil Green, with her *Romance in the Dark* and *Why Don'tcha Do Right?* was a particularly successful singer in the 1940s; her discs still sound good. Young Timi Yuro of Los Angeles, only twenty, could become a singer of prominence should she learn to be more selective in her material and accompaniment. She has the voice.

BASS NOTES

Ray Charles is undisputably the kingpin among men jazz singers but is hardly the "genius" that he is billed. Joe Williams, for several years featured with the Basie band, is in many ways Charles' equal and employs fewer attention-grabbing affectations. Nat Cole's income as a singer tops Charles' every year, but Cole is arbitrarily rated a pop singer by jazz fans and is excluded from the "inner circle" by many. Cole, nevertheless, can sing a jazz vocal unmatched by any man in the world when he wants to. He also can—and sometimes does—rip off a scintillating piano solo equal to anything being played by any jazzman today. His appeal is, of course, far more cerebral than Charles' bobbing, weaving, nervous, perspiring approach.

Billy Eckstine, like Cole, is a jazz singer of unlimited ability when he cares to prove it. His singing with the old Earl Hines band during World War II, and with his own band later, typified the finest in the vocal art. Louis Armstrong, Jimmy Rushing, and Joe Turner have been noted already as early jazz vocalists; they remain excellent entertainers.

Men singers seem far more inclined to gimmicks, or unnatural mannerisms, than the women. Babs Gonzales, Oscar Brown, Jr., and Jon Hendricks depend exclusively on unorthodox lyrics. Mark Murphy, Mel Torme, and Jackie Paris attempt self-conscious improvisations so hip they often come off as hilariously corny.

Frank Sinatra—before his superb voice declined so measurably in the late 1950s—Vic Damone, Buddy Greco, and Perry Como have all sung jazz, at least occasionally. Bing Crosby was a truly inspired and inspiring singer through the 1930s, recording dozens of timeless jazz vocals before his pipes deteriorated. The misguided attempt of his four sons to sing jazz a generation later can charitably be described as pitiable.

Infinitely more musical are the efforts of Aaron (T-Bone) Walker, a Texan who sang with Les Hite's band in California nearly a quarter of a century ago. His amplified guitar complements his dramatic baritone voice ideally. Sonny Terry; the late Roosevelt (The Honey Dripper) Sykes; the late Walter (*Confessin' the Blues*) Brown; Brownie McGhee, the guitar-playing partner of Terry; John Lee Hooker, the Mississippian; Champion Jack Dupree, the former boxer, out of New Orleans; Sam Lightnin' Hopkins, another talented Texan with an extremely commercial sound—these singers boast none of the sophistication and polish of the Hollywood and New York big names, but they are more exciting with their honest, country-styled approach to a song.

Also worth hearing is Smokey Hogg, still another of the Lone Star State blues shouters. Peatie Wheatstraw, the Devil's Son in Law; the pianist Mose Allison, who appeals to younger listeners with his old-fashioned manner; William (Jazz) Gillum, who like Sonny Terry plays hot harmonica as well; Sonny Boy Williamson; Lou Rawls, a Los Angeles youngster with a future as brilliant as he chooses to make it; Jimmy

Witherspoon, the big-shouldered shouter whose idol is Joe Turner; Arthur (Big Boy) Crudup; Crown Prince Waterford—these are additional jazz and blues singers of the 1960s whom the neophyte musician or beginning record collector might enjoy sampling. None sings like Johnny Mathis.

B. B. King carries his own combo with him, playing Negro clubs, ballrooms, and ball parks almost exclusively and selling far more records and albums (mostly on Crown) than anyone realizes. King also works as a radio jockey in the Memphis area. He pays guitar along with his singing.

This has become a singers' era. Youngsters seek out the rock 'n' roll vocalists and vocal groups. Older audiences have swung to the folk field since the Kingston Trio and the Weavers broke through in the 1950s. And although Bailey, Holiday, and a long line of talented singers are gone, more are coming up the ladder in the jazz field. And like Mamie Smith, one just may hit the bull's eye momentarily with another *Crazy Blues*. We're waiting.

9

Everything's Swinging

The early '30s were difficult days for everyone. Fletcher Henderson's pioneering band had been forced to toss in the towel in the winter of 1934. Duke Ellington, returned from a tour of England and France, was awaiting bookings at a time when hundreds of ballrooms and theaters had closed their doors. King Louis Armstrong concentrated on records at a dismal time when a sale of 1,000 copies was considered exceptional. In short, Americans on all levels fought bankruptcy.

In New York, a 25-year-old clarinet and saxophone player named Benjamin David Goodman was forming a new band comprised of radio studio musicians, the only ones around who were prospering. Benny had survived long road trips with the old Ben Pollack orchestra, and was still young enough to face the challenge of attempting to click with an unknown new organization. He hired Smack Henderson to write a library of jazz-oriented arrangements at a time when the "name" orchestras were

ILLUSTRATION: William "Count" Basie, at the piano, with Benny Goodman. This photograph was made on a World War II "Command Performance" by the Armed Forces Radio Service.

George Olsen, Vincent Lopez, Wayne King, Jan Garber, Guy Lombardo, B. A. Rolfe (on the Lucky Strike *Hit Parade* broadcasts), and Isham Jones. Only Jones' group was of unusual musical interest. Henderson's brother Horace—Little Smack—also did Goodman arrangements.

Within weeks, in the spring of 1935, another era had begun. Jazzmen who had been hibernating in radio studios, and playing their own music behind closed doors, came up for air as Goodman's NBC broadcasts for a cookie sponsor began to attract a vast new audience of young listeners who were eager to acclaim a new music. No one could define it. Not even Goodman or Henderson could describe it in words. They merely called it "swing."

Swing changed the nation, to a certain extent. Goodman went into the Los Angeles Palomar Ballroom and near-riots ensued. Tommy and Jimmy Dorsey's new swing band was an instant success in the East. Glen Gray and the Casa Lomans junked some of their earlier "sweet" charts and quickly steered into a swing course. Joe Haymes formed a band somewhat like Goodman's. The English arranger-conductor Ray Noble, playing high atop the RCA Building in Radio City, hired Glenn Miller away from the Dorseys and built still another organization which boomed the swing movement along.

The public's eager acceptance of jazz under the guise of a new name put Smack and Horace Henderson back with a new and exceptional band that featured men like Chu Berry, Roy Eldridge, John Kirby, Buster Bailey, Sid Catlett, and Fernando Arbello by the time it moved into Chicago's Grand Terrace in early 1936. *Christopher Columbus* was just one of the tunes waxed by this group.

Gil Rodin, a Pollack saxophonist, formed another orchestra and got Bob Crosby, a Dorsey Brothers singer, to front it. With an emphatic and unique Dixieland flavor, the Crosby band caught on with its great sidemen, Eddie Miller, Yank Lawson, Ray Bauduc, Bobby Haggart, Nappy Lamare, Matty Matlock, and others.

The enthusiasm and inspiration of swing musicians and addicts gave even the old master, Duke Ellington, a new incentive and drive. Back in 1932, he had composed and recorded *It Don't Mean a Thing If It Ain't Got That Swing*, and along with Armstrong and Henderson, had done more for jazz than anyone. Now he kept pace as a swing leader. He and his band appeared in Paramount's *Murder at the Vanities* movie, in which *Cocktails for Two* and *Live and Love Tonight* were introduced, and a Mae West flicker also for Paramount, *Belle of the Nineties*, in which Duke introduced *My Old Flame* and *Troubled Waters*. A prestige engagement in the Urban room of the Congress Hotel in early 1935 also helped put Ellington's name back in the hopper. He was rolling again, and composing some of his finest music at the same time.

From Memphis—Handy's town, they called it then—Jimmie Lunceford took a band into international prominence starting with a series of Decca blue label records in September 1934. A graduate of Fisk University, Lunceford was articulate, urbane, and a musician of the first rank. His billing was "The Harlem Express." Sy Oliver set the tone of the group with his highly original arranging style and solo trumpet, but men like Eddie Tompkins and Paul Webster of Kansas City, trumpets; Eddie Wilcox, piano; Willie Smith and Joe Thomas, reeds; Eddie Durham, trombone; and powerful Jim Crawford, drums; helped make Lunceford a bellwether of the swing period.

Ben Pollack, ever skilled in finding young musicians of exceptional promise, launched a new aggregation in which Harry James, Irving (Fazola) Prestopnik, Stan Wrightsman, Clarence (Shorty) Cherock, Freddie Slack, Thurman Teague, and Dave Matthews were sidemen. But within months Jimmy Dorsey, splitting with brother Tommy and forming his own band, stole Cherock and Slack. Goodman grabbed James. And Prestopnik went with the Crosby band.

In Chicago, Earl Hines was alternating at the Grand Terrace with the Henderson brothers. His flashy piano, for nearly a decade the pride of Chicago's South Side, was flanked by Walter Fuller's trumpet, Wally Bishop on drums, Budd Johnson's tenor sax, Quinn Wilson's bass, and Darnell Howard and Omer Simeon doubling reeds.

Claude Hopkins, another jazz pianist, likewise commanded respect from musicians with a New York band in which Ovie Alston, Ed Hall, Vic Dickenson, Fred Norman, and the ballad singer Orlando Roberson played.

Chick Webb, a fixture at the Track in Harlem—the Savoy—was leading as exciting a band in 1934-35 as Goodman, with sidemen like Taft Jordan, Sandy Williams, Edgar Sampson, Wayman Carver (the first jazz flute soloist), and Bobby Stark, and with Ella Fitzgerald on the bandstand as vocalist. Webb played a lot of commercial, non-jazz stuff in the early evening and oftimes lulled rival musicians into a false security, but when the lights went down after midnight and another band set up on the opposite stand, the mighty little percussionist could kick his troupe into a frenzy and chase the competition out into Lenox Avenue.

Glenn Miller left Noble and formed a new band. It failed.

Teddy Hill featured Bill Coleman, Dicky Wells, Russ Procope, and his own alto sax in still another swing band of the 1935 period. It was known only in New York. None of its records was particularly notable. By 1938 Hill had disbanded.

Coleman Hawkins of the big-toned tenor saxophone had moved to England in 1934 at the invitation of Jack Hylton, the popular British maestro. McKinney's Cotton Pickers had disbanded, victims of the depression.

The Dorseys had a private competition going among themselves, Tommy having stomped off the stand in 1935 when Jimmy kicked off a too-fast tempo on *I'll Never Say 'Never Again' Again*. That was at the Glen Island Casino just outside New York City on Long Island Sound. Jimmy retained the band, in which Ray McKinley, Arthur (Skeets) Herfurt, Jack Stacy, Bobby Van Epps, and Roc Hillman were featured. Tommy took over Joe Haymes' group and almost immediately enjoyed surprising success on records and personal appearances. With Tommy were Sterling Bose, Noni Bernardi, Gene Traxler, Dave Tough, Max Kaminsky, and Joe Dixon that first year. Not until 1939 did Jimmy catch his younger brother income-wise, although Jimmy's band was in every sense as good a jazz organization as Tommy's from the start.

Tommy asked 100 per cent of everyone with whom he had contact. Musicians, song publishers, trade paper men, singers and even swing fans were quickly placed on the dreaded "TD list" if they liked Jimmy, or Jimmy's band, or anybody else's music. I was an outspoken admirer of Jimmy Dorsey's unit verbally and in print, and paid for it by being barred from Tommy's confidence until a decade later. The younger Dorsey, who screamed first and considered later, never seemed to realize that *many* fine bands and soloists could be appreciated. Jimmy was far more tolerant.

Casa Loma was a cooperative group, with leader Glen Gray fronting the band expertly. A one-time Illinois freight hustler, he was surrounded by immaculately-dressed, first-rate sidemen including a sensational clarinetist, Clarence Hutchenrider, and trombonists Billy Rauch and Walter Pee-Wee Hunt, pianist Joe Hall, guitarist and arranger Gene Gifford, and Grady Watts, Sonny Dunham, and Frank Zullo, trumpets.

Critics charged the Casa Loma rhythm section with being "stiff," "mechanized," and other deprecatory adjectives, but the band all the same did much to popularize and exploit jazz and swing all over the world. Its Brunswick *White Jazz, Buji, Casa Loma Stomp*, and *Maniacs' Ball* proved potent tonics to youngsters bored with the three-tenor hotel orchestras of the day. Its complicated charts required the finest musicianship, moreover. And some of the band's ballad arrangements made use of bassoon, bass clarinet, and flute, all revolutionary writing thirty years ago.

No jazz historian yet has given proper credit to Cab Calloway for the music his orchestra purveyed in the 1930s. His Alabamians were one of the Middle West's finest ensembles when Cab took them over, and in later years he strived to improve the group with new and younger men. By the late '30s, Calloway's crew featured men like Hilton Jefferson, Cosy Cole, Chu Berry, Chauncey Haughton, Benny Payne, Jonah Jones, Claude Jones, Keg Johnson, and Milt Hinton, and when Calloway wasn't being pressed to record inane vocal novelties about Minnie the Moocher, the band turned out numerous jazz instrumentals which are valued today, notably *Ghost of a Chance, Ratamacue, Willow Weep for Me,* and *Blue Interlude.*

Irving Mills, the music publisher, who managed Ellington and others, occasionally put together swing bands which left a legacy of memorable masters on a half-dozen labels, most of them under the title of the Mills Blue Rhythm Band. Benny Carter, Lucky Millinder, and Baron Lee served as leaders; the personnel was made up from whatever bands happened to be in Manhattan when a record session was being planned. They made few inferior sides.

Charlie Barnet was an Ellington fanatic who had organized a full-sized orchestra in 1933 and recorded four mediocre sides with Helen Heath and Harry Von Zell, vocalists, and young sidemen including Toots Camarata, Chris Griffin, Pete Peterson, and Billy Miller. *I Want You, I Need You* reveals clearly why Von Zell quit music and became one of the world's best radio announcers. The band folded, but Charlie— with unlimited financial backing from his grandparents—stuck around, and by persisting caught on with a good band in 1937 and later swept the swing tides with *Cherokee, Redskin Rhumba,* and others. Rich boy or no, Barnet played gutty, moving tenor sax, soprano sax, and occasional alto and clarinet. Some of the alumni of his band include Bobby Burnet, Johnny Mendell, Nat Jaffe, Phil Stephens, Irving Goodman, Buddy Schutz, and Kurt Bloom.

Barnet still idolizes Ellington twenty-five years later.

Louis Armstrong by 1935 was fronting Luis Russell's orchestra and enjoying the swing craze along with every other musician. It was right after his return from England and France, and a few of the titles he recorded in this period included *You Are My Lucky Star, I'm in the Mood For Love, On Treasure Island, Red Sails in the Sunset,* and *Shoe Shine Boy,* all on Decca. Between Christmas and New Year's Eve of that year an insipid novelty called *The Music Goes 'Round and 'Round* swept the nation with its zany "you press the first valve down" lyrics and Louis recorded that, too. He was probably at his artistic peak, thirty-five years old and a world-famous figure.

The swing wagon rolled even faster in 1936. What else happened then?

In Nevada, the Hoover Dam was completed.

Roosevelt inundated Alf Landon of Kansas in the November presidential election.

Life magazine was introduced.

German pro-Nazi clubs, or *Bunds*, made their appearance in various states, ostensibly devoted to sports and social activities.

For kidnapping the infant son of Charles A. Lindbergh, Bruno Richard Hauptmann died in the New Jersey electric chair.

Big motion pictures included *Anthony Adverse, Modern Times, The Great Ziegfeld, San Francisco, Mr. Deeds Goes to Town*, and *The Story of Louis Pasteur*. Broadway successes were *Idiot's Delight, The Women, Red, Hot and Blue, Brother Rat, You Can't Take It With You*, and *On Your Toes*.

Hit songs of the year were *When My Dream Boat Comes Home, Until the Real Thing Comes Along, The Touch of Your Lips, Pennies From Heaven, I Can't Get Started*, and *There's a Small Hotel*.

That was 1936. On the horizon were signs of better times, more jobs, an improved economy for all. Two former musicians in Chicago, Glenn Burrs and Carl Cons, were struggling with a two-year-old monthly publication called *Down Beat*. Some months it failed to appear; but when it did, musicians and jazz fans liked it, bought it, passed it around, and ultimately made it the most widely read of all popular music publications.

Down Beat not only rode the swing bandwagon, but greased the wheels and steered it along its rocky, rollicking course. A Benny Goodman backache was page one copy. Ellington was a maharajah. Henderson was presidential material. Both Dorseys were invincible. And every year Burrs and Cons invited their readers to select, by mailed votes, a grotesque all-star band of non-swinging musicians which they headlined:

THIS YEAR'S CORN CROP

Musicians like Guy Lombardo, who was grossing more than $250,000 annually, and Clyde McCoy, Henry Busse, Abe Lyman, Wayne King, and a half-dozen more were ridiculed in the swing-crazy era.

New York's West Fifty-Second Street became a mecca for swing musicians as Joe Helbock made his little downstairs Onyx Club a swing shrine with Stuff Smith's hot fiddle and jam sessions in which the nation's best joined in. The Hickory House and Famous Door followed with more swing. Artie Shaw introduced his new swing band (with strings) at the Imperial Theater in May, won a record contract, and was on his way as Goodman's chief rival.

Musicians called each other "gates," if not for long. Some called their clarinets "licorice sticks." Slang became jive. *Life* published a picture story on swing and swingmen. Armstrong's book, *Swing That Music*, was published. Hollywood made movies with "swing" in the title using studio orchestras with ninety-eight violins. And Fats Waller made fun of the entire scene on his records.

Benny Carter and Coleman Hawkins, in Europe, didn't know what they were missing.

From New Orleans a decade before, Sidney Bechet had taken his clarinet and soprano saxophone to Chicago and, later, New York. Now he was playing in Noble Sissle's orchestra, a commercial, run-of-the-mill aggregation which barely qualified as a swing band. Sissle, never a favorite in New York nor in a class with Ellington, Lunceford, and Armstrong, toured the hinterlands into the Far West. In Kansas City, Harlan Leonard had taken over the Thamon Hayes musicians and book, an offshoot of Moten, and was building an excellent orchestra in the swing idiom.

Jay McShann, a piano-playing immigrant from Oklahoma, also was forming his first band about this time in the Pendergast city. One of his saxophone players showed promise, but had difficulty showing up. He was, of course, Charlie Parker.

From the sordid Reno Club on Twelfth Street, Count Basie and an augmented band (Buck Clayton took Lips Page's trumpet chair; Caughey Roberts replaced Buster Smith on alto) had moved into the Grand Terrace on Chicago's South Side. Basie began his enviable recording career, on Decca, shortly after. So did Andy Kirk, whose *Until the Real Thing Comes Along* with Pha Terrell singing had become a surprise '36 hit, also on Decca.

They left just before the house—the Pendergast house—fell down. Convicted for illegal insurance payola and federal income tax evasion, barrel-bellied Tom Pendergast was sentenced to Leavenworth and died shortly after his probationary release. A reform city government moved in, threw out city manager Henry McElroy, who also died shortly thereafter, and the booming, colorful Kansas City era had ended.

Nor has it resumed.

Don Redman in New York was now on his own, a refugee from McKinney's Cotton Pickers, with a crack band that comprised, in the summer of 1936, Renald Jones, Shirley Clay, Sidney DeParis, trumpets; Benny Morton, Gene Simon, trombones; Eugene Porter, Ed Inge, Rupert Cole,

Harvey Boone, and Redman, saxes; Don Kirkpatrick, piano; Talcott Reeves, guitar; Bob Ysaguire, bass; and Manzie Johnson, drums.

Bernard (Bunny) Berigan, a Wisconsin trumpeter who had played with Hal Kemp, moved into his proper bailiwick and became a leader, first with a small jazz combo, then with a large, Goodman-sized band that was responsible for a score of fine swing records (in addition to his *I Can't Get Started* epic) but which lacked something for the public. Bunny wound up in Tommy Dorsey's brass section. There probably has not been a more refreshing, inventive white soloist since, and only Beiderbecke could match Berigan earlier.

Artie Shaw's first band featured two fiddles, a cello, and a viola; with Sammy Weiss on drums; Hank Wayland, bass; Willie Kelly, trumpet; and Mark Bennett, trombone. Tony Pastor came in two months after Shaw cut his first record in June 1938, and remained on tenor with the New Haven clarinetist for many years. In 1937, Shaw abandoned his strings and went all out with another Goodman-styled band. By '39 Artie was commanding as much money in theaters as Goodman. Artie's liquid clarinet was never the hot, swinging instrument that Benny played, but he had assets of his own. He never made a poor record in all the years he recorded.

One of the important studio musicians in radio was Mark Warnow, who had only a superficial interest in swing music. But his little brother Harry became a swing buff early, changed his name to Raymond Scott and created wide attention with his quintet playing originals like *Powerhouse, Dinner Music for a Pack of Hungry Cannibals*, and *In an Eighteenth Century Drawing Room*. Scott later formed a full-sized orchestra, hired Dorothy Collins as his singer, and toured the nation in the late '30s.

Still another entry in the swing sweepstakes of 1936 was Woody Herman's "band that played the blues." A clarinet and sax virtuoso from Milwaukee who had been a member of Tom Gerun's California dance band, in which Tony Martin also played saxophone, Woody and his co-op swing group were two years on the road, half-starved and without presentable uniforms, before their luck turned and they won acceptance.

Woody and his sidemen were left over when Isham Jones disbanded his fine dance orchestra. They voted to remain together with Herman as leader. Eventually, Woody with an entirely different jazz group was to lead the world's number one band. In the late 1930s his was just another Swing crew—though a good one.

Red Norvo's subtle, musicianly orchestra with Mildred Bailey singing and arrangements by Eddie Sauter has been recalled previously. It was ahead of its time. It had no eye-opening gimmicks. And perhaps Red's xylophone wasn't commercial in those raucous days of hot trumpet and tenor sax solos. Sadly, Norvo's orchestra never became a big winner as did Goodman's and Shaw's. Red and Mildred deserved more for the superior music they so consistently produced in person and on records through the '30s.

From the campus that tobacco built, Duke University in North Carolina, Les Brown in 1936 emerged with a collegiate swing band that made several impressive sides for Decca. But like Glenn Miller, Brown's first orchestra lacked management and, perhaps, that certain style that made a leader immediately identifiable. After working as a free-lance arranger around New York, Brown tried it again in 1938 and made it big his second time around.

Miller, too, had all the competitive spirit and professional skill of a champion, and refused to quit in the face of early reverses. With financial help from the New England ballroom operators Charlie and Sy Shribman, he wrote dozens of new arrangements, recruited a new orchestra and became an even more popular swing maestro than Goodman, Shaw, Basie, Lunceford, Ellington, and the Dorseys, even though four out of five of his charts were slow ballads of a non-jazz nature. Lunceford was Miller's favorite orchestra, and some of his arrangements had a touch of Sy Oliver. Others were cleffed by Jimmy Mundy, Edgar Sampson, Bill Finegan, Horace Henderson, Billy May, and Jerry Gray, as well as by Miller himself.

Glenn made no claims to having a great swing band. Often, in the Cafe Rouge of the Hotel Pennsylvania—now known as the New York Statler —he talked jazz between sets, delighting in arguing the merits of a new Ellington or Basie record while avoiding the hordes of songpluggers seeking radio exposure for their pop tunes. Miller knew jazz, and the blues, and had recorded in his younger days with Coleman Hawkins, Red Nichols' Pennies and Ben Pollack. Had he not died in the English Channel in 1944—the plane in which he was flying from London to Paris disappeared—he almost certainly would have offered more in the way of jazz on his return to civilian life following World War II. Miller was as exemplary a man as he was a musician. He still is sorely missed twenty years later.

John Kirby, a taciturn bassist with Fletcher Henderson, formed his own little swing combo with Charlie Shavers on trumpet, Billy Kyle at the piano, O'Neil Spencer on drums, Buster Bailey, clarinet, and Russell Procope, alto, and became a prominent leader on records and in deluxe night clubs.

From Alabama State College, Erskine Hawkins, like Les Brown, headed north with a band of collegiates in which Avery Parrish, pianist, and Julian Dash, tenor sax, were outstanding jazzmen. Hawkins played trumpet, enjoyed a hit record with *Tuxedo Junction,* but contributed little to the jazz-swing archives.

Jan Savitt, a classical violinist in his youth, likewise leaped aboard the swing wagon. For a brief period, Savitt conducted a shuffle-beat swing group in which Georgie Auld's booting tenor and Al Leopold's daring trombone vied with Bon-Bon Tunnell's scatty vocals.

Teddy Powell, a songwriter, was much like Savitt. He contributed little to his own orchestra, but employed first-rate musicians and turned out several swing records of merit. Larry Clinton, the arranger, featured Bea Wain's vocals and original instrumental compositions of a semi-jazz nature like *A Study in Brown* and *The Dipsy-Doodle* and was able to work America's top theaters and ballrooms for several years. Saxophonist Bob Chester fronted still another of the large swing bands of the 1938-39 period.

Through it all, quiet, reflective Benny Goodman rode the crest as top man. He made motion pictures in Hollywood, his weekly broadcasts for Camel cigarettes were aired from whatever city he happened to be playing, and his records were steady best-sellers for RCA-Victor. His trio, with Teddy Wilson at the piano and Gene Krupa on drums, was matched for artistic excellence only by the Goodman quartet, in which smiling, bouncing Lionel Hampton played vibes.

At Carnegie Hall in New York, Benny and his musicians not only made swing respectable in the eyes of millions, but also produced a magnificent set of spontaneous records which were issued by Columbia some fifteen years later in LP form. At the Paramount Theater in New York, home of the better swing bands for years, Benny's jumping Henderson arrangements and superior soloists (Harry James, Ziggy Elman, Vernon Brown, Jess Stacy, and Vido Musso, in addition to Wilson, Hampton, and Krupa) caused youngsters in the audience to dance wild jitterbug routines in the aisles, as they did everywhere he played.

Goodman was never an easy man to work for. Drummers were his particular Achilles' heel. After Krupa left him in 1938 to form his own band, Benny seemed unable to work with Gene's many successors. A quick look at the drums while Benny was blowing up a blizzard on his clarinet was known throughout the land as a "death ray." Yet Goodman often did generous things, and his courage in mixing Negroes with what was essentially an all-white orchestra and touring the Southern states can never be underestimated. He achieved as much in smashing segregation in the arts as anybody in history.

Through the years, Goodman's clarinet remained the model for all beginners. Shaw could play "prettier" notes at times, Barney Bigard added an elusive coloring to Ellington's ensemble and big Irving Prestopnik wove glorious improvisations above the Dixieland blowings of the Bob Crosbyites, but Goodman had a sound all his own, a technique no other could top and a swinging, rhythmic approach that was irresistible. With the Smack and Horace arrangements that gave Goodman's band class, Benny's playing was like Bob Feller's pitching at the time—the best.

By 1938, swing had become a major part of the national scene. Sidemen in the better swing bands became so well known that many had their own fan clubs. Harry James, Teddy Wilson, and Bud Freeman left the Goodman band, à la Krupa, to form swing orchestras of their own. Freeman called his the Summa Cum Laude Combo and featured a Dixieland style. Wilson had a sleek, polished, big band that somehow never seemed to hit any kind of excitement peak despite Teddy's superlative efforts at the Steinway. James at first led a Basie-styled band that lost a fortune; later he added violins, hired Helen Forrest to sing, and cranked out a dozen smash records in a row. He now lives in semi-retirement in Las Vegas, playing only when he feels like it with a 1940-styled swing band.

Bob Zurke and Muggsy Spanier quit the Crosby band, but Zurke had no success at all with his own orchestra and ended up in the Hangover, a tiny Hollywood bar, where he was working as a piano soloist when he died in 1944. Spanier fared better, but the war depleted the supply of capable musicians and he was forced to drop down to a seven-piece combo which he has led successfully with his plunger-filled cornet since the early 1940s.

Few will remember how Ozzie Nelson, in the spring of 1940, feared for his future as an orchestra leader and turned to a book loaded with Count Basie stock arrangements and other swing charts to attract young fans. His wife, the singer Harriet Hilliard, was trying to rear their four-year-old son David and was pregnant with Eric during Ozzie's engagement at the Blackhawk Restaurant in Chicago's Loop. Bo Ashford played Bix-influenced trumpet and Charlie Bubeck fine baritone saxophone in that Nelson band. Eric turned out to be Ricky Nelson, and Ozzie and Harriet astoundingly developed into astute radio and television producers and actors. They forgot about Basie.

Down Beat taunted Horace Heidt, like a picador tormenting a raging bull, until its criticism of Heidt's schmalzy electric guitars and battery of vocalists spurred the California maestro to make a couple of record sides featuring Benny Carter on alto sax. Benny had returned home, as did Coleman Hawkins, with the outbreak of World War II in September 1939. The Heidt Columbia discing of *Seven Years With the Wrong Band* turned out well; *Down Beat* credited Heidt with a sterling performance and the record today remains a rare item for collectors.

Carter's own orchestra had everything—clean, danceable arrangements featuring sensational scoring for saxophones, and excellent sidemen including Eddie Heywood at the piano; Tyree Glenn, doubling vibes and trombone; Joe Thomas on trumpet; Hayes Alvis, bass; and Ulysses Livingston, guitar. Benny's alto and trumpet solos were eminently listenable and his handsome, confident appearance enhanced his band's effectiveness. But in retrospect, Carter probably returned home too late, for there were so many swing bands being booked by 1939 that his great organization never seemed to get the right bookings, nor the national radio time necessary to make it a favorite.

Hawkins' experience was somewhat similar. His big band was an almost instant failure despite the leader's impeccable tenoring and the attention focused on him because of his immensely popular *Body and Soul* record on Victor-Bluebird. But "Bean," as he has been called since his Henderson days, kept himself available for all kinds of gigs—theaters, niteries, concerts, records, and trips abroad (after the war ended) so that he has probably earned more money, and honors, than most of his colleagues. He is still free-lancing today in his fifth decade as one of the world's outstanding saxophonists, a long, long road from the days when, as a fifteen-year-old, he left his home in St. Joseph, Missouri, to travel with Mamie Smith's Jazzhounds.

Jack Teagarden, free of a long-term contract with Paul Whiteman, formed his own swing band, went into bankruptcy, then reorganized and carried on successfully until the mid-1940s when he joined the Armstrong combo.

Teagarden's trombone occupies a special niche in history. He had a hot, extremely melodic style which proved inimitable through the years. Young musicians have been inspired by his fat-toned manner since the '20s, and only Tommy Dorsey, before his death in 1956, won as many musicians' polls for favorite trombonist. With his own small group, affable Jack appeared all over the world exhibiting his undeniably brilliant musicianship every night. He was easily qualified for anyone's jazz hall of fame. Jack's death in January 1964, left a void in the ranks of all-time superior jazzmen.

Down Beat and *Metronome*, an older, more conservative monthly magazine headed by George T. Simon and Barry Ulanov, reported the swing era well month after month through its halcyon period. *Down Beat*, a hybrid product that was part newspaper and part magazine, yet madly enthusiastic and gutsy as its many libel suits attest, consistently mirrored the big name swingmen with Hearst-like headlines.

Once established, *Down Beat* rolled along with its twice-monthly issues to about 50,000-an-issue circulation as Burrs and Cons, the co-owners, left its operation in the hands of younger employees. Five years spent editing the colorful, bawdy rag in Chicago and New York gave me an acquaintanceship with everyone in the popular music profession, from the union's all-powerful dictator, James Caesar Petrillo, down to the third altoist in Shep Fields' gurgling reed section. It takes more than good musicians to produce jazz; they must have personal managers, bookers, publicists, and all the working personnel involved in the making of a record.

The trade paper writer-editor works with all these persons. It is, at least, an 18-hour-a-day job. There are certain newsworthy folk, moreover, who for one reason or another refuse to welcome one as he makes the rounds of his work. Kid Ory, Tommy Dorsey, Artie Shaw, and Frank Sinatra come to mind as artists who required several meetings before they accepted a writer unreservedly, and in my case Ory and Sinatra never did quite come down off their thrones 100 per cent. But Rudy Vallee was the most uncivil interviewee I ever tackled. Sinatra could take lessons from him on how to infuriate the press.

The swing era, looking back, lasted only briefly. From Goodman's triumphs in early 1935, swing reigned for exactly one decade. Many musicians were forced to leave the top bands for service in the military during World War II. Leaders who kept their bands together were allowed a minimum of gasoline for road trips. Few buses were available; the ones that were had old, over-worn tires that could not be replaced because the armed forces had first call.

Swing music put the record industry back on its feet after it had virtually expired in 1931-32. It created an unprecedented increase in the sale of all musical instruments, including accordions and pianos, and revived a reeling, ailing industry that even now, thirty years later, continues to benefit.

Before the period ended, a long list of one-time sidemen formed their own bands with varying degrees of success. The pianist Claude Thornhill, for one, built an orchestra that featured French horns, five clarinets, and his own light but tasteful piano. Glenn Miller assisted him financially shortly before Miller entered the army. Miller also was instrumental in putting trumpeter Charlie Spivak and saxophonist Hal McIntyre in front of their own bands.

Lionel Hampton quit Benny Goodman right after Pearl Harbor and has enjoyed more success with a big, brass-heavy orchestra than any of the Goodman alumni, James excepted. The athletic Hamp and his men have played everywhere since 1941, and in 1963 rang up phenomenal triumphs in Japan.

Will Bradley and Ray McKinley, for a time, scored big with their orchestra. Freddie Slack quit Jimmy Dorsey and helped the Bradley-McKinley band record a series of hit records with a flashy boogie-woogie piano style, but the war broke up the group as it did many others.

Duke Ellington's trumpet soloist, Cootie Williams, spent more than fifteen years as a leader but failed to achieve the success he sought. In 1963 he returned to the Ellington fold. Ellington's Johnny Hodges, Lawrence Brown, and Cat Anderson also checked out to try it on their own, but returned and are helping Duke maintain his leadership in the thinning ranks of jazz orchestras. Unlike Basie, Goodman, Herman, and many others, Ellington has never disbanded his unique organization even temporarily. It is his life.

Not all the able, popular swing men led orchestras.

Art Tatum was a constant Fifty-Second Street attraction in Gotham as a solo pianist. Blind in one eye, he came out of Ohio in 1932 and immediately established an enviable reputation for his prodigious technique and his ability to play anything once heard perfectly, from memory.

Tatum worked as a single, recorded prolifically, and in 1943 began appearing in a trio with Tiny Grimes, guitar, and Slam Stewart, bass. He died of uremic poisoning in 1956. Tatum's stature as a jazzman increases as the years go by. One may play any of his long-play records (Decca, Capitol, Verve) and hear something fresh and innerving each time.

Nat Cole, the son of a Chicago Protestant Minister, played more in the Earl Hines groove than Tatum, and likewise became a fixture along "the street" and in Los Angeles with his trio. Wesley Prince played bass and Oscar Moore electric guitar in the first Cole combo, but with an unprecedented series of hit vocal records (Capitol) Nat had no choice, eventually, but to concentrate as a singer and allow his classy, swing era piano to suffer. He has come a long way from Kelly's Stable, where, when I first met him, he was paid $35 a week and worked until four o'clock every morning.

The late Adrian Rollini, doubling xylophone and bass sax, always preferred working with a small group. He is heard on discs with Bix Beiderbecke and numerous others, including more than fifty titles under his own name. Not a steady Fifty-Second Street attraction, Rollini played for years in New York at the Piccadilly Hotel, a musicians' hangout like Plunkett's, Charley's and Local 802.

Not all good jazz was played on "the street" and in Harlem. One could prowl Greenwich Village and encounter a blues singer or two most any night. Eddie Condon and a fraternity of his friends which included Pee-Wee Russell, Dave Bowman, Bobby Hackett, Artie Shapiro, Max Kaminsky, Brad Gowans, and sometimes Bud Freeman and Joe Bushkin were always to be found at Nick's, or next door at Julius' bar. Condon became such a Village fixture that he opened his own club, hired and fired musicians himself and was regarded by visiting Ivy League students as being a sort of lower class Fiorello LaGuardia. His club prospered. It's still there, but Condon isn't.

There were other steadies along the swing alleys of Manhattan. After leaving Cab Calloway, Ben Webster and his tenor were frequently found in bistros where he had freedom to play as he pleased. In 1939, however, Ben took his axe into the Duke Ellington band for a four-year stint. Clarence Profit, like Tatum, wandered from club to club as a piano soloist. Guitarist Tiny Grimes; Roy Eldridge, out of the Henderson band, blowing a torrid trumpet before accepting a chair in Gene Krupa's brass section in the '40s; the brothers Sidney and Wilbur De Paris, playing trumpet and trombone; Teddy Bunn, a clever guitarist; Willie Bryant, a singer and promoter who became a radio jockey; Pete Brown, the alto saxophonist; Red Allen, for years buried in Louis Armstrong's band as a third trumpeter; Joe Marsala, a fixture at the Hickory House, along with his wife, Adele Girard, who played harp, and his brother, Marty Marsala, a highly competent trumpeter—all these able performers helped make swing the thing in New York.

Wingy Manone also played trumpet, Armstrong style, and shouted hoarse vocals on *Isle of Capri* and other pops. He favored the pure, small band Dixieland jazz of his native Louisiana and always used the best jazzmen on his record dates. One-armed, the patient Wingy had to listen time and time again, every night of his life on the bandstand, to the story of how one of his pals once gave him a single cuff-link for Christmas. Still around, most often in Las Vegas, Wingy hopes he has outlived the cuff-link anecdote. His ambition is to compose and conduct a serious suite based on his memories of New Orleans.

And what had happened with another Louisiana trumpet player, for years the King of all brass soloists—Joseph Oliver?

King Joe fell fast. Poor management, ailing health, and other factors had left the once-mighty King alone and lonely in Savannah, forgotten by all his old friends, his fans, and even the young musicians he had helped so graciously in the 1920s in New Orleans and Chicago. In April 1938, Oliver died in poverty, still writing pathetic letters seeking to line up engagements for an orchestra he no longer had.

Frankie Newton played a tasteful trumpet along Swing Street and Lips Page could be found blowing his powerful blues horn and singing indigo lyrics in any one of a dozen niteries, all of which served abominable food and watered drinks. Like Manone, Louis Prima went north from New Orleans playing Armstrong-like trumpet and singing in the same Louis-like manner. With the years, though, Prima became increasingly commercial and few of his many records are today highly valued by collectors.

Fifty-Second Street began to fade in 1945 when many of the buildings housing swing clubs were condemned to make way for new structures. The very word "swing" became so trite, and so misused, that most professionals no longer employed it. We of *Down Beat* actually banned it in the sheet's columns. The day of the big band, and the commercial dance bands as well, was dimming rapidly as World War II blazed in Europe and the Pacific. And so jazz became the thing again.

Cessation of hostilities, as the newspapers called it, saw another unexpected development within the jazz circle. A group of younger musicians, most of them unknowns, were eager to be heard. They had new ideas as to how jazz should be played. Few of the new school acknowledged any debt to the old masters, the Olivers and Mortons. Rather, they preferred to admit no identification with the older generation. A revolution in jazz was beginning.

10

Comes

the

Revolution

Suddenly, not long after the start of World War II, musicians were playing and talking about *rebop*. It was a new music. Some said it had no connection with jazz, or swing. Few of the older musicians enjoyed or understood it. Most young musicians delighted in it. The war was on, and everyone chose sides.

Most historians now agree that the new music was conceived at a Harlem night club called Minton's Playhouse. There, in modest surroundings, after hours, a small group of musicians, bored with swing music, experimented with new harmonies and rhythmic variations on standard tunes and the blues.

Thelonious Monk, a pianist, was one. He was in his early twenties and had held down the piano chair in Lucky Millinder's 1942 Savoy Ballroom band in which the featured solo trumpeter was Dizzy Gillespie. The late Trevor Bacon and Sister Rosetta Tharpe sang in the same band, and Tab Smith's fat-toned alto was still another plus. It was this band that broadcast over what was then the ABC radio network every Saturday afternoon in a special "script show" in which I was allowed precisely five minutes to announce the latest news and gossip of the swing world on the Savoy bandstand with Millinder's musicians.

ILLUSTRATION: Lester Young. (Photograph by Ivan Black.)

Monk, a quiet man, and Gillespie, an extrovert who had been fired by Cab Calloway for throwing spitballs during a theater performance, made an odd team. Yet they were similar musically. Gillespie had played not only with Calloway but with Benny Carter's big band and, frustrated, sought more freedom to experiment. Numerous musicians called his daring, piercing solos "Chinese jazz." Few understood what he was trying to accomplish.

Like Monk, one who did was Kenny (Klook) Clarke, a drummer from Pittsburgh who had worked in the Claude Hopkins, Teddy Hill, and Carter orchestras, and who had prepared for a professional career by studying trombone, piano, vibes, drums, theory, and harmony as a high school student.

Monk, Gillespie, and Clarke were acutely aware of the advanced technique and broad conceptions of the Texas-Oklahoma virtuoso of the guitar, Charlie Christian, who worked for a couple of years with Benny Goodman, contracted tuberculosis, and died in March of 1942. They, of course, had played with Charlie on gigs and bashes throughout the New York area. Minton's, however, was the ideal spot. Located next door to Harlem's Hotel Cecil on West 118th Street, it was owned by a man who had once led a band and who had worked as a Harlem representative of New York's powerful and integrated Local 802 of the musicians' union. Henry Minton served good food, kept his place clean, and welcomed musicians even when they had no money to spend. The manager of Minton's was the former bandleader, Teddy Hill, who had toured Europe with his own band in the '30s. He, too, understood musicians.

Joe Guy, another Millinder trumpeter; Mary Lou Williams of the Kirk orchestra; Earl Hines and members of his band including his manager, Charlie Carpenter; Roy Eldridge, Gillespie's favorite trumpet player; Idrees Sulliman, an extremely advanced musician; Lester Young of the Basie band—all these and others became frequent Minton's visitors. And when incompetent youngsters dropped by and asked to sit in, Monk and Diz would start playing something so difficult the interlopers would quickly pack their horns and sneak out the side door to avoid embarrassment.

"Chinese music" or no, the new sounds which Monk, Diz and Klook conceived began to attract attention, and by the time Jay McShann's riffing, blues-oriented swing crew arrived in Harlem from Kansas City in the summer of 1942 for a brief run at the Savoy, the unique rebop jazz had its followers.

On July 30 of that year, the musicians' union, through its national president James Caesar Petrillo, ordered all its members to cease and desist in the recording of phonograph records. For sixteen months record companies carefully issued the few masters remaining in their vaults until, in November of 1943, a settlement was made (Petrillo took a frightful beating but refused to admit it) and musicians happily resumed waxing sessions. Because of the long lull, none of the Minton experimenters had their music recorded.

An impish, eccentric alto saxophonist in McShann's rough orchestra at the Savory, Charlie Parker was known throughout the Middle West as the Yardbird (but mostly, just Bird) in the latter part of the 1930s. While he was traveling with McShann in Nebraska, the car in which they were riding struck and killed a chicken. Parker, leaping out of the vehicle, retrieved the fowl, returned to the car, carried it to the next town and enjoyed it for dinner after carefully instructing the cook how to prepare the yardbird. From then on, Parker was Bird. Like Gillespie, he was unanimously considered to be an erratic, clinker-hitting musician with a penchant for blowing screwy "Chinese notes."

In New York, during the Savoy engagement, Parker found his soulmates at Minton's. There, in comfortable surroundings among sympathetic ears, the Bird flew high with his new friends. Gone forever were his nutmeg days in Kansas City.

Clarke's newly-devised offbeats and accents had a sort of klook-mop sound, a rebop feel, and at first the new Minton's music was called rebop. Later, as Diz sang an occasional vocal break, it became bebop. Musicians detested the term and whenever they were asked to describe it, they testily shortened it to just bop. Trade paper writers disagreed violently over the merits of the music. Musicians, particularly those living outside New York City and those older than thirty, dismissed it rudely. But a great number of young musicians, many of them just coming out of military service, were intrigued and inspired with what they heard. And so the controversy, bitter at times, raged.

The pro-bop crowd took to wearing dark glasses, even in the dark, and goatees. Many wore insipid-looking little berets. Art Blakey, the young drummer; Clyde Hart, the pianist who had laboriously copied McKinney's Cotton Picker arrangements back in Kansas City; Earl (Bud) Powell, a native New Yorker who played exceptional piano and displayed unusual ability as a composer; Tadd Dameron, another young arranger, also an arrival from Kansas City where he had worked briefly with Harlan Leonard; Max Roach, the drummer; Oscar Pettiford, the bassist; J. J. Johnson, the trombonist, another ex-Benny Carter sideman; Al Haig, a pianist fresh from the Coast Guard; Milt Jackson, the Detroit vibes ace; and Kenny Dorham, trumpet, were among the most voluble, and capable of playing the novel new jazz. There were, in retrospect, remarkably few persons as World War II ended who displayed the open mind of Mary Lou Williams:

> "*Right from the start, musical reactionaries have said the worst about bop. But after seeing the Savoy Ballroom kids fit dances to this kind of music, I felt it was destined to become the new era of music, 'though not taking anything away from Dixieland or swing or any of the great stars of jazz. I see no reason why there should be a battle in music. All of us aim to make our listeners happy.*" *

Parker remained in New York when McShann's musicians returned to Kansas City. He worked for tips at a place called Monroe's Uptown House where musicians often gathered after Minton's had closed. In 1943, Billy Eckstine, singing with Earl Hines, took his boss there. The Earl hired Bird for his new band as a tenor saxophonist and, although Parker never felt at ease blowing the larger horn, he played things that Hines and his musicians never heard before—or since.

It was not until 1944 that the new music was recorded. Parker had made records previously with McShann's band, in Dallas in 1941 on the well-known *Swingmatism* and *Dexter Blues*† session supervised by Dave Kapp. For more than three years I had endeavored to obtain a contract for McShann, not because of Parker, but because the band was deserving. Dave Kapp and his brother, the late Jack Kapp, agreed to give the band a shot on Decca's "Sepia Series" slanted to the booming Negro market. Once recorded, the band did not impress the Kapp brothers nearly so much as did McShann's nasal-voiced blues singer, the late Walter Brown. His *Confessin' the Blues* proved a surprise commercial hit, selling in excess of 750,000 copies. All subsequent McShann discs thus featured Brown's sing-songy vocals rather than McShann and Parker, unfortunately.

In September 1944, and with guitarist Tiny Grimes as leader, Parker made the first sides in which his fiery alto was featured. For Savoy, the titles included *Tiny's Tempo, I'll Always Love You Just the Same, Romance Without Finance,* and *Red Cross.* Doc West, drums; Clyde Hart, piano; and Jimmy Butts, bass, were the other musicians involved. Despite Grimes' awkward vocals on two titles, these four masters made jazz history. Now musicians living thousands of miles from Minton's could hear and study the radical new jazz they called bop.

* Nat Shapiro and Nat Hentoff, *Hear Me Talkin' to Ya* (New York: Holt, Rinehart & Winston, 1955), p. 351.
† Named for the author.—ED. NOTE

Gillespie made his first records in his new leader attire in 1945 for the Guild and Manor labels, both now defunct. Titles included *Blue 'n' Boogie, Groovin' High, Dizzy Atmosphere,* and *All the Things You Are,* in February, followed by *Shaw 'Nuff, Lover Man,* with an unimpressive Sarah Vaughan vocal, *Hot House, I Can't Get Started, Good Bait, Salt Peanuts,* and *Be-Bop.*

It was inevitable that Gillespie and Parker work together.

They had teamed in Eckstine's big, bopping band briefly after Billy and Bird had worked together with Hines. Eckstine fronted an extraordinary gathering of hipped young musicians, men with bright, novel ways of thinking and playing. Leo Parker (unrelated to Bird) played baritone sax; Fats Navarro, trumpet; J. J. Johnson, trombone; and Lucky Thompson, tenor; they sometimes blew sour in creating new music, but an enthralled Eckstine patiently allowed each sideman to play what he wanted and develop a style. Billy himself was busy singing and attempting modest trumpet and trombone solo contributions. Those who watched the band in action—and I did not—affirm that it was indeed one that made jazz history for a brief period and deserved better. It disbanded, as did scores of other orchestras, because of the war-induced musician shortages, travel restrictions, and other factors beyond Eckstine's control.

Diz and Bird then went all the way to California to play the late Billy Berg's Vine Street boîte in the heart of Hollywood on Vine Street in 1945. "Millions of busy Californians," Gillespie remarked to me later, "failed to drop by and enjoy our music." It was their worst booking. Bop had not caught on in the Far West.

Klook Clarke left the scene to serve three years in the army. Bud Powell went with the new Cootie Williams band, off to a good start with a wildly swinging record, *House of Joy.* Monk wandered about New York, becoming more and more exclusive, playing less frequently and composing more often. Dameron's advanced arranging conceptions made him a leader in the new movement. Trombonist Johnson and Freddy Webster, a Diz-like trumpeter now deceased, joined Benny Carter's orchestra. King Gillespie organized a big band in New York. And suddenly the flow of musicians into the world of bop became a raging flood.

Record companies all belatedly began recording the new jazz. Some of it was unbelievably bad. Many of the youngsters confidently trying to play the complex, difficult alto style of Parker, or Gillespie's dizzy horn improvisations, were naive and unskilled, but they too recorded prolifically as the jazz critics and record executives scrambled to salute and profit by anything short of Dixieland. Bitter schisms developed among writers, musicians, bookers, managers, night club operators, and recording men.

Yet, for all the headlines and verbal arguments within the jazz circle, the conflict was essentially that of the young man against the older man.

DISBANDING

The big bands were dying fast. Even Count Basie, who had enjoyed immense success, disbanded and worked for a time with a septet. Lester Young, the Prez, took his tenor and worked the clubs solo and with trios. His style was perhaps as modern as Gillespie's and Parker's, and of course had been for nearly fifteen years before the birth of bop. Now Young was hailed as some sort of new chieftain in the tribe.

Benny Goodman consented to work only sporadically, and kept no regular band employed. He was enjoying his semi-retirement with his daughters at his spacious Connecticut estate. Ellington kept going in a strange new world of bop that frankly puzzled him. Always ahead of the jazz pack musically, the venerable Duke continued to compose his lovely, moody works with a genius that has outlived almost all the highly-publicized 1942-50 bop compositions. Jimmie Lunceford, also puzzled—perhaps shocked—by what he was hearing, died in July of 1947, as recounted in my "Jazz in the West" chapter, after eating a king-sized bowl of tainted chili at an Oregon roadside inn. Berigan, too, was gone. He died in the summer of 1942, an irreparable loss to jazz.

Shaw and Thornhill served in the Navy as bandleaders, and after the war neither was able to return to the heights. Shaw eventually attempted a writing career, moved "permanently" to Spain for several years, and recently has been operating a shooting range in Connecticut—not far from Goodman's estate. Shaw no longer plays clarinet.

Jimmy Dorsey abandoned his orchestra and rejoined Tommy Dorsey's for several years, but neither brother was able to climb to the popularity peak he enjoyed before and during World War II. Jan Savitt was dead. Fletcher Henderson was ailing, and his eyes were failing. Casa Loma broke up its unique corporation ownership and disbanded, too. The Crosby band was no more. It had dissolved in 1942 when its leader went into the Marine Corps, and Eddie Miller's attempts to reorganize and direct it in California met with success only for about a year.

Pollack was operating a "rib joint" in Los Angeles. Hines forsook his big band reluctantly and turned to a small combo, which he still is leading in the San Francisco area. Hopkins was no longer a leader. Ella Fitzgerald had gamely attempted to keep the great Chick Webb orchestra active after his death, but failed. Calloway turned to a small group, then junked it in favor of an acting career. He was excellent in various road company editions of *Porgy and Bess.*

Barnet formed and disbanded a half-dozen orchestras through the frantic '40s and today leads a quartet. Armstrong, appalled not only at the "Chinese music" he heard in most top presentations, but also with the furor it was causing, dropped down to a seven-piece orchestra and has maintained it with spectacular success ever since. Andy Kirk became a hotel manager in Harlem.

Noble Sissle threw in the towel. His celebrated clarinetist and soprano saxophonist, Sidney Bechet, moved to France and became as influential—and popular—in his way as Edith Piaf. Bechet's death in 1959 made world-wide headlines in the lay press as well as in jazz journals.

Kansas City's Harlan Leonard, a musician and gentleman who deserved far better, had to take a non-musical job with the federal government in Los Angeles. Don Redman, the mighty mite who sparked McKinney's and Henderson's orchestras in the 1920s and 1930s, became an arranger and still works as one in New York. Raymond Scott also defected from the jazz scene to become a professional sound engineer and electronics fanatic. Red Norvo, another whose matchless orchestra never made it big with the public, turned to a trio and has worked consistently ever since. His inherently excellent musicianship has allowed him to keep pace with all the young musicians. Anything they play, he can play as well. Coleman Hawkins, gigging about New York and recording almost constantly, is another of the "over fifty" soloists who has kept pace.

Les Brown followed a rigid schedule until the 1960s. Part of the year, from April through August, he would travel with a big band from his home in California to New England and back, playing college dances and summer resorts. From September to April, Brown, a much better clarinet and alto soloist than most musicians realize, would lead the same band on Bob Hope's television shows in Hollywood. Now, Les sticks to California the year round. His son Butch Brown is leading a good little jazz combo in Southern California clubs.

Sad to recall is the death of Smack Henderson. The once-great pianist and arranger, a gentleman and scholar always, had organized his last band in 1941 and opened at the Roseland on Broadway—where he had played so triumphantly earlier. Ed Flynn of *Down Beat* on February 27, 1941, awarded Henderson a special trophy in honor of his seventeenth anniversary as an orchestra leader. In the audience, which was delighted to honor the affable Georgian, were Benny Goodman, Jimmy Dorsey, Woody Herman, Vincent Lopez and jazz writers George T. Simon, George Avakian, Leonard Feather, Robert Goffin, and myself. In April, Smack recorded four mediocre titles for Columbia. By 1945, unable to keep his musicians together because of wartime rigors and restrictions, the gentle Smack went back to work as an arranger for Goodman.

But old Smack wasn't through. He hit the road with Ethel Waters, just as he had in the 1920s, but blood pressure troubles forced him to return to New York and rest for several months. Briefly, he led another combo at Bop City, then a fine sextet at Cafe Society, a New York club. Jimmy Crawford, Lucky Thompson, John Brown, Dick Vance, and Eddie Barefield were in that group. Then came the near-fatal stroke, which bedded Henderson for more than a year. Old Smack, his eyesight all but gone, hung on courageously, then died on December 24, 1952. Of Henderson, Frank Driggs has lovingly written:

"He lived and worked far—perhaps too far—in advance of his time. He never profited from his own ideas. Yet he built a musicians' band, a swinging band, years before the word came into general usage. It was a Henderson style and arrangements that precipitated the swing era which was then paced by Benny Goodman's orchestra. Even with his subsequent bands, Goodman clung to the Henderson style. Basie's band, too, continued the Henderson tradition of great soloists and settings. Fletcher Henderson's approach remains the foundation for big bands in jazz." *

Little Smack, Horace Henderson, moved to Los Angeles and today frequently works clubs there and in Las Vegas. He can still write the beat-filled charts which so many bands used or imitated through the 1930s and 1940s.

And what was the fate of other maestros of the swing period?

Hal McIntyre, the handsome lead altoist with Glenn Miller's pre-war orchestra, died in a Hollywood hotel fire in 1959. He was still trying to keep his orchestra active. John Kirby, whose immaculately dressed little sextet stands as the most precise and showmanly of all bands, also is dead. Diabetes killed him in 1952. Bob Chester, Larry Clinton, and Teddy Powell, all ranked well within the Top Twenty bands of the golden swing period, are alive but no longer active as leaders. Teddy Wilson works in New York without an orchestra and Bud Freeman gigs in the East, sometimes with Slick Condon's clique.

Benny Carter long ago junked his sophisticated orchestra, preferring to arrange and conduct in the motion picture, television, and recording studios of Hollywood. Frequently, however, the versatile "amazing man of music," as he was billed by his bookers for two decades, teams up with favorite musicians for jazz albums that are dear to his heart. I unhesitatingly recommend his 1962 *Further Definitions*, on Impulse, in which he

* From Driggs' booklet accompanying the Columbia album *A Study in Frustration—The Fletcher Henderson Story* (New York: Columbia Records, 1962-63), p. 12.

frolics on alto with Coleman Hawkins, Jo Jones, Phil Woods, Charlie Rouse, Dick Katz, Jimmy Garrison, and John Collins. Like Red Norvo and Hawkins—and few others—Carter plays anything the youngsters play, and often even better.

Red Nichols, another giant, still gigs here and there, and always with a slick, well-disciplined combo. Smiling Lionel Hampton carries on with a big band, jetting about from Tokyo to New York and always working. He is the exception.

Like Hampton, Ellington, and Basie today, another who resumed leading a full-sized aggregation was Woody Herman. A modest man of many talents, he left his home in Milwaukee early, and after a checkered career, awoke one afternoon in 1945 to find that his orchestra had become the most popular in the world. A series of records on Columbia showcasing his revamped personnel not only became best-sellers, but set new artistic standards for big bands at a time when most were disbanding. *Laura*, *Apple Honey*, *Caldonia*, *Northwest Passage*, *The Good Earth*, *Bijou*, *Wildroot*, *Panacea*, and *Blowin' Up a Storm* were among Woody's smashes. They showed the bop influence, and the undeniable musicianship of Herman's men, including Ray Wetzel, Pete Candoli, Neil Hefti, and Sonny Berman, trumpets; Bill Harris, trombone; Sam Marowitz, John LaPorta, Flip Phillips, Sam Rubinwitch, saxes; Davey Tough, Don Lamond, drums; Ralph Burns and Tony Aless, piano; Billy Bauer, guitar; and Chubby Jackson and Joe Mondragon, basses.

So great was the Herman herd's influence on music that Igor Stravinsky commissioned it to record and introduce his dissonant, nonjazz work, *Ebony Concerto*.

Another man who bravely bucked the tide of folding bands, and who energetically strove for even more progressive, bop-tinged jazz than Herman's, was Stan Kenton. Roaring out of California in 1942 with what was perhaps the most dedicated group of youngsters ever to one-night it together, Kenton's first engagement at the New York Roseland laid an egg, as *Variety* reported, on a frigid, miserable night when the temperature dropped well below zero and only a half-dozen of his friends showed up.

It was the same night that a Japanese submarine lobbed shells, harmlessly, onto the shore of the Pacific Ocean at Santa Barbara. Kenton, aware that his New York debut was unspectacular, said that even the Japs were out to get him.

Devoted friends, Kenton and Herman worked together to open new sites for big bands to play. With the end of World War II, ballrooms in every state went dark as Americans of every age stopped dancing. Thus did concerts come about. Coupling a top act like the King Cole Trio with a girl singer of the caliber of Anita O'Day or June Christy, Kenton could attract lucrative box-office grosses in any city, or on any college campus. So could Herman, Basie, Ellington, and Hampton.

Kenton turned out a series of records, on Capitol, which in their way proved as memorable as Herman's Columbias. *Eager Beaver* was the first; *Artistry in Rhythm, Balboa Bash, Intermission Riff, Lover,* and *Peanut Vendor* were among those that followed. In Stan's band in those early days—and working closely with him was my pleasure—were Stan Getz, Bob Gioga, Boots Mussulli, Vido Musso, Al Anthony, saxes; Buddy Childers, Karl George, Ray Borden, Mel Green, trumpets; Bob Ahern, guitar; Max Wayne and Ed Safranski, bass; Shelly Manne, drums; Milt Bernhart, Bart Varsalona, Kai Winding, trombones; and Kenton, piano.

Woody and Stan in the last half of the 1940s were considerably hotter attractions than Ellington, Basie, and what few other bands were remaining from the swing era, but they, too, were suffering severe frustrations and from time to time they disbanded temporarily. At one point, Kenton thought he was cracking up mentally. In my office at that time, he once demanded that I look up his guitarist's phone number. I gave it to Stan and he grabbed the phone and frantically dialed A–H–E–R–N, then couldn't understand why he failed to get a connection. He then fled to Brazil to avert a complete wig-out and returned refreshed and eager to resume with his orchestra. Herman, exhausted after some fifteen years on the road, attempted to settle down in Hollywood as a vocalist and master of ceremonies (he even tried a disc jockey job for a few days) but it didn't work out for him and, like Kenton, he reorganized and to this day is holding up well as a traveling maestro.

With Parker remaining in California mentally ill, and confined to a state institution in Camarillo outside Los Angeles, Dizzy Gillespie in 1946 organized his first full-sized orchestra and recorded eight sides for Musicraft with it, including *Things to Come, Emanon,* and *Ray's Idea.* Ray Brown, the bassist who wed Ella Fitzgerald; Klook Clarke, drums; and John Lewis at the piano comprised Diz's rhythm section.

By 1947, Gillespie's bop glasses, goatee, and beret had become the visual trademark of the bop movement and for a time the situation became laughable as hundreds of untried, inept musicians and bop devotees walked the streets in their odd attire, seeking identification and employment. Many of the records of the period were grotesque imitations of Diz, Bird, and other bop chiefs, and most of the imitations were so hopelessly bad that bop and its capable players were libeled. A surprising number of serious "critics" in *Saturday Review, Down Beat,* and *Metronome* glibly wrote ludicrous reviews praising the meaningless musical gibberish served up so brazenly by the incompetents. Some even rated high in the 1947-48 polls of *Down Beat, Metronome,* and *Esquire.*

The 1940s—may they not be forgotten—also will be remembered for the fresh concepts of a former UCLA student and jazz fan, Norman Granz, who eagerly violated every known rule of record-making by stringing up microphones on concert stages and waxing jazz while it was actually being played "live." All record men viewed Granz's early efforts with scorn—this writer was one—because of bad balance of instruments, coughing in the audience, long empty pauses, bum notes, reed squeaks and a dozen other bugs, but record buyers rallied to Granz's first albums and helped him become a millionaire concert promoter, entrepreneur, and resident of Switzerland with their purchases and support. Granz has spent hundreds of thousands of dollars employing jazz musicians since 1944. He also has helped lead the battle for integration.

The new half-century bowed in as Count Basie bowed to disappearing dancers and reduced his orchestra to a septet in which Clark Terry, Buddy De Franco, and the late Wardell Gray were featured. Young Theodore (Fats) Navarro, whom some musicians rated in a class with Gillespie, died of tuberculosis.

BACK TO DIXIE

It seems incongruous now that another movement in jazz paralleled the bop movement, and yet more Dixieland combos were formed during the Parker-Gillespie era than in any other period in history. Perhaps it was a reaction against what many musicians called "wrong-note jazz."

A San Francisco trumpet player, Lu Watters, had formed a New Orleans-oriented jazz combo in 1939. It broke up with the war. In 1947, Watters launched it again, and playing nothing but King Oliver-styled jazz of the 1920s, he succeeded quickly in attracting national attention to a New Orleans revival.

Watters' second trumpeter, Bob Scobey, split from Lu's group in 1950 and formed another Dixie band, one which was not so ancient in style as Watters' Yerba Buena unit. A third band, led by the trombonist Turk Murphy, gave the Golden Gate City a big lead in founding and nurturing a revival movement which spread not only throughout the states but to Europe, Australia, and South America as well.

Ben Pollack came out of retirement and re-formed his little Dixie group in Los Angeles. Pete Daily, a pint-sized Chicago cornetist, not only found work in the same city with a new Dixie band, but cut a hit version of the old Moten and Moten jazz classic, *South,* for Capitol. Rosey McHargue, the tall clarinetist for so many years with Ted Weems and

Kay Kyser, likewise fronted a fine Dixie group. Wingy Manone swept back into business with his jiving, nonsensical but humorous vocals and trumpet. Ray Bauduc and Nappy Lamare of the old Crosby band teamed together to lead their "Strawhat Five" on Los Angeles' new television station, KTLA, which boasted in its advertising a "guaranteed nightly audience in excess of 25,000 Californians."

A Disney studio artist, Harper Goff, played rhythm banjo and sparked the formation of the Firehouse Five Plus Two, all of whom wore red firemen's uniforms. Their records and albums, on Lester Koenig's Good Time Jazz label, reportedly outsold Gillespie's at the height of the bop craze.

Capitol quickly bought brilliant blue policemen's suits and outfitted the tenor saxophonist Dave Cavanaugh and his men so that they could be billed, on records, as Cavanaugh's Curbstone Cops.

If the dark-rimmed glasses and berets of the boppers were ridiculous, then so were the identification gimmicks of the revival orchestras. One wore striped prisoners' suits. Another, in California, was attired in surgeons' smocks—more than a decade before Dr. Ben Casey appeared. Nor was their music impressive. It had all been heard before. How many ways can *Muskrat* be served?

Assisted by Orson Welles, who genuinely loves jazz and whose knowledge of it is formidable, Kid Ory, Mutt Carey, Zutty Singleton, Bud Scott, Ed Garland, and other Louisiana pioneers reorganized and broadcast a series of programs sponsored by Standard Oil. Ory kept the group together and for years they worked at the Beverly Cavern, a small Los Angeles nitery that was a magnet for Dixieland buffs.

Trumpeter Teddy Buckner also entered the revival race. So did the Castle Jazz Band of Portland, Oregon. While back in the home of jazz, New Orleans, Joe (Sharkey) Bonano got together an outstanding combo in which Monk Hazel, Lester Bouchon, Santo Pecora, Harry Shields, Jeff Riddick, and George Girard were featured. It was perhaps the best of all the contemporary "revivalist" jazz bands. Preacher Rollo Laylon, now a Floridian as is Phil Napoleon, the veteran Memphis Five trumpeter, also attracted national attention.

But it was still a period of modernism, of experimentation—the battle of old versus new. The Dixie revival was a mere sideshow. The three rings under the big top, the main tent, were entirely modern.

THE COOL SCHOOL

As the fantastic '40s faded and a new and promising half-century approached, raw bop began to dim. An even newer manner of playing began to be noticed. It was the cool school. Soft-spoken Lester Young, who wore a porkpie hat instead of a beret, had been around for some twenty years. Now he suddenly and inexplicably became the trend-setter, although a good many musicians and fans had adored and applauded his effortless, easy tenoring throughout his five years with Count Basie. Young, more so in 1949 than ever, was hailed as the undisputed "prez" of the tenor saxophone.

In New York, the Royal Roost was now, in 1949, the focal point of modern jazz. Birdland opened December 15. Gillespie, high priest of modernism, returned with his band from a tour of Scandinavia to find a young trumpet player, Miles Dewey Davis, being acclaimed for an unorthodox solo style that epitomized the cool school. A St. Louisan, Davis had attended Juilliard in New York, then trekked to Los Angeles where he recorded with Parker on the infamous Dial session that saw a critically sick Bird trying to carry on before he collapsed.

Davis had worked Fifty-Second Street clubs before they were converted into strip joints and then leveled. He now worked the Roost with Parker, trombonist Kai Winding, and Allen Eager, saxophonist. He also recorded, for Capitol, four instrumentals that immediately became the most popular records of the new period.

The titles, in the order they were recorded, were *Jeru, Move, Godchild*, and *Budo* on the first session and *Boplicity, Israel, Venus de Milo*, and *Rouge* on the second. *The Coop, Moon Dreams,* and *Darn That Dream*, later, were not so successful musically.

Davis remains an enigma to many. On the stand, neatly dressed, professionally poised, and the master of his horn, Miles seems to dare his audiences to like him. He is unsmiling, unemotional, unshowmanly; many watching him work become bored because he appears bored. On numerous solos he sullenly turns his back to the paying customers. For all his unquestioned musicianship, it is obvious why he has achieved so little in all the years he has worked as a leader and recording artist. Young musicians who emulate his frigid, condescending personality are traveling down a one-way alley. Even erratic performers like Gillespie and Parker nonetheless enjoyed their own playing and were capable of transmitting their pleasure in creative, competitive work to those who paid to watch and hear them.

Gerry Mulligan, another native New Yorker, had worked in Gene Krupa's band before joining Davis on baritone saxophone. After a hitch with Thornhill's ill-fated orchestra, Gerry moved to California and gradually became a name leader with his own quartet in which no piano was heard. He also wrote cool, advanced jazz charts for the big Kenton band and others.

The Chicago pianist, Lennie Tristano, moved into New York with an inordinately advanced way of playing. Virtually blind, Lennie had earned a Bachelor of Music degree at the American Conservatory in Chicago in three years, and now was prepared to teach his new techniques to young musicians.

Esquire's *World of Jazz*, published in October of 1963, quotes Tristano:

> *"Bebop is diametrically opposed to the jazz that preceded it (swing as applied to large groups and Dixieland as applied to small ones). Swing was hot, heavy and loud. Bebop is cool, light and soft. The former bumped and chugged along like a beat locomotive; this was known in some quarters as drive. The latter has a more subtle beat which becomes more pronounced by implication."* *

One might argue with Tristano. Rarely does Ellington "bump" and "chug" along. His slow-tempo originals are cooler than Lennie's own creations. But we will happily concede that Tristano and his mates, Warne Marsh, Lee Konitz, Arnold Fishkind and Billy Bauer among them, helped bring in the cool school. So did Dave Brubeck, a pianist who appeals to the cerebral. But for all his front cover publicity in *Time*, Brubeck has contributed embarrassingly little to jazz. One suspects, the more he hears of Brubeck's mechanically-perfect, gutless quartet, that his altoist Paul Desmond and his drummer Joe Morello will be more vividly remembered in jazz a decade from now than Dave himself. To many, he perhaps studied too long and too academically with Darius Milhaud and Arnold Schoenberg. A transfusion from a Hines or a Garner might help.

Erroll Garner falls into no single classification. He's a million staves away from Dixieland. He is hardly a swing or a bop soloist and he is in no way a cool pianist. Pittsburgh's hybridish Erroll, who does not read music, pleases everyone with his dexterous digital ability and his Satan-like facial expressions as he explores the fine old standards and improvises on new ones of his own.

Garner, moreover, plays with a beat and an enthusiasm that many of the cool musicians lack. Oscar Peterson, the Canadian, is another who has never forsaken a rhythmic pulse. He won the 1962 poll of *Down Beat*'s readers with almost twice as many votes as young, diffident, super-sensitive Bill Evans received in second place. Peterson manages to serve up harmonically modern figures while playing—and swinging. Hollywood's André Previn, whom I first enjoyed hearing when he was a

* New York: Grosset & Dunlap, Inc., p. 60.

fifteen-year-old student at Beverly Hills High School during World War II, is another whose versatility on a keyboard becomes more and more impressive with the years.

George Shearing came in with the cool period from Great Britain, where he was a recognized boogie-woogie pianist in the Meade Lux Lewis–Pete Johnson mold. He cleverly evolved a new voicing for his piano, electric guitar (Chuck Wayne), vibes (Margie Hyams), bass (John Levy), and drums (Denzil Best), and became, for a period of several years, the favorite combo leader in America. His rare and ingratiating sense of humor, despite his total blindness, and high musical standards keep him, even today, in the front rank of internationally-known jazz purveyors.

Gil Evans, for many years a run-of-the-mill arranger, has spectacularly risen to the heights with the cool school after many years in obscurity as an arranger for Claude Thornhill and the late Skinnay Ennis. It was Evans who charted *Boplicity* for Miles Davis, and again in '57 he arranged *Miles Ahead* for the same trumpeter. Recently, the unusually gifted Evans, who like Bill Evans plays piano, has free-lanced for the world's best jazzmen in New York. He is in his fifties, but a bright future lies ahead. He may very well be the number one jazz arranger in the world today, Ellington excepted; yet he retains respect for the jazz and jazzmen who were heard before his time.

Red Norvo, divorced from Mildred Bailey, formed a new trio in which Tal Farlow played electric guitar and Charlie Mingus, bass. Then 42, the Illinois xylophonist had long since switched over to the more modern sounding vibes and was able to ingeniously incorporate cool bop, swing and cocktail lounge music into his fascinating repertoire.

Stan Getz, a young Philadelphian so strikingly handsome that he might easily have achieved success as an actor, began at sixteen with dance bands as a tenor saxophonist, and after working with Kenton—where he was first recorded—and a dozen others, he became a name with Woody Herman via a cool record of *Early Autumn* in which he played two gorgeous solos. He also played on the Herman basketball team with Chubby Jackson and others against our Capitol quintet (featuring Lee Young as a forward) at the Hollywood YMCA. The Hermans lost.

Stan's quartet played various New York clubs, as did so many others. He toured with Norman Granz. And as he matured he developed an easy, lyrical tenor style not far from Lester Young's, and yet highly personal. For several years he battled a narcotics problem. Today, Getz is perhaps the favorite of most tenor saxophonists. He is young enough, born in 1927, to develop even more. Herbie Steward, Al Cohn, and Gene

Ammons were other cool, influential saxophonists, as were Sonny Stitt, Paul Desmond, Bud Shank, Art Pepper, Zoot Sims, and Yusef Lateef. None matched Getz in 1950; none matches him today.

The early '50s saw more and more musicians making trips to Europe. Only Louis Armstrong and Kid Ory of the old, original New Orleans school remained active. Armstrong, a true phenomenon, actually became more and more popular. Television provided him with a medium for moving into the private homes of every American family with his simple but forceful trumpet and his smiling, raucous vocals. His price, never low, doubled, trebled, and increased again with his long-time Chicago mentor, Joe Glaser, still aggressively and loyally serving as his manager.

There are all too few good bands around these days. Basie, of course, led a mediocre septet only briefly. It wasn't successful, but his big bands of the last twelve years or so have been astoundingly so.

Ellington, the master, has watched his orchestra go through rich periods, and lean, disappointing phases, for forty momentous, unforgettable years. He has never had a poor or even average organization, and today his elegant, versatile orchestra is again in the ascendency with Cootie Williams back in the fold, on trumpet, where he belongs. A listen, live, in any ballroom or auditorium (not a theater, please) will confirm that Duke's men swing as excitingly as any. The hoary canard that Ellington is unable to go, that his is strictly a harmony book, is as patently ludicrous today as it was when it was started in the 1930s by a disgruntled jazz critic. No band, not even Basie's, outswings Duke's when it is *on*—and that's most all the time.

Kenton's men blow hot and cold, as they always have since his Balboa Beach start in 1941. At times, Stan's is a brilliant ensemble. Herman in 1964 again was fronting a strong entry, the best since his 1954 unit in which Nat Pierce, Bill Perkins, Jack Nimitz, Cy Touff, Red Kelly, Al Porcino, Dick Collins, and Charlie Walp distinguished themselves. Quincy Jones, the arranger; Terry Gibbs, the vibes soloist in Los Angeles; Gerald Wilson, the likable ex-Lunceford trumpeter; Gerry Mulligan's big band; and Shorty Rogers, the agile, versatile trumpeter, are others to be watched in the future. They face pitfalls in this era of nondancing youngsters that none of the swing bands faced in 1935-45, however.

Maynard Ferguson, from Montreal, plays not only the loudest trumpet but for several years has been leading what must easily be the loudest of all bands. Ferguson is vastly improved as a soloist, however, since he blew tasteless, screeching horn solos with Kenton and Charlie Barnet more than a decade ago. He also is capable of playing agreeable solos on other instruments, including saxophone, valve trombone, French horn, clarinet, oboe, and baritone horn.

New Talent

More young musicians began to make their mark as hundreds of new record companies were formed. Almost anybody who could run scales on a saxophone or a trumpet could get a record date from one of the little one-man record firms. Milt Gabler's Commodore label, at one time the only all-jazz concern, suddenly had competition from a couple hundred or more jazz companies. The majors, too, took a good, long look at jazz and increased their recording budgets. In the 1950s, remember, there were many kinds of jazz to be recorded and sold. Dixieland, ragtime, swing, bop, cool, and vocal all had their supporters.

About the time that Dave Brubeck teed off his California quartet, John Lewis, the pianist, was struggling to get off the ground with his pretentious Modern Jazz Quartet, a combo appealing exclusively to the intellectuals. The group had no beat, but Lewis' novel compositions, arrangements, and piano, combined with Milt Jackson's vibes, Percy Heath's bass, and Connie Kay's drums—all ultra-modern in concept—had a novel, built-in snob appeal that attracted dilettantes in droves. In 1963, the MJQ made an attempt to combine its far-out, unmelodic, nonswinging music with a string section.

Along with the MJQ came the Jazz Messengers headed by the drummer, Art Blakey, who possessed an enviable reputation for his work with Fletcher Henderson's 1939 orchestra, with Mary Lou Williams after she had left Andy Kirk to head up her own group, with Billy Eckstine during Billy's short-lived leader period, and with Lucky Millinder and Buddy De Franco as well. Horace Silver, one of the truly extraordinary musicians of the '50s, played piano with the Messengers. Kenny Dorham, trumpet, Hank Mobley on tenor, and Doug Watkins, bass, filled out the group. Unlike the Modern Jazz Quartet, Blakey's Messengers swung, exhibited superior soloists—and contributed infinitely more to jazz.

Blakey, too, had to make personnel changes, but his replacements were uniformly excellent with men like Junior Mance, Bobby Timmons, Walter Davis, and Sam Dockery at the piano; Benny Golson, Wayne Shorter, and Johnny Griffin, tenor sax; Donald Byrd and Lee Morgan, trumpet; and Jackie McLean on alto sax. The Messengers, moreover, are even more popular in Europe than here.

Horace Silver has long since been on his own, and enjoying one success after another, including records. Preferring to work with a quintet, Silver, a Connecticut musician who played saxophone as a youth, could make it big as a composer alone. He is one of the outstanding younger talents of the modern period.

A year older than Silver, born in 1928 in Tampa, Florida, Julian (Cannonball) Adderley comes from a musical family and plays trumpet, clarinet, flute, and tenor in addition to the alto sax for which he is most noted. With his brother Nat on trumpet, Adderley today ranks among the most "in demand" attractions in jazz with his quintet. Cannonball's pyrotechnical alto smacks of Parker at times, and he is pegged as a hard bop blower by fellow musicians. Unlike most jazzmen today, he has recorded with happy results with singers, such as Dinah Washington, Nancy Wilson, and Sarah Vaughan. He, too, like Blakey and Silver, is an artist to watch carefully.

Ramsey Lewis, born in 1935 in Chicago, is on record as tabbing Bud Powell and the late Art Tatum as his favorite musicians, yet his piano-playing and composing talents are distinctly his own. His combo increases its popularity and standing among professionals every year.

John William Coltrane, "Trane," is a North Carolinian who has studied music formally for many years and whose savage tenor piping is regarded as one of the more controversial topics of jazz these days in the New York area. He leads his own combo now, but worked as a Miles Davis sideman for several seasons before branching out for himself. Coltrane's soprano sax also is noteworthy.

Equally controversial, in some circles, is the tenor of New Yorker Theodore (Sonny) Rollins, who also worked, but briefly, with Miles Davis in 1951. Rollins, unfortunately, has experienced periods recently in which he felt incapable of playing. His return to records in 1963 on RCA-Victor after a long silence indicated he might require even more rest before attempting to seriously pursue his career. He, too, is a "hard bop" saxophonist with much to say and an unlimited imagination—when he is "right." Only time will tell if Rollins is to occupy a high place in jazz tenor annals. He is far from it today despite his occasional periods of technical brilliance.

George Russell, a Cincinnatian, also enjoyed formal musical training as so many of today's jazz leaders have. It is said that Russell first heard jazz when Fate Marable, in whose riverboat band Louis Armstrong played, visited the Ohio city. The youngster learned drums first and arranging later, but recurring illnesses have kept him from advancing in jazz as rapidly as he deserved.

It was during a despairing sixteen-month hiatus in a Manhattan hospital that Russell devised tonal principles based on the Lydian mode, which in a select circle of progressive younger jazz musicians were regarded as highly original and valuable—but hardly understood by most. George has recently been leading his own group of extreme modernists and, his health permitting, will almost certainly attain even greater stature in time. He was forty in 1963.

Shelly Manne, another of the native-born New Yorkers, deserted his home to resettle in Los Angeles in 1952, and has sparked much of the jazz action there since. As a modern drummer, he is perhaps as gifted as anyone. For several years now, Manne has owned and operated his own Hollywood night spot (the Manne Hole) profitably, and is giving many of America's finest jazzmen a place to work and be heard on the West Coast. Shelly is unique among modernists because he has played drums with Dixieland groups (Joe Marsala), swing bands (Bobby Byrne, Will Bradley, Les Brown), and more progressive, daring units including Stan Kenton, Woody Herman, and Shorty Rogers—all in addition to radio, motion picture and television assignments. He has recorded several thousand tracks.

Yet Shelly remains a warm and humble man, an amiable and cooperative performer who apparently has no need for psychiatrists. A man of his caliber does much for jazz, as much in his numerous trips outside the nation, particularly Europe, as for the U.S.A. In the summer of 1963 while I was in Mexico City I was hardly surprised to see Manne chasing about the capital looking for Mexican jazz.

Like Manne, J. J. Johnson is in his forties and well-adjusted. My first encounter with him was in San Francisco in 1944 when he took the 'bone solos on a Benny Carter session I was producing. For a time it was Bill Harris who was influencing the young musicians (just as the late Miff Mole, Teagarden, and Tom Dorsey exerted influences earlier) but since 1950 the man with the big slide—the important slide to embryonic trombonists—has been Johnson. From Indianapolis, he went on to play with Basie, Herman, Gillespie, and the late great bassist, Oscar Pettiford. Teaming with another trombonist, Danish-born Kai Winding, Jay and Kai for two years successfully worked clubs and made the jazz trombone even more popular. J. J. has been blowing with Miles Davis and his combo in recent years, and winning the *Down Beat* poll the last eight or nine.

Bob Brookmeyer is almost certainly the only white musician born in Kansas City who got out of Jackson County and made a name for himself, Leith Stevens of the Hollywood film studios excepted. His fame as a trombonist, especially with Gerry Mulligan's band, is remarkable in the extreme when one considers that Bob played piano until he was an adult. Curtis Fuller, Jimmy Knepper, Locksley Wellington Hampton—who shrewdly changed his name to Slide Hampton—Al Grey, Urbie Green, Jim Cleveland, Benny Green, and Dave Baker are youngsters on the instrument on their way up.

They, too, may reach the heights enjoyed at various times by Jack Teagarden, Bill Harris, Lawrence Brown, Vic Dickenson, Frank Rosolino, Dicky Wells, Benny Morton, Melba Liston, Bob Brookmeyer, the late Jimmy Harrison, and Joe (Tricky Sam) Nanton, and today's favorite, Johnson.

There are more. The veterans die, and young men, each seeking to express himself, move in and take their shots at the target. Few of the hundreds of neophytes make an impression at all.

THE SOLOISTS

The newer soloists? There are many. Today, they don't play in big bands. The trio, or quartet, or combo up to eight men is the thing. Red Norvo, Lionel Hampton, and Milt Jackson, all of whom go back to the 1930s, retain their popularity in the face of capable young vibes soloists on the way up: Mike Mainieri, Bobby Hutcherson, Dave Pike, Vic Feldman, Terry Gibbs, Cal Tjader, Teddy Charles, Gary Burton, and Walter Dickerson all merit encouragement.

Clarinet? Here there are fewer young men in the race. Benny Goodman remains semi-active (his Mexico City engagement in June 1963 with Bobby Hackett playing cornet alongside him was one of his most sensational successes in twenty years) and Jimmy Giuffre, Tony Scott, Pete Fountain, Marshall Royal, Jimmy Hamilton, Pee-Wee Russell, Albert Nicholas, Woody Herman, Buddy De Franco, and Edmond Hall are all older than thirty. Where are the "hard boppers" here?

The piano obviously is more suited to the new crop. Tommy Flanagan, Wynton Kelly, McCoy Tyner, Ramsey Lewis, Martial Solal—the Algerian now in New York—Bobby Timmons, Don Friedman, Les McCann, Ahmad Jamal, Phineus Newborn, Clare Fischer, Cecil Taylor, and Bill Evans, in particular, have already impressed. All record consistently. Basie, Ellington, Hines, Wilson, Silver, Brubeck, Tristano, Previn, Shearing, Garner, Monk, Red Garland, Hank Jones, Walter Bishop, Bud Powell, John Lewis, Hank Jones, Jimmy Rowles, Arnold Ross, Jerry Wiggins, Jay McShann, and Oscar Peterson are not about to turn in their cards, however.

Wes Montgomery is another who has succeeded in the difficult and overcrowded field of guitarists. Charlie Christian was the last great and uniquely original soloist. Today, with Montgomery, there are Barney Kessel, Charlie Byrd, Herb Ellis, Joe Pass, Jack Marshall, John Gray, Tal Farlow, Gabor Szabo, Les Spann, Howard Robbins, Grant Green, Johnny Smith, Al Casey, Jimmy Raney, the veteran Freddie Green with Basie, Laurindo Almeida (a Brazilian-born modern who is equally skilled in playing classical literature), Kenny Burrell, and Jim Hall, who may become the best of them all.

During the swing era, Chick Webb's Wayman Carver was the only flutist playing jazz; today there are more than a dozen. Frank Wess, Yusef Lateef, Roland Kirk, Eric Dolphy, Leo Wright, Herbie Mann, Jerome Richardson, Bud Shank, Prince Lasha, Paul Horn, James Moody, and Buddy Collette are probably the best known and liked.

Ray Brown, with Oscar Peterson for so long, is almost certainly the most renowned bassist playing today. He wins *Down Beat*'s readers' poll every year, as regularly as the swallows return to the Capistrano Mission. Charlie Mingus, a broad-shouldered Red Callender protégé who doubles piano, rates highly and is slowly winning recognition as a composer as well. Percy Heath, Jimmy Garrison, John Ore, Leroy Vinnegar, Gene Wright, Ron Carter, Paul Chambers, Bob Cranshaw, Gene Ramey, Sonny Dallas, Sam Jones, Red Mitchell, Pat Senatore, Charles Haden, El Dee Young, Gary Peacock, Harry Babasin, Art Davis; and the more mature Milton Hinton, Red Callender, Pops Foster, and George Duvivier are other popular men on their instrument.

The trumpet was the lead horn in early New Orleans bands; it is a lead horn today regardless of the school of jazz. Davis, Gillespie, Armstrong, Ferguson, and Nat Adderley have been noted in previous pages. Clark Terry, Art Farmer, Thad Jones, Shorty Rogers, Don Ellis, Don Cherry, Blue Mitchell, Don Byrd, Don Ferrara, Lee Morgan, Wilbur Harden, Kenny Dorham, Gene Shaw, Marvin Stamm, Carmel Jones, Shorty Cherock, Ray Nance, Buck Clayton, Jack Sheldon, Joe Graves, and Al Hirt have been reaping the most votes in musicians' polls and in record sales, but there are some who will deny that Hirt plays jazz. His many-note, explosive, flag-waving style is better suited to the carnival circuit.

The saxophone family has its stars as well. On alto, Cannonball Adderley, Paul Desmond, Sonny Simmons, Phil Woods, Jimmy Woods, Jackie McLean, Ornette Coleman, Frank Strozier, Eric Dolphy, Lanny Morgan, and Charlie Mariano are the bellwethers among the younger jazzmen; but Benny Carter, Johnny Hodges, Bud Shank, Sonny Stitt, Art Pepper, Paul Horn, Lee Konitz, Earl Bostic, and Russ Procope, all older, remain active and popular.

Harry Carney, the dependable and still-exciting Ellington anchor man; Gerry Mulligan, Jay Cameron, Cecil Payne, Al Beutler, Pepper Adams, Les Rout, Charles Davis, Sahib Shihab, and Frank Hittner are the best-known baritone saxophonists in jazz today. It is a difficult, cumbersome instrument, but an important one.

Handsome Stan Getz, as noted previously, has consistently rated as the favorite tenor saxophonist among musicians since the death of Lester Young in 1959 in Paris. Coleman Hawkins, the incredible old "Bean" whose big, gutsy sound has thrilled listeners for forty years, remains sharp, hip, and quickly adaptable to modern sounds and techniques, as does Ben Webster, who has been playing almost as long. Ellington's Paul Gonsalves, John Coltrane, Zoot Sims, Bud Freeman, Gene Ammons, Buddy Tate, Johnny Griffin, Sonny Stitt, Plas Johnson, Harold Land, Eddie Miller, James Moody, Sonny Rollins, Archie Shepp, Teddy Edwards, Bill Perkins, Yusef Lateef, Wayne Shorter, Stanley Turrentine, Dexter Gordon, Richie Kamuca, Paul Renzi, Charlie Rouse, Buddy Arnold, and Sam Donahue are additional tenor stars who enjoy wide followings.

Johnny Hodges never plays it any more and Sidney Bechet is deceased. So John Coltrane stands as the world's foremost soprano saxophonist though there are those who might vote, instead, for Pony Poindexter or Steve Lacy.

The drums are ever-identified with jazz. At one time, Gene Krupa was the most popular and highest paid drummer in the profession. He is still active. Now, the men who win and place high in the polls are Art Blakey, Joe Morello, Charlie Persip, Max Roach, Jo Jones, Philly Joe Jones, Elvin Jones, Shelly Manne, Mel Lewis, Buddy Rich, Sam Woodyard, Sonny Payne, Dan Richmond, Chico Hamilton, Roy Haynes, Ed Thigpen, Connie Kay, Klook Clarke, who now resides in Paris; Rufus Jones, Louis Hayes, Jimmy Cobb, Al Heath, Jerry McKenzie, Gus Johnson, Walter Perkins, Chuck Flores, Mickey Sheen, Dave Bailey, Rudy Collins, Ben Riley, Frankie Dunlop, Jake Hanna, Pete LaRoca, Frank Butler, Ed Blackwell, and Billy Higgins.

Jazz organ? Like the accordion, it is a difficult instrument for jazz. Jimmy (Chicken Shack) Smith is perhaps the best at the moment, even though he has been playing only since 1952.

Roland Kirk deserves more than a solitary paragraph all to himself. "I constantly think about music," he told Burt Korall in the English *Melody Maker*, February 9, 1963. "When I go to sleep I actually dream about music and hear things which I try to play during my waking hours. One night about five years ago, I dreamed I was playing three reed instruments at once—the sounds and feeling created coincided with what I had been seeking on one instrument."

Unable to find the proper horn in a music store in Columbus, Ohio, the proprietor searched his own home, near Kirk's, and came upon a manzello. Kirk tried it. It had the exact sound he had "heard" while dreaming. A year later, the same friend found a stritch and showed it to Roland. "I worked out on it," he told Korall, "and realized my search was over. I got the exact sounds I wanted."

Blind, Kirk is one of the strangest of jazzmen in appearance because of the three horns (tenor sax is the third) that he plays simultaneously. A siren whistle hangs from his neck as well. During an evening, he will also play nose flute, humming box, and a small slide trombone with a reed mouthpiece called a suolophone. He has recorded all these instruments, including the three played at the same time, on Mercury.

Don Elliott, mellophone; Ray Starling, mellophonium; Julius Watkins, French horn; Ray Nance and the veterans, Stuff Smith and Joe Venuti, violin; Tommy Gumina, Ernie Felice, and Art Van Damme, accordion; Candido on conga drum—all received votes in *Down Beat*'s 1963 readers' poll for "miscellaneous instruments."

Take Oliver Nelson of St. Louis as an example of the young, modern musician. He plays fine flute, alto and tenor saxophones, and has composed excellent modern jazz. He studied the piano when he was six. In the marines, he served in Japan. He attended Washington University and Lincoln University, then in New York played in the orchestras of Erskine Hawkins, Wild Bill Davis, and Louie Bellson after being employed in the Mound City as a streetcar pilot and bus driver. A wild career for a man who was only thirty in 1962? Yes, but keep in mind that Nelson also is qualified to practice taxidermy and embalming. *Down Beat* may yet have to open a voting classification for flute-blowing morticians.

CHAOS AND STUDIED BOREDOM

In jazz, revolution is relative. Arrangements by Stan Kenton and Pete Rugolo were regarded as "far out" in the 1940s; today both are considered conservative chart-writers. Parker's alto was the ultimate in 1950. Today, Ornette Coleman of Fort Worth, Texas, plays a revolutionary "free form" alto sax that heeds no meter, no continuity and no relationship with what other musicians in Coleman's combo may be playing. To many ears—most ears—it is a chaotic sound, but there are some who enjoy it. Like Coleman, Eric Dolphy is the complete individualist, playing whatever notes he feels like playing with no regard for tempo, key, or accompaniment. Coleman and Dolphy lead what musicians call "the new thing." It makes the cool phase old-fashioned.

Charlie Mingus similarly composes and plays music that is often understandable to no one but himself. He, too, is thus identified with "the new thing."

Today's jazz buffs soberly reflect the unemotional, studied boredom of their musician idols. They never dance. They don't tap feet. Some don't even applaud. *Time* in its issue of June 23, 1963, commented on the listeners attending temperamental old ex-bopper Thelonious Monk's sessions at the Five Spot in New York:

> "*Few jazz disciples know much about the music. Since they are given more to worship than appreciation, they seldom develop an ear—only an attitude. Often, Monk, for one, will spend a whole night horsing around on his piano while his sidemen accompany with him with all the enthusiasm of cops fighting drunks. On other nights he plays brilliantly and the sidemen follow with insight and devotion —but the applause is just the same. Monk's audience is far too devoted to him to worry about his music.*"

Time's jazz notes are more often wrong than right, but its description of the sophomoric attitude of jazz listeners (and some musicians as well) can generally be applied to those who follow the Modern Jazz Quartet, Miles Davis, Charlie Mingus, Ornette Coleman, Eric Dolphy, and others of the contemporary crop. Personable Shelly Manne, dissenting from behind his drums, shakes his head and grins:

> "*Listeners to jazz should participate if they want to appreciate it to the fullest. Most musicians invite enthusiasm. Tap your foot, clap your hands, drum on the table, sing along if you like. Or else go listen to a string quartet play Bach.*"

11

The BIRD

Charlie Parker was a spoiled brat. In Kansas City, when he was grow-ing up in the 1930s, he was called a "mommy's boy" by musicians who quickly tired of his thinking only of Parker. And years later, in New York at Birdland when he reigned as the uncontested king of the alto saxophone throughout the world, an advertising agency executive* hur-ried into the club one night, did not see Parker on the bandstand and prepared to leave and return later. But then he saw Charlie, in a telephone booth with the door wide open: the Bird was urinating.

Writers for every jazz magazine and music trade paper as well as those for mass-circulation magazines have wasted hundreds of thousands of words concluding that Bird died of frustration because (1) his genius was appreciated by only a few, and (2) his colleague Dizzy Gillespie got all the credit for introducing modern jazz and became bop's high priest.

Parker may indeed have been frustrated. Most everyone is today. But Parker's miseries started much earlier, perhaps as far back as 1933, cer-

---

* Cy Schneider, account executive of Carson-Roberts, Inc., an extremely knowl-edgeable jazz buff who has written many liner notes for Norman Granz down through the years.

ILLUSTRATION: Charlie "Bird" Parker.

tainly by 1934, when he was fourteen years old and attending Lincoln High in Kansas City. There he played a baritone horn, whenever he showed up. Ed Mayfield and other of his schoolmates at Lincoln have always tried to be tactful in speaking of little Charlie's childhood, but that he tried to bully others, borrow "lunch money" that was never repaid, and brush off schoolmates who tried to be friendly in favor of older boys who took him on benzedrine parties, is documented.

Those who played alongside Parker say he was smoking marijuana in high school, where he was a perpetual freshman until he quit and turned to music full time. The late Bob Simpson, a fine trombonist, and Lawrence Keyes, the pianist who is still active, were both more advanced musicians than Parker at fourteen. Parker demanded, never graciously, that they teach him chords. The late and lovable Freddie Culliver, who in 1940 recorded beautiful tenor solos with Harlan Leonard's band on Victor-Bluebird, was a far more polished and musicianly saxophonist. Little Franz Bruce, alto, Johnny Jackson, alto, and Jimmy Ross, another Leonard sideman, likewise were regarded as far more skillful jazzmen than Parker. They were all his age.

But Charlie, for all his surliness and bad habits, could charm the leaves from the trees. When he wanted something, he got it. His mother, Mrs. Addie Bailey Parker, widowed when her son was seventeen, went without necessities to provide for him. She also supported Charlie's half-brother, John Parker, although he was not her son. But Charles, as she always called him, was the pet.

Parker married his first wife, Rebecca Ruffin, when he was sixteen. Their marriage lasted two years and in that time young Charlie turned to narcotics. A sleazy little crumbum named "Little Phil," whom we constantly encountered in jazz clubs and at rehearsals, was the salesman. He was locked up later, but much too late to deter Parker and certain other youngsters from acquiring the most despicable, deadly habit there is.

Mrs. Parker worked first at a Western Union telegraph office as a cleaning woman and then became a practical nurse at Kansas City's General Hospital, cheerfully surviving long, black-breaking days and nights of hard physical labor to dress Charlie well, supply him with cigarette money (and, unknowingly, narcotics funds) and all the other things youngsters in their late teens require. Charlie was never wrong.

Mrs. Parker told Robert George Reisner for his enchanting book, *Bird*:

> *"Charles got into serious trouble one night when he kept a taxi for six or seven hours and ran up a $10 bill which he couldn't pay. The taxi driver tried to snatch his horn, and Charles stabbed him with a dagger. They took him off to the farm. I told the police, 'How dare*

you treat my son like that? Bring him back!' He came home the next day. They'd taken the dagger away from him." *

I did not meet Parker until he started working with Jay McShann and the Harlan Leonard band in Kansas City in 1937-38 (neither was employed regularly, so Parker rehearsed and gigged with both) while I was a reporter-rewrite man on the Kansas City *Journal-Post*, a correspondent for *Down Beat*, *Metronome*, and *Orchestra World*, and a stringer for *The Billboard*. Parker was ever the personality kid, and he would pick your billfold from a rear pocket while showing you how to finger a high E on the side keys of his alto. If you caught him, he would laugh it off and hand the billfold back.

"Little Phil" not only lurked about, furtively, but there were girl-pushers as well. McShann and Leonard chased them away. They would meet with the personable Parker later. Apparently his mother still was unaware of his use of heroin, but she knew how he beat his first wife, Rebecca. And she eventually learned how he would constantly hock the new saxophone she had bought him with money earned from scrubbing floors, then get it back with money he "borrowed" from McShann, Leonard, and the musicians with whom he worked.

Parker also played with Buster Smith, Kansas City's "little jazz professor," who along with Tommy Douglas unquestionably exerted a powerful, style-shaping influence on the youngster. Charlie had watched Smith in the little Basie band at the Reno. But for all his admiration of the older "professor," he felt more at ease with the McShann group. They, like him, were just kids.

It was a memorable outfit, on a modest, local scale. Never did a group of young musicians work harder, or enjoy playing more, than at the daily and sometimes nightly rehearsals McShann called. Skinny Gene Ramey, who looked somewhat professorial himself, was a warm, intelligent and humor-blessed bassist who acted as a sort of volunteer guardian for Charlie. He asserts that Parker—not yet nicknamed Bird—was one of the least impressive saxophonists in the two Kansas Citys until the summer of 1938, when he went out with the kind old former leader George E. Lee to the Ozark hills around Lake Taneycomo in southern Missouri and spent all his spare time playing the first Basie records and digging every Lester Young note on each side repeatedly.

Ramey recalls:

> *"When he came back, he was a different musician. Nobody put him down any more. He knew the changes, he knew the fingering of his*

* *Bird: The Legend of Charlie Parker* (New York: Citadel Press, 1961), p. 163.

horn, and even his tone was better. From that summer on he had it made with all of us around Kansas City. By that time Basie had gone to Chicago and Andy Kirk, Mary Lou Williams, Dick Wilson, and all the other fine Kirk musicians were ever on the road. So we had to play for our own kicks."

Ramey's extreme liking for the tormented Parker was somewhat like Mrs. Parker's. But Ramey looks back now and wonders how he was consistently "taken" by Parker night after night. He calls Charlie the "greatest of all the con men."

Playing his saxophone, he was anything but a con man. At first he was a slow, unsure reader, but his musician friends all helped him, Keyes in particular. Efferge Ware, the guitarist who recorded with Julia Lee and other Kaycee artists, remembers tutoring not only Charlie but most of the McShann musicians out in the big park on the Paseo, a wide tree-lined boulevard, on warm nights. Scholarly William Scott, a tenor man who composed *Swingmatism* and *Dexter Blues* on the band's first record date in Texas later, needed no teacher. He was a first-rate arranger with an unlimited future until his sudden death in 1955, only a week or so before Parker's.

Charlie and the McShanns toured the Middle West and South throughout 1938. Parker kept getting better. On a one-nighter in Chicago about that time, after I had moved there to edit *Down Beat* for owners Carl Cons and Glenn Burrs, it was Charlie who took the alto solos instead of Jackson. By now he was the Bird, named by the McShann musicians.* And in all honesty, his playing, to me, was reminiscent—perhaps even a copy—of Buster Smith's in Kansas City. Good, yes. Great, no. And he still behaved like an only child who needs his backside paddled.

McShann chased away the dope pushers, but Jay had a weakness for whiskey or a tasty domestic wine. The musicians called alcoholic beverages "billiards." There were nights when McShann was "hootie" on "billiards"—jive for high on alcohol. And to this day the likable McShann, a clever, original pianist who deserved better than he got, is known as "Hootie McShann" through the Middle West. He is still playing—and superbly—in Kansas City.

Parker many times tried the patience of McShann and everyone with whom he had contact. By the time he was twenty (1940) he was irretrievably hooked by narcotics, and often unable to play at all. He became less gregarious, more serious in his attitude, and he found less time for fun, gags, and horseplay with musicians. He played tenor for a while

* For an account of the Bird's nicknaming, see page 123.

with McShann (after having left Jay for a few months in 1939 when he bummed his way to New York, worked as a dishwasher, and earned a half-dollar a night in gratuities at John Williams' Chicken Shack) and made his first sides with the band under Dave Kapp's supervision, in the session described in the previous chapter.

It was a vocal side by the late Walter Brown, *Confessin' the Blues,* which immediately became the hit—which provided the band and me with a major disappointment. Brown was a highly original blues singer and a deserving artist, but McShann and his musicians and those of us who had boomed the band and publicized it and helped it get the Decca contract knew that a band must have a click instrumental disc to make the big time. *Blues* sold more than 500,000 copies, however, and gave John B. Tumino, McShann's manager, the weapon he needed to put the group into New York's famous Savoy Ballroom in Harlem in 1942.

Parker never returned West. He gigged about Manhattan, played for a few months in the Noble Sissle band—one of the dullest in America—and his specialty was *Cherokee,* just as it had been with McShann. His period with Earl Hines followed. Abandoning his conventional swing-styled outfit, Earl had also hired Sarah Vaughan as his singer and a fired-up, Minton's-inspired Diz Gillespie on horn. They never recorded. The union's ban on recording was on and few got to hear a band that has since become a legend.

Tired of the road by now, Bird continued his con man traits. He frequently used a dime store ring to lure young girls to his pad. Sometimes, Hines' sidemen say, the Bird actually went through a marriage ceremony to get what he wanted. That ruse has, of course, been used by musicians, salesmen, and travelers for a thousand years. But Bird bragged about his deception. Hines' musicians desperately tried to keep him straight, but it was a losing cause. He missed shows in theaters. In ballrooms he failed to show, or fell asleep on the stand, his cheeks puffed out as if he were blowing his horn.

Billy Eckstine of the Hines band later went out on his own with a new orchestra in which nine members of the Hines group played, including Parker, in whom Eckstine still had faith, and Gillespie. But it was too late. The era of the big swing bands was fast passing, and although Eckstine recorded several sides after the record strike ended, there were no places for a band his size to work during those difficult World War II days.

Art Blakey, Tommy Potter, the doomed Fats Navarro, Sonny Stitt, Gene Ammons, Dexter Gordon, Lucky Thompson, and Bird's old buddy from Harlan Leonard's band, Tadd Dameron, also worked with Eckstine. Ironically, a few years after he disbanded, Eckstine became the nation's number one pop singer with vapid studio orchestras in Hollywood and New York. Sometimes, it seems, there ain't no justice.

Parker's next phase already has been touched on in the previous chapter. He worked the joints and boîtes of New York's Fifty-Second Street with scores of musicians, made his first bop records, formed his own groups, left his second wife Gerry and wed Doris Sydnor, made his first trip to California for the ill-advised and egglaying run at Billy Berg's nitery and, sadly, more and more demanded narcotics.

In Los Angeles, depressed as he had never been before because of the Californians' apathy, Bird returned to his hotel room one evening, set fire to it and wound up in the Camarillo sanitarium northwest of Los Angeles.

He was there for more than six months. His incarceration, of course, was page one streamer news in all the music sheets. Most musicians assumed he was through. The late Freddy Webster had come out of Benny Carter's band and lost his mind. So had Bobby Moore, a promising young trumpeter with Basie. Back in the 1920s Leon Rapollo had wigged-out and spent the remainder of his life in an asylum. Other cases musicians knew about were purposely unpublicized.

At Camarillo, Bird was allowed to meet his wife Doris three times a week. They fixed his teeth, which had always been bad. But mostly, he rested.

There followed the greatest, most illustrious, and most creative period of the Bird's short life. He still "borrowed" money from everyone with whom he had contact. No one ever recalls his reimbursing anybody. But he was as straight as he had ever been. Camarillo had benefited him. His records of this period on Dial included *Bird's Nest, Cool Blues, Relaxin' at Camarillo, Cheers, Carvin' the Bird,* and *Stupendous*—all made in Hollywood after his release—and on Savoy *Chasin' the Bird, Cheryl, Buzzy,* and *Donna Lee,* cut in June 1947, after he returned to New York.

Charlie had always been a heavy drinker, even while dependent on narcotics. And musicians who were working with him in this pre-1950 period will sadly relate how junkies and pushers of heroin flocked around the Bird almost constantly. Charlie frequently warned young musicians of the horrors of narcotics and sometimes missed work drinking himself into a stupor, apparently trying to evade the "horse" habit. But, like so many addicts, he gave in, and was back on the treadmill to hell by the summer of 1947. There was, his friends apologized, just too much pressure to resist.

In '48, when the union again enforced a ten-month musicians' strike against all record companies, Parker received the first warning from a doctor that his health was not good. He had ulcers, his blood pressure was too high, and the ravages of alcohol and heroin were beginning to be evident.

Most of the time, Bird worked at a place called Bop City. He played at the Royal Roost too. In February 1948, he felt "hurt" because he had not been invited to the First International Jazz Festival at Nice, France. Under the auspices of the French writer, Hugues Panassié, the program starred Louis Armstrong's sextet with the late Velma Middleton as vocalist, Rex Stewart's little combo with Sandy Williams' trombone, Mezz Mezzrow's orchestra, and the popular Django Reinhardt, gypsy jazz guitarist.

But the following year, Bird got the call to Nice, making his first trip outside the U.S.A. except for a quick visit to Mexico, where he and Doris Sydnor had been married. He switched over to Mercury and resumed recording with the end of the strike. (Union chief James C. Petrillo learned after a month or so that thousands of musicians were recording as if there was no restriction; his union was defeated so decisively by the numerous record companies—and its own membership—that there has never been a strike since.)

It is evident now, years later, that Charlie's Savoy series including *Barbados, Ah-Lou-Cha, Constellation, Parker's Mood, Perhaps, Marmaduke, Steeplechase,* and *Merry-go-Round* were all recorded during the strike. His Mercurys were recorded after the ban had been lifted by the shell-shocked Petrillo. On the new label, Bird concentrated on Afro-Cuban and Latin-American things like *Mango Mangue, No Noise,* and *Okiedoke Rhumba* which emphasized conga drum, timbals, and maracas. But the exotic rhythms somehow did not enhance his gyrating, fleetly-fingered alto as they did his colleague Diz Gillespie's trumpet.

In 1949, he happily recorded with strings for the first time, initially with Neil Hefti's orchestra, then in November with a studio ensemble with which he made *Just Friends* and *April in Paris.* Jimmy Carroll inked the charts and conducted.

The French jazz buffs Panassié and Charles Delaunay, long-time guiding lights of the Hot Club of France, split about this time in violent disagreement over the course jazz was taking. Delaunay, son of a brilliant French artist, forthwith produced the 1950 International Jazz Festival in Paris himself, intending to concentrate on the newer bop and cool musicians. Bird got an invitation.

Delighted, eager, and perhaps inspired, he went to Sweden first, played about a week there, then went to Paris and soared off on a mad, wailing, drunken binge of at least three days and missed the festival completely. Delaunay, it seems, had paid the Bird in advance!

His marriage to Doris Parker ended, he began a common-law marriage with the beauteous Chan Richardson. She bore him a daughter, Pree, who died at two, and a son, Charles Baird. Bird also had an older son, Leon, born of his first marriage to Rebecca Ruffin in 1937.

Occasionally, he would fly to Kansas City, visit his mother briefly, jam around town with his old musician buddies of Local 627, and leave abruptly. Tootie Clarkin, who operated a club called the Mayfair on the South Side of the Missouri city where Parker had played long engagements years before with McShann, remained a close friend, and Bird sometimes telephoned him from cities a thousand or more miles away.

"He usually wanted money," Clarkin says, "but I'll give him credit. When he was ready to hang up he would always ask me to tell his mother he was fine. He had a lot of character for all his weaknesses."

Bird had even more stiffs hanging around him by 1950. His fatalistic philosophy attracted all kinds of nuts. Alcoholics, junkies, girls, matrons, musicians, singers, writers, artists—they all pursued Parker. Some of the musicians who worked with him regularly have told me that while Charlie always tried to assist young musicians, and would often give bums generous handouts, he retained his mother fixation and behaved like an illogical, pampered brat during most of his hours off the bandstand.

Norman Granz, by now operating his own Norgran label, made every effort to keep Bird straight. He paid him well to perform in his various *Jazz at the Philharmonic* troupes, as he had for many years. But Parker used Granz every way he could. Heroin took all his income. He could and did spend $1,000 a night. He could and did repeatedly go without sleep for 72 hours. He could do and did do things no normal musician or human being would do.

Confidential, a disgusting scandal sheet that attracted almost hysterical attention and a bi-monthly readership of millions for a time in the early 1950s, ran a raw, sensational article about Parker and his narcotic-filled life that is said to have upset the Bird terribly. His manager, Teddy Bloom, always devoted, persuaded him not to sue. "The article is true," he told Bird. Bloom saved enough of Parker's income to purchase him a dazzling Cadillac. When Bird went into one of his common tantrums that Teddy was "stealing my money," Bloom took him to a garage, pointed to the car, and gave him the keys. Parker picked him up, kissed him, jumped into the car . . . and in two weeks, had hocked it. His record of *Bloomido* was named for his mentor, who played violin.

By 1954, Bird was without any question the most publicized musician alive, in the trade mags. The public still knew nothing of his phenomenal talent, or his eccentric behavior, but musicians throughout the world carefully followed his every move. Yet, he endured periods when he had no money in his pockets, none in the bank, and none in sight. He survived another trip to California in 1952 but failed to attract patronage aside from musicians in both Los Angeles and San Francisco.

He said he would turn atheist, but they didn't have holidays.

There are some who insist that Parker's suicide attempt (drinking iodine) was an act, and that he merely smeared iodine on his tongue with cotton in September 1954. It gave him admission to New York's public Bellevue Hospital (for the second time) and perhaps a rest and a chance to think things out for two weeks.

Robert George Reisner's research (see his *Bird* book, mentioned above) reveals that Bird's record at Bellevue was eye-opening: Psychometric testing indicated a high average intelligence with paranoid tendencies, a hostile and evasive personality with manifestations of primitive and sexual fantasies associated with hostility and gross evidence of paranoid thinking. The diagnosis during his second stay was simple: acute alcoholism and undifferentiated schizophrenia. A spinal tap was performed. Colloidal gold curve proved negative, and blood Wasserman was two-plus positive. Notes on his medical chart indicated that the patient was "lazy" and kept bothering nurses for doses of paraldehyde, Reisner's findings showed.

So much for the Bird's pathetic physical condition just six months before his death. His ulcers were painful and he had survived at least two heart attacks, one a blockbuster. His liver was bad. He had gained sixty to seventy pounds over his early days in New York.

Parker's last days were not happy ones. Like Bolden, Oliver, Beiderbecke, Berigan, and other outstanding jazzmen before him, Bird had nothing to show for all his ability, and the long arm-jabbing years of music and addiction. More and more he was seen around New York looking aged, and shabbily dressed. More and more did musicians and fans "lend" him money. He knew his time was limited, and he told some of his friends he wouldn't be around much longer.

The following March, preparing to leave for Boston and a job at Storyville, he stopped by the Stanhope Hotel suite that his friend—and the friend of numerous musicians and artists—Baroness Pannonica de Koenigswarter, called "Nica" by her friends, shared with her small daughter. The baroness has many times been asked to clarify Bird's last night on earth because of inept, inaccurate reporting by the New York newspapers three full days after Parker died.

With his horn and clothing in a car outside, Parker came in, sat down, looking ill, and refused a drink ("which was unusual," she adds). Within minutes, Bird started vomiting blood. Genuinely alarmed, Nica called her physician. He arived promptly, examined Bird, and urged that he go to a hospital immediately. But Charlie protested that he would be "okay" in a half-hour and refused. The baroness and her little girl suggested that he remain in their suite, where they waited on him around the clock, mostly bringing him astounding quantities of ice water.

Robert Freymann, M.D., visited Parker two and three times a day on March 10, 11, and 12, 1955. He warned the baroness that Bird, whom he had never heard of, was critically ill of advanced cyrrhosis and stomach ulcers. But Bird felt better every hour, except for occasional coughing and vomiting spells. On Saturday the 12th, he, Nica, and her daughter sat watching Tommy and Jimmy Dorsey's CBS television show produced by the Jackie Gleason staff. Bird commented on Tommy's skill as a trombonist, rose from his chair, appeared to gasp and choke, and then fell back in his chair. He was dead.*

Dr. Freymann arrived shortly thereafter and ordered the body to be taken to the Bellevue morgue. There was nothing irregular.

Not for three days was anything printed about the death of Bird. Then, from municipal records, the New York papers came out with inaccurate, distorted news stories that listed Parker's age as 53 (he was actually just five months short of being 35) and stated that his body had lain unidentified for forty-eight hours at Bellevue. The reports were untrue. But the baroness faced criticism from certain quarters because she had taken in a dying man and tried to help him.

Bird's tired, abused body was at rest. But the end was not yet in sight. His wives argued about the services. Chan claimed the body at Bellevue, but Doris roared in, threatened to sue, and had the body removed from one funeral home to another. Gerry (his second wife) demanded his alto.

Services were held, finally, at the Abyssinian Baptist Church in Harlem, where Fats Waller's funeral had been held twelve years previously. Parker's body then was shipped to the town he both loved and hated, Kansas City, for burial. A striking, almost hypnotic color photograph of his grave by Art Kane is featured on one full page of the magnificent *Esquire's World of Jazz* book (page 105). Two small birds are pictured on the headstone. But to make the setting all the more moving and sad, the date of his death is mistakenly engraved as March 23. That was two days *after* his funeral.

Parker's estate, consisting almost entirely of royalties still accruing to him as a composer and recorded performer, is being contested and fought over by various parties. But the Yardbird is gone. His mother—and never was one more devoted to a son—mourns him as she did in 1955. With

---

* Tommy Dorsey choked to death in November of the following year at his home in Greenwich, Connecticut.

the years, the Parker legend, like Beiderbecke's, spreads to every corner of the world:

How he would line up six to eight doubles of Old Grand Dad on a bar and gulp them all down just before going on the bandstand . . .

How he answered Dr. Freymann, three days before he died, when the physician asked him if he drank liquor. "Sometimes," the ailing Parker answered straight-faced, "I sip a little sherry before dinner" . . .

How he horsed around in Kansas City, in his late teens, goosing musicians on the stand, stealing packs of cigarets from their cases, and invariably greeting a cub *Journal-Post* reporter who didn't think Parker was anything special with a smiling but sarcastic, "Greetings, Dexterious!" . . .

How his appetite for the opposite sex was inexhaustible, averaging out three "servings" a day, according to his loyal and attentive manager, Teddy Bloom . . .

How Norman Granz, whom Parker never spoke of in complimentary terms, paid all expenses of the funeral, shipment of body, and burial, and hoped to keep it quiet . . .

How he was listed in magazines and music books for twenty years as "Charles Christopher Parker" until his mother finally protested and vehemently denied the middle name ever existed. His headstone simply lists his name as "Charles Parker, Jr." . . .

How Bird's revolutionary playing will live forever, although there were as many musicians who disliked it, didn't understand it, and didn't want to hear any more of it as there were those who called Parker a genius.

There will never be another like him.

12

Internationally Speaking

Jazz commands more attention throughout the world today than it has at any previous time, the golden era of the 1930s not excluded.

Dave Brubeck, who has been travelling the continents consistently for more than a decade, found that jazz was banned in those nations governed by rigid dictatorships, but whenever partial freedom returned to such countries, playing jazz in public was invariably permitted. In Poland, where once jazz could be heard only privately, Brubeck and his musicians were met at the Cracow railroad station by a Polish jazz combo. They cheerfully played *Yankee Doodle*.

Jazz may be heard within Russia today, the strict ban against it having been eased following the death of Joseph Stalin, but Americans who have visited Moscow report that the Russians are perhaps fifteen years behind the West in jazz musicianship. Benny Goodman and his musicians proved a first-rate attraction on their 1962 tour of the Soviet Union, but a few months later the Russians rejected both Duke Ellington and Count Basie as cultural exchange attractions, preferring a troupe of marionettes and selected performers from American circuses.

Ellington and his orchestra, instead, undertook a memorable tour of the Middle East and India under the auspices of the State Department. Basie, who previously had played Japan, substituted another concert tour of Europe, at his regular fee, for the rejected Russian trek.

Jazz is important to the people of Russia, however. Joseph Vinestain's band is said to be their outstanding jazz ensemble. It recorded an album called *American Jazz* featuring the compositions of Horace Silver, John Lewis, and Cannonball Adderley, with Gennady Golstein, alto, and Constantin Nosov, trumpet.

ILLUSTRATION: Django Reinhardt of France. (Photograph by Studio Tronchet, Paris.)

Every American jazzman who has ever broadcast or had his records beamed internationally has received mail not only from musicians and fans in Russia but from those in other Iron Curtain nations as well. Willis Conover's government jazz programs have created and sustained an immense audience for many years. The television series, *Jazz Scene, U.S.A.*, produced by Jimmie Baker and Steve Allen, was being programmed regularly in fourteen countries as of 1964. On film, each sequence stars America's best-known jazz musicians. Mexico, Cyprus, Finland, France, Great Britain, New Zealand, the Netherlands, Portugal, Puerto Rico, the Philippines, Ireland, Sweden, and Nigeria all report *Jazz Scene* to be successful in attracting and holding viewers.

In the Congo, François Luambo and the O.K. Jazz Band are favorite entertainers, although they read no music. They, too, record frequently and travel extensively just as do their idols in the U.S.A.

For centuries, the sensitive Filipinos have been acknowledged as the finest (and most popular) musicians in the Orient. The Japanese, however, are probably even more adept in the jazz idiom. Tokyo has become the jazz center of the Eastern world. Every child, even the poorest, plays some sort of an instrument. The Nippon Gakki firm is the largest manufacturer of pianos in the world.

American artists visit the Islands frequently. Oddly, an American musician, Russ Gary, is one of the most popular orchestra leaders in Tokyo. His sidemen are all Japanese.

Before World War II, France and England led the world in appreciating and furthering American jazz. England maintains its predominance. France has slumped somewhat.

In Paris, I watched an outfit led by drummer Klook Clarke and pianist Bud Powell excite French musicians and fans—and tourists as well—with shockingly lackadaisical performances at the Blue Note on the dark and narrow rue d'Artois just off the Champs-Élysées. Several nights later, with Kenny Drew and Johnny Griffin billed as the "outstanding new attractions," the same naive enthusiasm greeted what obviously were drab, uninspired efforts by the American pianist and tenor saxist, respectively.

Another basement bistro, as unattractive as the Blue Note, is the Chat Qui Pêche. There, Chet Baker, on trumpet, displayed more apathy than musicianship to the scattered but alert young patrons. Paris clubs prosper with girlie shows, it seems, and most of the jazz available is on records or at infrequent concerts.

Yet, at one time, France was regarded as *the* jazz beehive with Hugues Panassié and Charles Delaunay, the esteemed writers and critics, unquestionably rating among the top five jazz authorities in the world. Django Reinhardt, Stéphane Grappelly and their scintillating Hot Club of France combo were universally renowned; even today their 1930s records remain brisk sellers in album form.

France still has its writers, its fans, and its musicians. But the visiting *aficionado* will not see them unless he happens into the City of Light on the night of a special concert.

André Ekyan, Hubert Rostaing, Lou Viola, Lulu Gaste, Roger Chaput, Alix Combelle, and Django's brother, the guitarist Joseph Reinhardt, were perhaps the outstanding French pioneers. Thirty years later, two pianists are carrying the Gallic modern jazz banner most prominently: Martial Solal and Bernard Peiffer, both of whom now reside in the United States. French traditionalist leaders would include Maxime Saury, Claude Luter, and possibly the saxophonist Guy LaFitte.

France remains a large, ever-hungry devourer of jazz records, and more are said to be purchased there per person than in the States. André Hodéir stands as one of the world's most literate and authoritative critics.

Great Britain has far more "live" jazz to offer than any other nation outside North America. There are more jazz clubs, too.

There are old-fashioned "trad" bands in abundance, and several ultramodern groups. The Dixieland combos are paced by Chris Barber, Kenny Ball, Terry Lightfoot, Alan Elsdon, Ken Colyer, Alex Welsh, Acker Bilk, and a Scots group led by Pete Kerr. The moderns acknowledge as their leaders Tubby Hayes, Johnny Dankworth, Ronnie Ross, Bill Le Sage, Jim Deuchar, Ronnie Scott, Shake Keane, Tom Whittle, Don Rendell, and the astounding alto saxophonist Joe Harriott, who is by far the most advanced jazzman in the United Kingdom.

Victor Feldman, a child jazz prodigy, has long since become an American citizen, as did Dizzy Reece and George Shearing before him. Ted Heath's big band occasionally plays jazz and there are others, like Humphrey Lyttleton and his group, who prefer the middle-of-the-road.

A weekly newspaper, *The Melody Maker*, continues to encourage jazz intelligently and effectively with superior pictures and feature stories on the subject, and is possibly the most influential periodical on the subject in the world.

Sweden, year by year, becomes more and more prominent in the international jazz picture. There is only one professional Dixieland group of note, Anders Hassler's Cave Stompers; Hassler estimates there are ten other traditional combos, all comprised of amateurs.

Sweden's most popular writer and radio commentator on jazz, Hans

Fridlund, rates two modern pianists, Jan Johansson and Nils Lindberg, as the finest in Scandinavia. Lars Gullin, Bengt Hallberg, Arne Domnerus, Ake Persson, Eie Thelin, Rune Karlsson, Bengt-Arne Wallin, Lars Fernlof, Bernd Rosengran, George Riedel, Bjorn Alke, Borje Fredrickson, and the veteran Putte Wickman round out the Svenska scene. All are moderns. Most are in their early twenties. Each is known in North America via records.

Fridlund's articles in the Stockholm newspaper, *Aftonbladet,* are doing much to increase the popularity and serious study of jazz throughout Sweden.

In nearby Copenhagen, a restaurant called the Montmartre regularly features American and Danish jazzmen, and amid surroundings considerably more attractive than those found in Paris.

I found little jazz activity in Finland. Radio and recording musicians frequently practice and record jazz together on an informal basis for personal pleasure, but there are no clubs offering jazz.

Germany is fast becoming a major site for jazz, although most of the groups I saw in 1955-57-59-63 were amateur. Friedrich Gulda, the classical pianist, is becoming Deutschland's most noted performer because of his ability to compose and play refreshingly different, contemporary jazz. He is an Austrian.

Joachim E. Berendt and Dr. Dietrich Schulz-Koehn have, since World War II, won recognition as Germany's most perceptive and knowledgeable jazz authorities. Hans Koller, tenor, and Albert Mangelsdorff, trombone, are regarded as West Germany's most gifted instrumentalists. Frankfurt, West Berlin and Cologne are the leading jazz centers. Most of the clubs, *bier* taverns and ballrooms I visited, however, were featuring yodelers and Bavarian-type oompah bands.

The Netherlands, as all buffs know, is the home of the Dutch Swing College Band directed by Peter Schilperoort. It is strictly a New Orleans combo, but it imitates no other groups. Holland, like England, is proud of its numerous jazz organizations—fan clubs—unknown in the United States among jazz followers. But there are no "live" places where jazz may be enjoyed regularly.

Belgium is known for its annual festival at Comblain la Tour, a village near Liège. Italy, unlike the northern European nations, favors traditional bands. Spain and Portugal apparently hear jazz exclusively on imported records. So do the citizens of many other nations.

South America has not kept pace with Europe, and Japan, in fostering jazz.

Argentina and Brazil have small and vociferous corps of musicians and devotees, but ones that can in no way be ranked with those of the leading jazz nations. In Argentina and Brazil there is a modicum of interest in jazz, but despite the synthetic bossa nova boom of several seasons ago, little of merit in jazz has emanated from there.

But in Mexico City there is a surging, healthy jazz movement that reminds an American visitor of the mid-1930s in America. Tino Contreras, drums; Mario Contreras, trumpet; Al Zuniga, piano; Pepe Solis, trumpet; Hector Hallal, tenor; Mario Ballina, bass; Boaulio Guaderrama, drums; and Chucho Zarzosa, the pianist, are regarded as the leading Mexican jazz musicians. How odd it is to drop into a Mexico City nitery to hear modern jazz and encounter Nancy Wilson, Shelly Manne, Jack Sheldon, Jack Marshall, Howard Roberts, and Jimmy Rowles also present at adjacent tables!

The affable drummer Cosy Cole, a professional jazzman for more than three decades, may or may not have attracted more members to the jazz cause during his tour of Africa. When one of Cosy's musicians accidentally cut his finger on the stage of a Uganda theater while playing to a standing room only audience, Cole quickly got attention with a loud cymbal break and solemnly inquired of the crowd: "Is there a witch doctor in the house?"

How much good will has been engendered by the frequent visits of American musicians to scores of foreign lands in recent years cannot accurately be gauged, but Louis Armstrong alone has unquestionably made millions of friends for the U.S.A. simply by playing his golden trumpet, singing a bit, smiling a lot, and demonstrating his love of people of every race and creed.

One conclusion is obvious: American jazz, for nearly fifty years indigenous to North America alone, now is global music. Global, too, are the musicians who compose and play jazz. Ellington is as prominent in Thailand as Queen Elizabeth is in Singapore. Basie, Armstrong, Gillespie —these Americans command artistic respect the world over as do the Oistrakhs, Callas, and Klemperer. They are infinitely more popular with the people, moreover.

Time will tell whether jazz continues to become a more potent force for good throughout the world. From its humble start in the deep South before the turn of the century to the remarkably high degree of acceptance and popularity it enjoys on every continent today, jazz most certainly emerges as a major social and artistic phenomenon of the twentieth century. How much farther it progresses will depend on youth—the world's youth.

Charlie Parker's bebop alto saxophone solo

Ornithology

By CHARLIE PARKER
and BENNY HARRIS
(Based on Dial Record 1002)

A

Modern Jazz

Bibliography

More words have been written on the subject of jazz in the last decade than in all the previous years.

Books on the subject were few and far between before World War II. *Hot Discography*, compiled in Paris by Charles Delaunay (revised and reissued in 1963 as *New Hot Discography;* New York: Criterion Music Corp.); a couple of critical treatises by Hugues Panassié, also written in Paris; the Frederick Ramsey–Charles E. Smith *Jazzmen* (New York: Harcourt Brace and World, Inc., 1959; Harvest Book HB30), first of the better American volumes; a Benny Goodman biography, *Kingdom of Swing* (New York: Frederick Ungar Publishing Co., n.d.), written by Irving Kolodin of the *Saturday Review*, at that time a critic on the old *New York Sun;* the *Jazz Record Book* (New York: A. S. Barnes & Co., n.d.) by the foursome of Charles E. Smith, Frederic Ramsey, Jr., William Russell and Charles Payne Rogers; and Winthrop Sargeant's *Jazz, Hot and Hybrid* (New York: Arrow Editions Co-operative Association, Inc., 1938). These virtually comprised the lot.

There was another source of good writing. The booklets issued inside all the old 78 r.p.m. shellac record albums sometimes were crammed with new and exclusive information on jazz. Those who were paid from $25 to $50 for weeks of researching, compiling personnels, writing, and copying their efforts performed a highly valuable service to jazz and jazzmen. Much of that material is today included in books by writers who were of kindergarten age when all the difficult, poorly-paid work was being achieved as a labor of love by men like George T. Simon, Leonard Feather, Timme Rosenkrantz, Inez Cavanaugh, Charles Edward Smith, George Frazier, George Avakian, Irving Kolodin, Warren W. Scholl, Eugene Williams, and myself.

Today's stodgy, assembly-line notes on the back covers of albums rarely if ever offer anything new and valuable to jazz literature. But the pay has surely improved.

Dozens of jazz magazines, unfortunately, have discontinued publication down through the years. Even *Metronome*, a leader in the field with *Down Beat* through the swing, bop, and cool periods, has recently ceased publishing. *Down Beat*, subdued and elderly in its format and spirit, continues twice-monthly publication, but without enthusiasm in its writing, topography, or artwork.

Best of the publications is the revamped, revised, and regenerated *Jazz*, edited by Pauline Rivelli in New York and published whenever she gets around to it. London's *Jazz Journal* also merits the support of every musician and buff. Paul E. Affeldt and his improving *Jazz Report* from Ventura, California, just about rounds out the list of serious jazz periodicals available in 1964 to American readers.

Saturday Review devotes more space to jazz every year. Wilder Hobson, Helen and Stanley Dance, and other competent writers and critics regularly review new albums and contribute articles.

Most of the books published in the last two decades are now out of print, or severely outdated if still available. The bibliography that follows, therefore, is limited to those books written no earlier than 1957. All were available as of the end of 1963:

Bird: The Legend of Charlie Parker, by Robert George Reisner. Invaluable, definitive story of the late Charles Parker, Jr., as told by his mother, friends, and Reisner, who knew him well. New York: Citadel Press, 1961.

The Book of the Blues, edited by Kay Shirley, with notes by Frank Driggs. A handsomely produced volume that reproduces in full, sheet-music size pages 100 great blues songs replete with melodies and lyrics. New York: Crown Publishers, Inc., and Leeds Music Corp., 1963.

Collector's Jazz: Modern (1959) and *Collector's Jazz: Traditional and Swing* (1958), by John S. Wilson. A serious presentation by the New York writer with emphasis on available records. Philadelphia: J. B. Lippincott Co.

Dinosaurs in the Morning, by Whitney Balliett. A series of articles originally published in *The New Yorker* neatly collated into one volume. Philadelphia: J. B. Lippincott Co., 1963.

Down Beat *Record Reviews* and Down Beat *Yearbook.* Volumes published every year since 1956 by Maher Publications, Inc., of Chicago, the publishers of *Down Beat.*

Esquire's *World of Jazz,* by the editors of *Esquire.* By far the most artistic jazz book ever to be conceived. Its 224 big pages feature superb color paintings and photography, informative text, and striking layouts—a graphic arts masterpiece. Lewis W. Gillenson served as editor-in-chief. New York: Grosset & Dunlap, Inc., 1963.

The Encyclopedia of Jazz, by Leonard Feather. Another outstanding achievement, the Encyclopedia in 527 large pages offers biographies of 2,000 jazzmen, more than 200 photos, and a text by the English-born veteran writer that succinctly sums up the course of jazz, plus other valuable material. New York: Horizon Press Inc., 1960.

Jam Session: An Anthology of Jazz, edited by Ralph J. Gleason. Essays and other readable miscellany about jazz. New York: G. P. Putnam's Sons, Inc., 1958.

Jazz, edited by Nat Hentoff and Albert J. McCarthy. Twelve highly regarded contemporary writers contribute to this academic tome. New York: Holt, Rinehart & Winston, Inc., 1959.

Jazz, by Leonard Feather. A concise history of the music spanning the short period of 1942-59. Trend Books, 1959.

Jazz and the White Americans. The Acceptance of a New Art Form, by Neil Leonard. Longest title to date covers a book chiefly concerned with early jazz, its relationship to classical music and to musicians, and how it evolved into an art form in the 1930s. Chicago: University of Chicago Press, 1962.

The Jazz Makers, edited by Nat Shapiro and Nat Hentoff. Another compilation, this one featuring portraits of 21 musicians by 9 writers. New York: Grove Press, Inc., 1959.

Jazz Panorama, edited by Martin Williams. Contains 39 articles on jazz, including 21 record reviews, from the *Jazz Journal* of London. New York: The Crowell-Collier Publishing Co., 1962.

The Jazz Titans, by Robert George Reisner. Thirty-three additional profiles of musicians by the man who put together the *Bird* book. Garden City, N.Y.: Doubleday & Company, Inc., 1960.

The Jazz Word, edited by Dom Cerulli, Burt Korall, and Mort Nasatir. Still another compilation of poetry, fiction, and essays on the subject of jazz. New York: Ballantine Books, Inc., 1960.

My Life in Jazz, by Max Kaminsky, with V. E. Hughes. Kaminsky, the popular trumpeter, reminisces. His experiences with Artie Shaw in a World War II Navy band are particularly enlightening. New York: Harper & Row, Publishers, 1963.

The New Jazz Book, by Joachim Berendt, translated from the German by Dan Morgenstern. Jazz in eight sections, along with a well-conceived discography by Morgenstern. New York: Hill and Wang, Inc., 1962.

The Reluctant Art: The Growth of Jazz, by Benny Green. A brief readable book by the British critic, humorist, and tenor saxist. Built around his essays on Beiderbecke, Goodman, Holiday, Parker, and Young. New York: Horizon Press, Inc., 1963.

The Sound of Surprise: 46 Pieces on Jazz, by Whitney Balliett. Another cherry-picking trek into the pages of *The New Yorker* (see *Dinosaurs in the Morning*) with 46 of Balliett's articles represented. New York: E. P. Dutton & Co., Inc., 1959.

Toward Jazz, by André Hodéir, translated by Noel Burch. A difficult, rambling venture into jazz by the author of *Jazz: Its Evolution and Essence* (translated by David Noakes; New York: Grove Press, 1956). Some of Hodéir's murky, pseudo-arty theorizing I find down-right boring, although many critics and musicians hold him in high regard. New York: Grove Press, 1962.

What Jazz Is All About, by Lillian Erlich. A work carefully slanted to very young readers. Julian Messner, Inc., Publishers, 1963.

The
Jazz Story
on
Records

Released concurrently with this book is the Capitol Records long-playing album set *The Jazz Story*. Following is a list of the sixty selections included in this five-album recorded history of jazz.

VOLUME 1: CAPITOL ALBUM W-2137

The Original Dixieland Jazz Band: *Barnyard Blues*

Leadbelly: *Backwater Blues*

Zutty Singleton's Creole Band: *Oh, Didn't He Ramble*

Cora and Sallie Martin: *Satisfied*

Eddie Miller's Octet: *Muskrat Ramble*

Sharkey and His Kings of Dixieland: *The Eyes of Texas*

Lizzie Miles: *Lizzie's Blues*

Armand Hug's New Orleans Jazzmen: *That Old Gang of Mine*

Wingy Manone's Band: *Paper Doll*

Ray Bauduc–Nappy Lamare: *Savoy Blues*

Louis Armstrong: *Sugar*

Louis Armstrong: *I Want a Little Girl*

VOLUME 2: CAPITOL ALBUM W-2138

Phil Napoleon's Memphis Five: *Wang Wang Blues*

Blue Lu Barker: *When the Wagon Comes*
Red Nichols and His Pennies: *Ida*
Jimmie Noone's Orchestra: *The Blues Jumped a Rabbit*
Frankie Trumbauer: *Between the Devil and the Deep Blue Sea*
Julia Lee and Her Boy Friends: *I Was Wrong*
The Capitol Jazzmen: *I'm Sorry I Made You Cry*
Joshua Johnson: *Days*
Ray Turner: *The Entertainer's Rag*
Johnny Hodges' Orchestra: *Good to the Last Drop*
Earl Hines: *Deep Forest*
Bobby Hackett's Band: *Struttin' With Some Barbecue*

VOLUME 3: CAPITOL ALBUM W-2139

Joe Venuti and Eddie Lang: *Pink Elephants*
Duke Ellington's Famous Orchestra: *Sophisticated Lady*
Fats Waller: *The Flat-Foot Floogee*
Chocolate Dandies: *Blue Interlude*
Gene Krupa's Chicagoans: *Three Little Words*
Pete Daily's Chicagoans: *I Want to Linger*
Fletcher Henderson's Orchestra: *Nagasaki*
Fletcher Henderson's Orchestra: *It's the Talk of the Town*
Big Sid Catlett's Band: *I Never Knew*
Joe Sullivan: *My Silent Love*
Bunny Berigan's Boys: *You Took Advantage of Me*
Bunny Berigan's Boys: *I'm Coming Virginia*

VOLUME 4: CAPITOL ALBUM W-2140

Glen Gray and the Casa Loma Band: *Casa Loma Stomp*
Billie Holiday–Paul Whiteman: *Travelin' Light*
Art Tatum: *Would You Like to Take a Walk?*

Duke Ellington's Famous Orchestra: *Happy-Go-Lucky Local*
Don Byas: *Blue and Sentimental*
Cootie Williams' Orchestra: *House of Joy*
Benny Goodman's Orchestra: *Sometimes I'm Happy*
Benny Carter's Orchestra: *Hurry, Hurry*
Bob Crosby's Dixieland Band: *Maryland, My Maryland*
Jimmie Lunceford's Band (Led by Billy May): *For Dancers Only*
Django Reinhardt: *Nuages*
Harry James' Orchestra: *Two O'Clock Jump*

VOLUME 5: CAPITOL ALBUM W-2141

Kenny Clarke: *Be a Good Girl*
Tadd Dameron: *John's Delight*
Woody Herman's Herd: *Misty Morning*
George Shearing's Trio: *What's New*
Jimmy Giuffre: *Finger Snapper*
Dizzy Gillespie and the Metronome Stars: *Leap Here*
James Moody's Boptet: *Delsoney*
Miles Davis: *Moon Dreams*
Gerry Mulligan: *Taking a Chance on Love*
Cannonball Adderley: *I Can't Get Started*
Stan Kenton's Orchestra: *Commencement*
Joe Harriott's Free Form Jazz: *Shadows*

Index

Abadee brothers, 14
Adams, Pepper, 141
Adderley, Julian (Cannonball), 4, 100, 138, 141, 157, 167
Adderley, Nat, 138, 141
Advanced School of Contemporary Music, 5
Affeldt, Paul E., 162
Agnes, 41, 42 (illus.)
Ahern, Bob, 130
Albert, Don, 85
Alciatore, Antoine (Chef), 17
Aless, Tony, 129
Alexander, Ora and Texas, 95
Alexandria, Lorez, 101
Alke, Bjorn, 160
Allen, Eddie, 75
Allen, Henry (Red), 119
Allen, Jasper (Jap), 80
Allen, Steve, 158
Allison, Mose, 103
Almeida, Laurindo, 140
Alston, Ovie, 107
Alvis, Hayes, 116
American Federation of Musicians, 3
Ammons, Albert, 37
Ammons, Gene, 136, 142, 149
Amos, 95
"Amplivox," 39
Anderson, Ernestine, 101
Anderson, Gene, 26
Anderson, Ivie, 68, 91, 102
Anderson, Louella, 74
Anderson, Sonny, 74
Anderson, William (Cat), 118
Andy Boy, 95
Anthony, Al, 130
Arbello, Fernando, 106
Archey, Jimmy, 13
Arlington, Madame Josie, 15
Armstrong, Louis, 2, 4, 7, 11, 12, 13, 14, 16, 18, 20 (illus.), 20–29, 33, 36, 37, 38, 39, 46, 49, 51, 55, 58, 60, 61, 64, 66, 80, 89, 91, 94, 95, 99, 103, 105, 106, 109, 111, 116, 127, 136, 138, 141, 151, 161, 165
Armstrong, Shelley, 96
Armstrong family (Willie, Mary-Ann, Beatrice), 21
Arnheim, Gus, 86,87
Arnold, Buddy, 142
Arnold, Kokomo, 96
Ashford, Bo, 115
Atkins, Boyd, 38
Atkins, Ed, 32
Auld, Georgie, 114
Austin, Cuba, 69
Austin, Lovie, 89
Austin, Willie, 75

Avakian, George M., 41, 43, 127

Babasin, Harry, 5, 141
Bacon, Louis, 89
Bacon, Trevor, 121
Bacquet, George, 9, 11
Bailey, Dave, 142
Bailey, Mildred, 28, 82, 88 (illus.), 96–97, 99, 102, 104, 112–13, 135
Bailey, William (Buster), 23, 61, 89, 106, 113
Baker, Chet, 158
Baker, Dave, 139
Baker, Dorothy, 53
Baker, Harold (Shorty), 75
Baker, Jimmie, 158
Ball, Kenny, 159
Balliett, Whitney, 163, 164
Ballina, Mario, 161
Banks, Billy, 96
Banks, Paul, 78
Barbarin, Paul, 31
Barber, Chris, 159
Barefield, Eddie, 81, 83, 128
Barefoot Bill, 96
Barker, Blue Lu, 166
Barker, Danny, 14,
Barnes, Faye, 91
Barnet, Charlie, 109, 127, 136
Barris, Harry, 51
Bartlett, Viola, 92
Basie, William (Count), 4, 63, 73 (illus.), 78, 79, 81, 83, 84, 98, 101, 102, 103, 105 (illus.), 111, 113, 115, 118, 126, 128–29, 130–31, 133, 136, 139, 140, 147, 148, 150, 157, 161
Battle, Edgar, 85
Bauduc, Ray, 50, 106, 132, 165
Bauer, Billy, 129, 134
Baxter, Helen, 92
Beal, Eddie, 87
Beall, George, 35
Beaman, Lottie, 92
Bean, Floyd, 37, 41
Beatty, Josephine, 23, 91
Beaverbrook, Lord, 68
Bechet, Sidney, 7, 9, 16, 31, 111, 127, 142
Beckett, Freddy, 85
Beers, Sam, 38, 90
Beery, Wally, 27
Beiderbecke, Charles B., 54
Beiderbecke, Leon Bix, 36, 37, 46 (illus.), 46–55, 65, 71, 73, 74, 75, 112, 118, 153, 155
Belasco, David, 17
Bell, Anna, 92

Bell, Sweetie, 74
Bellson, Louis, 143
Bennett, Floyd, 25
Bennett, Mark, 112
Bennett-Sabin dance act, 44
Berendt, Joachim, 160, 164
Berg, Billy, 125, 150
Berger, Herbert (Ham), 75
Berigan, Bernard (Bunny), 97, 112, 126, 153, 166
Berman, Saul (Sonny), 129
Bernardi, Noni, 108
Bernhart, Milt, 130
Bernie, Ben, 69
Berry, Chuck, 76
Berry, Leon (Chu), 63, 83, 90, 106, 109
Berry, Leroy (Buster), 73 (illus.), 81
Berton, Vic, 71
Best, Denzil, 135
Beutler, Al, 141
Bibb, Leonard, 41
Bigard, Barney, 13, 29, 67, 114
Bilk, Acker, 159
Billboard, The, 147
Bishop, Wally, 107
Bishop, Walter, 140
Black, Lew, 35
Blackburn, Lacy, 77
Blackwell, Ed, 142
Blackwell, Scrapper, 96
Blake, Eubie, 59
Blakey, Art, 123, 138, 142, 149
Bland, Jack, 75
Blanton, Jimmy, 33, 76
Blind blues singers, 95
Bloom, Kurt, 109
Bloom, Teddy, 152, 154
Blue, Thornton, 70
Blue Devils, 79, 81, 83
Blue Friars, 36
Blythe, Jimmy, 92
Bocage, Pete, 11
Bolar, Abe, 81
Bolden, Charles (Buddy), 10, 11, 12, 14, 25, 28, 35, 153
Bolden, Lela, 92
Boles, John, 52
Bonano, Joseph (Sharkey), 35, 48, 132, 165
Boone, Harvey, 112
Boots and his Buddies, 85
Borden, Ray, 130
Borders, Ben, 86
Bose, Sterling, 108
Bostic, Earl, 33, 141
Boswell, Connee, 50, 102
Bouchon, Lester, 132
Bowman, Dave, 118
Bowman, Euday L., 77

Index

171